The Mathematical Path

Despite what we generally think about mathematics, the system is not actually made up of numbers and the principles that express relationships between numbers. Rather, the mathematical system consists of the *idea* of numbers and the *idea* of principles. This is no hairsplitting distinction. Mathematics has no physical existence. The entire system is a mental concept—a tool of the mind—that we express with written symbols in order to make it easier to use. Its use can apply to anything having form. The term "form" is employed here in its broad philosophical meaning, which encompasses all that makes up the physical, manifested level of existence.

Mathematics does, of course, have structure, so it does itself have form. But this is an elastic, elusive, ethereal kind of form. It can assume any shape, so to speak, from the most concrete to the most abstract levels of earthly existence. Said another way, mathematics is capable of representing, or modeling, the inner and outer natures of anything.

Among the fields amenable to mathematical representation is the spiritual path. Although this way of life is far removed from the hustle and bustle of daily life, as well as being eternally enshrouded in mystery, it has form nonetheless, with an identifiable structure to it. Part of its mystique arises from the belief that the spiritual path is profoundly not-of-this-world, and that it originates in the Realms of Spirit, giving it an unfathomable and impenetrable quality. The initial inspiration of spiritual belief systems may well be from a transcendent source, but the concepts and symbols developed to represent the Way of Spirit are human conclusions. Thus, while the ultimate goal of the spiritual quest is unpredictable and unknowable, the path that leads toward it is quite well known. That path can be represented mathematically.

—Steven Scott Pither

About the Author

Steven Pither holds a masters degree in French and Spanish from Ball State University. He has lived in France, England, and Brazil, and was in the Peace Corps in Tunisia. Mr. Pither has traveled widely in Europe, North Africa, and North and South America. He is married, and resides in Tulsa, Oklahoma. He has avidly pursued the spiritual and psychological meanings of numbers since 1985, and has given over seven hundred numerology readings.

To Write to the Author

If you wish to contact the author or would like more information about this book, please write to the author in care of Llewellyn Worldwide and we will forward your request. Both the author and publisher appreciate hearing from you and learning of your enjoyment of this book and how it has helped you. Llewellyn Worldwide cannot guarantee that every letter written to the author can be answered, but all will be forwarded. Please write to:

Steven Scott Pither
℅ Llewellyn Worldwide
P.O. Box 64383, Dept. 0-7387-0218-8
St. Paul, MN 55164-0383, U.S.A.

Please enclose a self-addressed stamped envelope for reply, or $1.00 to cover costs. If outside U.S.A., enclose international postal reply coupon.

Many of Llewellyn's authors have websites with additional information and resources. For more information, please visit our website at
http://www.llewellyn.com

THE COMPLETE BOOK OF NUMBERS

The Power of Number Symbols to Shape Reality

Steven Scott Pither

2002
Llewellyn Publications
St. Paul, Minnesota 55164-0383, U.S.A.

First Edition
First Printing, 2002

Designed and edited by Karin Simoneau
Cover design by Gavin Dayton Duffy
Cover image © 2002 Rubberball Productions

Library of Congress Cataloging-in-Publication Data
Pither, Steven Scott, 1942–
    The complete book of numbers: the power of number symbols to shape reality /
Steven Scott Pither
        p. cm.
    Includes bibliographical references and index.
    ISBN 0-7387-0218-8
    1. Numerology. 2. Symbolism of numbers. I. Title.

BF1623.P9 P58 2002
133.3'35—dc21   2002016127

Llewellyn Worldwide does not participate in, endorse, or have any authority or responsibility concerning private business transactions between our authors and the public.

All mail addressed to the author is forwarded but the publisher cannot, unless specifically instructed by the author, give out an address or phone number.

Any Internet references contained in this work are current at publication time, but the publisher cannot guarantee that a specific location will continue to be maintained. Please refer to the publisher's website for links to authors' websites and other sources.

Llewellyn Publications
A Division of Llewellyn Worldwide, Ltd.
P.O. Box 64383, Dept. 0-7387-0218-8
St. Paul, MN 55164-0383, U.S.A.
www.llewellyn.com

Printed in the United States of America

This book is dedicated to my wife, Eve, whose Spirit Communication,
Spirit Teachings, loving support, and understanding provided the inspiration
and environment for me to see, hear, and write more clearly;
and also to Dion Fortune and Rudolf Steiner,
two of the most important occult teachers ever.
I am grateful they are always with me.

Contents

Acknowledgments

A book like this cannot be written alone. With deep gratitude I honor my Spiritual Source, which showed me that numbers are love, and also how vast and deep that love is. I am indebted to the giants of humankind who created the Divine Science of Number Symbolism, to the mathematical geniuses who have developed and proven our amazing system of mathematics, as well as to the many authors who have made their thoughts available through books. Thanks go to Daniel Lee Fulkerson, who taught me to use the computer and who gave me editorial advice. Thanks also to Juliana Fulkerson, who offered her computer in the beginning and provided occasional helpful comments. Finally, I give special thanks to my beloved wife, Evelyn Moss Pither, whose loving support and inborn understanding of numbers have helped make this book possible.

Introduction

On an evening in the autumn of 1985, I was dragged to a seminar at the Tulsa School of Metaphysics. The subject of the seminar was numerology. Although I was familiar with the term "numerology," I had no knowledge of its workings and was even less interested in learning about it. As the first hour of lecture plodded on, my thoughts wandered dreamily, only occasionally returning to the seminar in progress. At length, the discussion focused on the meanings of the nine numbers of numerology. When the woman giving the presentation came to the number two, she repeated over and over, "Two is the number of pure receptivity, pure receptivity." After the sixth or seventh time, something strange happened. I heard a clear, distinct voice inside my head, and it said, "Well, shoot, I know what that is. I know *exactly* what that is!" Both that moment and that voice have since, to this day, been an utter mystery to me. But from that night on, I have been stimulated by an intense need to know about numerology as deeply as possible.

Over the next five years, I studied one book after another. I learned that numerology is part of an incredibly ancient system used for understanding oneself and other people, for divination, and even for spirituality. Most civilizations back to the beginnings of recorded history used some type of numerology or number symbolism, as far back as Sumer, when writing was invented in 3200 B.C.E. I realized there had been a great many forms of number symbolism, perhaps hundreds, and that the modern variant, the so-called Pythagorean numerology, was a relatively recent development of the twentieth century. Even the venerable Kabalistic numerology did not come into being until the early centuries of the Common Era. Number symbolism has changed over time, and has not always been the sophisticated tool it is today. In its developing stages, it often took form in ways that are now dismissed. During the Middle Ages, for example, winners of contests were predicted on the basis of totaling numbers corresponding to the letters of the names, the higher count supposedly foretelling the victor. These kinds of misfires notwithstanding, there have been and presently are many valid forms of number symbolism, ranging from the Kabalistic Tree of Life to the I Ching, which is the Chinese Book of Changes said to be a "mathematical model" of the universe. And, of course, Pythagorean numerology.

During my studies of Pythagorean numerology, it became apparent there are many discrepancies, contradictions, and limitations among today's practitioners of the art. A glaring case in point concerns the number zero. At the present time, there exists no consensus as to whether this is a valid number in numerology. Some say it is; many say it cannot be (now . . . either it is or it is not). Still, on this and other fundamental questions there is no attempt being made in the pertinent literature to determine validity or even to justify this or that concept. Yet without some rationale to support an author's ideas, we are left in the unenviable position of having to accept someone else's understanding on faith, however limited or inaccurate that may be. The alternative to blind acceptance is to formulate our own ideas and understandings through research, meditation, and analysis. We can work to discover for ourselves a conclusive system of number symbolism that is "self-consistent," as scientists and theoreticians would say. As much as anything, that is my purpose in this book. In a self-consistent symbol system, all parts are interdependent and necessary to the functioning of the whole. As Fritjof Capra writes, ". . . self-consistency is the essence of all laws of nature."[1]

But consistent in what way? For number symbolism, the obvious answer is in terms of the axioms, postulates, principles, and theorems of that great body of knowledge that has been designed specifically to handle and manipulate numbers: our system of mathematics. Many centuries ago, number symbolism was mathematical practice, right alongside arithmetic and geometry. The mathematical techniques of the day were applied fully to number symbolism. But that was also during eras when mathematics was in its infancy. Most systems of number symbolism were fully developed on the basis of primitive mathematical knowledge, and they have never been updated. Consider the "controversial" zero. Apart from the Mayan Indians and astronomers of Sumer, no European, African, or Asian civilization had the true zero until relatively modern times, just before the beginning of the twentieth century! Consequently, when those early peoples created their sacred numbers, naturally they did it without the zero. Today, all of those number symbol systems, as well as their offspring, still operate that way—the old-fashioned way.

This is a curious anachronism in a world in which the zero is so fundamental to the use of numbers. Numbers, which are used symbolically for psychological or spiritual purposes, are no different from numbers used to measure and quantify. However, the course of mathematics and that of number symbolism separated definitively around 1600 c.e., about the same time the scientific method took hold. I began wondering how these two methodologies tie together nowadays. I felt a deep intuitive conviction that they were cut from the same fabric. But how? What would the connection be beyond their shared use of numbers? I found there were many connections.

This book contains a great many of my conclusions. In order to present them in a cogent manner, I begin by tracing the remarkable and often strange history of mathematics, with an emphasis on its cultural and philosophical development. This discussion concludes with a fascinating shift in mathematical understanding that occurred during the twentieth century. As a result of spectacular advances in physics, many concepts (particularly in subatomic physics) come breathtakingly close to metaphysical understanding! And why not? Transcendent number symbolism was developed by the ancients using *mathematics,* as they understood it. Why would it not be so today?

Throughout this book, I extend the work of the ancients by transliterating (with the utmost respect) their techniques and terminology into current mathematical practice. This allows a far greater depth and complexity of understanding and use of number symbolism than is currently the case, especially with Pythagorean numerology. Kabalistic numerology is considerably more mathematical and spiritual in its conceptualization than is its Pythagorean brother. Still, it also would profit, I believe, from such an update. I know of no work now in print whose purpose it is to regenerate number symbolism for our time. Although many writers have reported what they learned from their researches into the past, few, if any, have attempted to make the ancient symbology speak to us moderns in the language of our thinking. However fascinating and alluring the symbols of the distant past may be, they are not, and can never be, fully meaningful to us now. For example, what can the numerologist of today, or anyone, for that matter, understand from the ancient Greek notion that 6 is a perfect number? It was so considered because the numbers that divide evenly into 6—1, 2, and 3—also total 6 when added together. Perfect numbers had utmost significance in the time of Pythagoras, but the meaning for us in the present time may be unknowable or perhaps even irrelevant.

It is my earnest hope that mathematicians and scientists will consider the contents of these pages with what might be called scientific objectivity. The prevailing scientific attitude toward number symbolism and metaphysics in general seems to be a desire to ". . . clear away the debris of millennia, including all the myths and false cosmologies that encumber humanity's self-image."[2] People committed to the scientific search for "objective truth" may, however, benefit from exploring the analogous metaphysical search for the true nature of reality presented here. I agree with Edward Wilson in some respects when he writes: "Science offers the boldest metaphysics of the age."[3] The potential for number symbolism to enhance living is also bold, however. The metaphysical terms, images, and techniques we have inherited from the inspired agrarian societies of long ago need to be translated, at the very least, and to a great extent reinvented, in the light of present-day understanding and knowledge, or else they will remain impenetrable.

For the scientist to switch to a metaphysical model of reality from a scientific one involves more than finding common ground or common language, or even being genuinely receptive to a radically different approach. This present volume is packed with metaphysical concepts expressed mathematically. I do not believe, however, that this alone will enable mathematicians to bridge the gulf. There is too much intellectual and emotional investment in the mathematical mindset to permit an easy apprehension of mystical subject matter. What we have here are two fundamentally different perceptions of reality that are not talking to each other.

An illustration taken from biology makes a marvelous metaphor for this conundrum: butterflies see a different range of the light spectrum than do humans, and so they ". . . find flowers and pinpoint pollen and nectar sources by the pattern of ultraviolet rays reflected off the petals. Where we see a plain yellow or white blossom, they see spots and concentric circles in light and dark."[4]

I believe it is fully worthwhile to find out what the "magical, mystical butterfly" sees. The promise and the real purpose of numerology, or any metaphysical symbol system for that matter, is a deepening of the spiritual life, including an enhanced ability in the art of living. Unfortunately, as I was completing my research into Pythagorean numerology in 1990, I found virtually nothing of a spiritual nature in it. Apart from a few references to karmic numbers and karmic lessons, this discipline is devoted exclusively to dealing with the life and affairs of this world. For all its wonderful potential to inform the soul, Pythagorean numerology amounts to little more than a supernatural tease. Such notions as karmic numbers are, in my opinion, baseless speculations, a position I will explore in mathematical terms later in the book.

Numerology is an exceptional tool for the analysis of character in subtle detail . . . with one limitation: there is no numerical way to determine from a numerology chart how an individual is living his life or how far he has advanced spiritually. Virtually the same combination of numbers could be those of a destitute beggar or of a prosperous businessperson; of a debased career criminal or of a committed idealist working for the betterment of humankind. Numerologists across the land will no doubt object strenuously to this assertion. It is my surmise, however, that consistency in interpretations of numerology charts is due to the fact that, in the main, only certain types of people seek this out. Destitute beggars, debased criminals, and a variety of others outside the conventional range will probably not be in that group.

Ultimately, I *knew* number symbolism would prove to be spiritual in nature. The ancients knew it. The Kabalists today know it. I was determined to find it in modern mathematics. After prolonged investigation and effort, I have been able to identify a process of spiritual advancement, and other aspects of spiritual living, through the interpretation of certain numbers and mathematical usage. Our mathematical system is the epitome of logic and order. Based on a small number of axioms, which are propositions accepted as true without proof, the entire system of mathematics is built up, step by step, by constructing a perfectly consistent structure. It begins with, and never deviates from, the initial assumptions. For the most part, my method of development has been to use what physicists call "thought experiments." In a thought experiment, the discovery process is carried out mentally with the same meticulous accuracy, precision, and attention to detail applied to any scientific experiment. To use the metaphysical term here, I meditated deeply each step along the way and only committed my findings to paper when I was completely certain of the correctness and the exactness of my conclusions.

Toward the end of the book I have listed a major part of this work, which consists of interpretations of ninety number combinations as well as ten different levels of those numbers. In this effort, truth has been everything. This section of interpretations required a year and a half to complete, involving intense concentration on the most subtle, mysterious, and elusive of meanings. The single most difficult interpretation for me to make was that of a "four digit number at the nine level,"[5] which necessitated a full four months before I knew I had it. The payoff was a single sentence consisting of eight words! What a feeling it was after those long months of digging to find a nugget of pure gold.

If you, the reader, are willing to put in the necessary time and effort to interpret these number combinations for yourself and to master the mathematics of this spiritual symbol system, the benefits will be very special. The sustained, creative practice of number symbolism can bring its practitioner insight, knowledge, and improved living that are unrecognized and undreamed of at this time. The act of discovering its subtle meanings and intricate inner workings is an exciting process in which knowledge, wisdom, and progress occur at every step of the way. Prepare yourself for a spiritual adventure.

(A note to the reader about the language usage in this book: I apologize to female readers for the use of "he," "his," and "him" to refer to either a female or a male. Although this is still grammatically correct, it is no longer an appropriate mode of expression, in my opinion. However, because there are no acceptable alternatives, I hope both female and male readers will bear with this antiquated phraseology.)

Endnotes

1. Fritjof Capra, *The Tao of Physics* (Boston, Mass.: Shambhala Publications, 1991), 290.
2. Edward O. Wilson, *Consilience: The Unity of knowledge* (New York: Alfred A. Knopf, 1998), 61.
3. Ibid., 12.
4. Ibid., 46.
5. The significance and meaning of this will be explained in chapter 12.

chapter 1

The Ancients Give Us Gifts

Mathematics: in its origin, this Greek word means all that one learns by lessons or by direct experience.

—Lucien Gérardin, *Le Mystère des Nombres*

This book is about a foreign language. Not a foreign language spoken by another people, but a language of mind that is foreign to our thinking. I speak of the spiritual language of sacred symbols. In the distant past, spiritual symbol systems were known as myths, and they functioned well in their time. At the present time, that same tradition continues in many forms, one of which is number symbolism. For the past hundred years or so, the name we have used for this discipline is *numerology*.

From earliest times, people have lived better and understood life more deeply as a result of using number symbolism. In the ancient days, numbers were held in reverence and the art of their use was better understood than it is today. Pythagoras, the renowned Greek mathematician and philosopher, believed numbers were magic. Plato held that mathematics, which at the time included number symbolism, was founded on infallible intuition as a sure source of knowledge. Likewise, Aristotle considered that truth, the axioms upon which mathematics is founded, were actual memories from the Spirit State before birth. These are strong statements. Yet, we have the wary feeling that they only spoke metaphorically, and the nagging suspicion that numbers can do little more than provide some insight and make predictions. If true, this is not the stuff of deep spirituality.

The ancients did not speak thoughtlessly or superficially about numbers, however. They recognized an inseparable bond between the mundane and the divine. Number symbolism was perceived as a means to bring Spirit and matter together as one. This concept was not limited to a certain region or to a particular people. Sages and mystics from all parts of the world used number symbolism for spiritual purposes, sometimes with impressive results. "Hindu mythology," for one example, "seems to have aimed at and achieved a total unity between the physical and metaphysical, with number theory providing the ground for an absolute certainty of viewpoint."[1]

These are strong and reassuring words. The question is: how might we in our time discover such an "absolute certainty of viewpoint?" This is a deep question with no quick or easy answers, but there *are* answers if the right kind of effort is made with sufficient persistence. Toward that end, we will inquire deeply into the nature of number symbols in the belief that perfect perception of numbers and their operations results in perfect understanding of the self and how to live in harmony with Spirit. We will use the language of our own time in this effort—not the mythic terminology of gods and supernatural powers, but the modern imagery of mathematics and science. As Dion Fortune wrote, "Occult science, rightly understood, is the link between science and religion; it gives the means of a spiritual approach to science, and a scientific approach to spiritual life."[2]

Spiritual symbol systems, including number symbolism, when examined at face value, make no sense. In their vocabulary, structure, and syntax, they appear to be about common, everyday things, but they are not. Or, they appear to be about divine beings and other worlds on a cosmic scale, but they are not. Rather, spiritual symbol systems give form to transcendent, eternal principles that seem initially far removed from the stresses and strains of everyday life, as well as describe living conditions on the cosmic level. To the uninitiated, spiritual symbol systems seem like abstract intellectual exercises with no bearing on reality or everyday life. Yet, they have the greatest imaginable relevance to all levels of a person's life when they are understood.

It is the elusive nature of spiritual symbols that makes their mastery such a long and patient process. They are Spirit based. This is why no form of thinking that is worldly or egocentric brings results, and also why we find them so ticklishly difficult to grasp. The knowledge is personal. It can be stated to others, but not communicated. There is no reference book, spiritual textbook, person, or even teacher that can give this learning to you. The only access each of us has is through a mysterious process of inner realization—a process this book was written to facilitate.

An example taken from the number symbolism of ancient Greece will demonstrate the problem of understanding symbolic numbers. In the sixth century before the Common Era, the Greeks had a fully developed system of number symbols. In one aspect of this, 5 was considered the number of marriage because it represented the union of two other numbers, 2 and 3. The first feminine number was 2, and 3 was the first masculine number. Now, having heard this much, what are we to make of it? The natural thing is to associate 5 with the marriage between two people of the opposite sex. Perhaps the first feminine and masculine numbers refer to a philosophical or archetypal concept of man and woman. We might then go one step further to suppose that 5 represents an ideal of marriage toward which each individual marriage should strive. Having settled on this as the gist of the matter, we are left with the hollow feeling, "So what?" Why would the Greeks have gone to all this trouble to state the obvious using abstract, unromantic numbers?

As reasonable as these thoughts about 2, 3, and 5 are, they miss the point completely. This is not about marital life. But the Greeks did the best they could to represent "something" using words and concepts available to them in their language. This is all *any* verbal language can do in the effort to discuss "something" that can not be put into words.

Okay, so we missed the first time through. Let's try again, this time using a more informed approach based on what is known about Greek number symbols. The Greeks were definitely of a philosophical bent. The numbers 2, 3, and 5 were abstract concepts. The feminine 2 and the masculine 3 were considered the two most basic principles, or laws, of life. Together, they covered all the polar opposites (all forms of duality) on the earth plane. The Greeks listed ten pairs of opposites, which included light and dark, male and female, and good and evil. They reasoned that if those kinds of fundamental conflicting qualities could be harmonized and made to function together (they used the term "married"), this would result in the ability to live one's life in a positive, productive, effective way. In this manner, 5 symbolized such a state of harmony.

This explanation is clearly an informed one. The point of it is as significant now as it was in ancient Greece: living harmoniously in a world filled with polarizing opposites. It is a marvelous statement of spiritual principles, and yet it gives us nothing except information. After all the pomp and ceremony of the discourse is over and we return to the privacy of our own thoughts, we are left to wonder, *So, what am I supposed to do now?* Normally when something is explained properly, we are able to act on our new understanding. That did not happen here because personal meaning was not communicated, and no experiential learning took place. The entire explanation merely expanded on symbols that were unintelligible in the first place and remained so. The language of these number symbols remains foreign to our thinking.

The art of interpretation is the key skill necessary to use number symbolism. To learn to interpret, we must go back to the very beginnings of mathematics to discover how and why numbers developed as metaphysical symbols. Numbers that are used symbolically are mathematical in every sense of the word. The history of number symbols and the history of mathematics were one and the same from the beginning until about 500 C.E. It is important to state at the outset of this brief historical excursion that numbers, in addition to being used to count, measure, and calculate, have always been given cultural and metaphysical attributes.

Today, mathematics is a purely abstract system. In the beginning, however, numbers were not abstract in the least. The first efforts thousands of years ago to count were almost unimaginably strange to the modern mind. There were no written numbers like we use today, or even words for numbers. Counting often meant carving lines into wood or stone, or making impressions in clay tablets. A given number was recorded by carving as many lines: 6 required six lines, and 28 required twenty-eight lines. The convenient diagonal slash to indicate multiples of five was unknown. Some early peoples counted by pointing to different parts of the body. An instance of this exists today in a tribe on the island of Papua: 1 is the right little finger; 2 is the right ring finger; 3 is the right middle finger; 4 is the right index finger; 5 is the right thumb; and so on until 12, which is the nose, 13, which is the mouth, 14, which is the left ear, and so on.[3] A more sophisticated version of this was finger counting, a counting method that persisted in Europe as late as the 1700s. The Romans were able to count from one to ten thousand using their fingers.

In the far distant past, there were often no separate words for counting. The quantity of something was a part of the word itself, just as in present-day English we change nouns to mean more than one by adding an *s* (for example, tree: trees). In Arabic prior to 700 B.C.E., *radjulun* meant man, *radjulan* meant two men, and *ridjalun* meant men.[4] Vestiges of this same practice can be seen in such current English expressions as a yoke of oxen and a team of horses. It may seem unimportant nowadays that some languages had words for one-of-a-thing and two-of-a-thing. But in the early development of mathematics, some cultures had no numbers beyond two or three. At different times and places, 2, 3, 4, and most commonly 10 (because we have ten fingers) were the limits of counting. This is close to unbelievable now, in a time in which schoolchildren are routinely familiar with numbers in the millions and billions. Yet even in today's world, there is a tribe of South Seas Islanders whose highest number is 2. They count from 1 to 5 in the following manner: 1, 2, 2'1, 2'2, 2'2'1.[5] Many early peoples knew how to count from 1 to 9, after which they simply said "many." The root meanings of German numbers show that at one time their highest number was 10. One hundred was expressed as "ten of tens," and thousand was "strong ten of tens." Our own word for million has the same type of history. It is a combination of the Latin word "mille," meaning thousand, and "one," which was a strengthening word. Joined together, milli-one means "many thousand."[6]

Today, our entire mathematical system consists of just ten different numbers: 0 and 1 through 9, after which we must combine digits in order to go higher. Consequently, we have what is called a base of 10. Mathematical bases other than ten have also been used in the past. The Chinese once had a base of 2. Five has been used as a base, as well as 20, which was used by the Mayas, Aztecs, and Druids. Evidence of this practice of the Druids can still be found in the modern French word for 80—*quatre-vingts*—which means four-twenties. In the mathematics of ancient Sumer, they had two different bases: for everyday counting they used a base of 10, and for astronomy they used the unusual base of 60. In other words, they had sixty numbers available to them before they had to combine numbers to express higher quantities.

In Sumer, as in every ancient culture, numbers had sacred and philosophical meanings. Numbers were identified with gods. Key relationships between gods were established, in part, by those numbers that divide evenly into 60. Today, in place of the term "gods," we would probably call them spiritual forces or cosmic laws. Numbers that divide evenly into 60 probably demonstrated relationships between the gods because the connections could be easily established in a straightforward, mathematical manner.

Sumerians derived their sacred numbers from nature, in particular from the length of the year and the objects they observed in the skies, as did so many civilizations of that era. The sun, moon, and stars were believed to be divine beings, and the cycles of their orbits were thought to be the gods in action. Now, the

Sumerians, along with many other peoples of ancient times, are known to have been excellent astronomers, far more accurate than we moderns generally think they could have been. In some cases (for instance, the predictions of lunar eclipses) they were nearly as accurate as we are! Despite this knowledge, the length of the Sumerian calendar year was an even 360 days, not the more accurate 365¼ we now know a year to be. This was certainly convenient because many numbers can evenly divide 360, whereas the actual length of the year cannot be divided by any whole numbers due to its extra ¼ day. At first, I found this discrepancy troubling. Their entire cosmology was based on the number 360. Yet the Sumerians were, in fact, well aware of the true length of the year, and they even established a method for adding in the extra five days so their year would stay on schedule. The same was practiced by other astronomer civilizations as well—the Druids, the Hindu Aryans, the Egyptians, the Mayans, the Incas, and the Chinese—which all had calendar years of 360 days and included the five extra days. I wondered if the Sumerians had deliberately manipulated the numbers in order to make their number symbolism work. Then I learned that ". . . at some point during the Age of Cancer we acquired the five extra days known as epagomenal, the earth having previously taken only 360 days to complete its annual cycle."[7] This was reassuring to me because spiritual symbol systems that lack integrity are without value. As it turns out, many civilizations were simply showing reverence for an earlier period in earth's history. It also demonstrates that reality in this world changes, and the entire premise of a wisdom system can be invalidated with sufficient passage of time—*if*, that is, it has its basis in physical reality. In our own time, there no longer exists any basis on which to make 60 or 360 sacred numbers.

It was a dream of the Sumerians to structure the universe by numbers, but this would not even be attempted for another 1400 years in the time of Pythagoras. By "structure the universe," they meant expand their knowledge of number symbolism to explain everything in their world. Although they did not succeed, there are, however, two legacies from the Sumerians that we retain to this day. Our measurement of 360° in a circle and our division of an hour into 60 minutes are cultural holdovers from that long-past civilization. Another inheritance is their invention of calculating the numerical value of names and words. This is essentially the basis on which modern numerology works, along with several other lesser known forms of number symbolism, like *gematria*. Gematria is a method of determining the hidden connections between words that have the same numerical value. It is amazing how strong the staying power of culture and tradition is!

With the advent of Sumer, we come into the purview of recorded history. Despite the many advances in mathematics up to that time, the state of the art was still very primitive by today's standards. Numbers were very cumbersome to write. Worse, they could not be used at all to make even the simplest of calculations like addition and subtraction. These kinds of limitations would continue to be the case the world over until some time after 700 C.E., when the so-called Arabic numbers, the numbers we use today, were invented in India.

Written numbers until then were only used to record quantities and the results of calculations. From the time of Sumer some 5000 years ago right up through the 1700s C.E., people relied on finger counting and counting boards to do their addition, subtraction, duplation (doubling), mediation (halving), multiplication, and division. Counting boards were constructed of wood or stone on which a set of parallel lines was drawn. Pebbles, carved counters, or other sorts of markers were used to make the calculations. The quantity of markers required to represent a number was equal to the number. The number 7 required seven markers, for example. In Europe, the columns on counting boards indicated the place-value of each number. This is to say that the column, or place, determined whether the number was units (1, 2, 3, and so on through 9), tens (10, 20, 30, and so on through 90), hundreds (100, 200, 300, and so on through 900), and so on. Zero played no part in counting boards. Columns representing zero were simply left blank. On the counting board, then, the number 204 was indicated as shown in Figure 1. As important as place-value was to the operation of counting boards, this technique was not incorporated into written numbers until well into the fifteenth century.

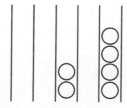

Figure 1. The number 204 represented on a counting board.

It is interesting to note that in China little wooden or bamboo sticks were used on counting boards instead of counters. This is perhaps related to the fact that sticks were originally thrown in order to consult the I Ching. Today, for simplicity, three coins are tossed in place of sticks. The theme of the I Ching revolves around 64 hexagrams. These are designs consisting of six lines that are either broken or unbroken (see Figure 2). The particular combination of lines and the order in which they occur are interpreted for meaning. The alternation of broken and unbroken lines clearly recalls the ancient Chinese mathematical base of 2, hence just the two symbols. This is another example of an early people using mathematics to express concepts of wisdom and spirituality.

An important advance in written numbers occurred when alphabets began to be used as numbering systems. This was a Greek innovation of about 450 B.C.E. that was later emulated by the Hebrews. In both alphabets, the first nine letters served additionally as the numbers 1 through 9. The next nine letters represented the tens, 10 through 90, while the last nine letters were the hundreds, 100 through 900. The striking advantage of alphabet numbers was simplification. Before alphabet numbers, there were often only written numbers for 1, 5, 10, 100, and so on. Other numbers were then written by repeating and combining the basic digits. Just as on the counting board, 4 (to cite an example) was written by putting down "1" four times. Forty was made by writing the "10" four times. In ancient Egypt, to make this example concrete, 1 was represented by a vertical line and 10 by an arch. Their method of writing 44 was: ||||ΩΩΩΩ. Alphabet numbers, on the other hand, had a letter/number for each of the units, each of the tens and each of the hundreds. So now 44 could be written 40'4 (using the proper Greek or Hebrew letters, of course). To write the number 404, which we now accomplish by inserting a zero, they wrote

Figure 2. This sample Hexagram number 17 entitled "Sui Following" is partially interpreted to mean: "Joy in movement induces following," and later, "The idea of following in the sense of adaption to the demands of time grows out of this image."

400'4, and never felt anything was lacking because there was nothing (that is, no zero) in the ten's column. "For the primitive reckoner, number is always *a number*, a quantity, and only a number can have a symbol."[10] This was how the Egyptians and most ancient peoples did it, and how they did it on the counting board. The Egyptian number for 100 was 9, so 404 was written: | | | |9999. With alphabet numbers, it became possible for the first time to use written numbers to make computations, as cumbersome as they were to use from the modern perspective.

Alphabet numbers were clearly the origin of the present-day numerological practice of associating letters with numerical values, in particular Pythagorean and Kabalistic numerology. Initially, alphabet numbers were purely a mathematical development. Soon, however, the symbolism of numbers was extended to letters and to the words that are made up of letters. Number symbolism, like all spiritual symbol systems, tends to develop in two ways. In the first way, a symbol system slowly matures over time as the people of a culture work with it generation after generation. Gradually, the timeworn elements are refined and purified through the telling and retelling. A kind of organic process of elimination occurs through which essential truths of human nature and life are distilled out in pure, archetypal form. At some point, somehow, this worthy work comes to sanctify the symbol system, producing wisdom and spiritual knowledge of a sacred nature. In the second way, a gifted individual makes a contribution of such depth and meaning that the entire symbol system acquires a more profound vision.

Such an individual stepped forward in Greece in the sixth century before the Common Era: Pythagoras. He was a mathematician, a philosopher, a mystic, a teacher, and one of the best-educated men in history. He developed the Pythagorean theorem of geometry, still studied by schoolchildren today. He founded a mystery school that was renowned in its day. Also, today's most popular form of numerology, Pythagorean numerology, is named after him. However, as we shall see in due course, virtually none of Pythagoras' teachings and mathematical practices are part of Pythagorean numerology today. The only elements that could possibly be considered common to both are, first, the use of a base 10 numbering system, and, second, placing prime importance on the first ten numbers. For modern numerologists, it is just the first nine numbers. With so little to connect Pythagoras with the numerology named after him, it is tempting to conclude that his name was picked at random in order to honor a great historical figure!

Be that as it may, Pythagoras' monumental contribution was the concept that everything in life has a mathematical basis, ". . . a principle by which art, psychology, philosophy, ritual, mathematics, and even athletics were to be recognized as aspects of a single science of harmony."[11] Now, there were in the time of ancient Greece five branches of mathematics: arithmetic and geometry (which the Greeks considered the same), astronomy, music, and stereometry (the measure of volumes). The task of structuring philosophy with mathematical principles required a spiritual vision of high order, one that was capable of organizing the principles of life in terms of numbers. This would appear to be essentially the same dream that modern physicists have for a Unified Theory that combines all the basic forces of the universe into a single explanation.

The key element of Pythagorean number symbolism was no doubt the beloved Tetraktys (Figure 3). This was the arrangement of ten dots in the shape of a triangle with four dots at the base, then three, then two, and finally one at the top, all of which symbolized the creation of the universe. It was also known as the Principle of Health. It was based on the idea that there are ten principles, or universal laws, that cause and maintain the existence of everything that is. This is a thought to which the modern mind can relate, the concept that there is a small number of basic elements from which everything issues forth. It is also the long forgotten reason that numbers in Pythagorean numerology are routinely reduced to a single digit. Single digit numbers represent the most primal meanings of all Natural Numbers (whole numbers from 1 to infinity). To reduce 39 to a single digit, for example, add the 3 and 9 to produce 12, then add the 1 and 2 to obtain 3. Thus, we say that 39 reduces to 3.

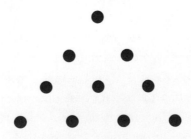

Figure 3. The Pythagorean Tetraktys.

The Tetraktys was actually made up of four key numbers that were responsible for all of creation: 1, 2, 3, and 4. One was Unity,[12] an indivisible unit called the Monad and the basis of all creation, represented geometrically by a dot. Two was the feminine (generative) principle, represented geometrically by a line. Three was the masculine (causative) principle, represented geometrically by a plane. Four was the measure of the universe, and it was represented geometrically by a cube. The Greeks saw profound connections between any two or more numbers and their sum total, as in the case of $1 + 2 + 3 + 4 = 10$. A curious aspect of numbers 1, 2, and 3 is that they were not considered to be numbers at all but instead principles or basic laws of the universe. Numbers were tangible, manifested things, and they began with 4. This was especially so for the 1 because of its unique role as the number from which all other numbers derive. The tradition of this belief was so strong that in 1585, a full two thousand years after Pythagoras, mathematician Michael Stevin devised a formal proof to establish that 1 is a number!

The sacred meaning of the Tetraktys was further deepened because the ten dots formed a triangle, and the Greeks called such numbers *triangular numbers*. Other triangular numbers were 3, 6, 15, and so on (Figure 4). They also esteemed *square numbers*, based on certain numbers of dots that form square shapes. Some square numbers are 4, 9, 16, and so on (Figure 5). Geometry was seen as a revelation from God, and any relationship they could establish between numbers and geometric figures demonstrated something of the sacred, as well as defined the underlying structures of life. The Pythagoreans believed everything to be physical. Even thoughts, feelings, and concepts like justice were considered to be physical to some degree. This may not be as silly as it first appears. Consider, for example, that today we have

Figure 4. Triangular Numbers 3, 6, and 15.

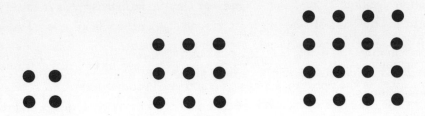

Figure 5. Square Numbers 4, 9, and 16.

instruments that can measure and record thoughts as electronic emissions from the brain. So, while we would not think of thoughts as physical to the same extent as, say, rocks and trees, we just might agree with the ancient Greeks that it is a matter of degree.

Nothing in the Greek cosmogony was abstract. For them, *everything* that existed, either physically or in their minds, was considered to be literally composed of Monads, also known as 1's or geometric dots. Pythagoras' famous dictum "All is number" did not have quite the meaning we attribute to it now. Today, from the perspective of physics, our understanding is that mathematical relationships explain the structure of physical reality. Modern number symbolists share the same understanding but from another point of view—they believe numbers express the nature of spiritual principles. Pythagoras, on the other hand, meant simply that any given thing or event is made up of a certain number of Monads. Everything was a number. Literally.

The ultimate goal of Pythagoras' number symbolism was harmony, unlike today, when the purpose is generally for psychological understanding, spiritual insight, or prediction. The Greeks did not emphasize the meanings of individual numbers as we do today. Harmony between numbers was established through addition, multiplication, and division, and this is what they worked so hard to understand. Some examples of their principles of harmony include:

Abundant numbers: These are numbers whose divisors total more than the number itself. Twelve is an abundant number because 1, 2, 3, 4, and 6, its divisors, add up to 16 (four more than 12).

Deficient numbers: These are numbers whose divisors add up to less than the number itself. Ten is a deficient number because its divisors, 1, 2, and 5, only total 8 (two less than 10).

Perfect numbers: These are numbers whose divisors exactly equal the number itself. Six is a perfect number because 1, 2, and 3, the numbers that divide evenly into 6, also total 6.

Amicable numbers: These are two different numbers whose divisors, when added, equal the other number. The numbers 220 and 284 are amicable because the eleven numbers that divide evenly into 220 add up to 284, and the five numbers that divide evenly into 284 total 220.

Evenly-even, oddly-odd, and evenly-odd numbers: These are numbers generated by the multiplication of even (feminine) and odd (masculine) numbers. Thus, 2 x 2 makes 4, an evenly-even number because both multipliers are even numbers. Ten is an evenly-odd number because it is the result of multiplying 2 (an even number) times 5 (an odd number). When two odd numbers like 5 and 7 are multiplied, this makes the result—35—an oddly-odd number.

This very brief examination of Pythagoras' ideas gives some insight into the origins of modern number symbolism. I have not made a thorough effort to interpret these ancient concepts for modern understanding or to evaluate the system as a whole. That would require a book in itself. My purpose here is to acquaint the reader with the little known origins of number symbolism, and to give a feel for the process that has produced modern mathematics and today's symbolic use of numbers. These are gifts from the ancients that enable us to be what we are today. It would be a mistake to take apart these Greek ideas point by point in order to bare their errors and inconsistencies, and there were many. It must be remembered that Pythagoras worked to develop a wisdom system. His wisdom cannot be evaluated on the basis of the mathematical methods he developed, or even our perception of his concepts. It is unlikely that anyone today understands Pythagoras' symbol system as a whole, or the spiritual wisdom he expressed mathematically. His methods were an attempt, and a very good attempt, to develop a system of numerical symbols. The fact that today we easily identify the flaws, limitations, and weaknesses of old mathematics does not diminish his achievement. It only shows how much we have to add to it.

Even during the era of Pythagoras, the time became ripe for change. It was apparent to some that certain elements of the philosophy did not add up.

> However far Pythagoras may have broken away from religion in the direction of pure science, it never became a dispassionate scientific study of the nature of number . . . but was always . . . on the lookout for symbolical significance. . . . The numerous symbolical meanings Pythagoreanism discovers are seldom . . . parts of any coherent system of rational thought.[13]

Major opposition to the ideas of Pythagoras first came from Parmenides, founder of the Eleatic School of Philosophy. This group included such Greek notables as Zeno, Empedocles, and Aristotle. Their fundamental disagreement concerned the nature of the number 1. If, they argued, 1 is Unity and indivisible, and if everything in the universe consists of some number of those basic building blocks (Monads), how could diversity (duality) come from that? It is akin to asking: if an artist uses only red to paint a picture, how is it possible to have the full spectrum of color? As a result of this line of reasoning, gravely serious in its day, 1 eventually came to be considered both odd and even, instead of being odd only. So then they thought, *Well, if 1 is both odd and even, it therefore has the capability of producing both odd and even numbers.* Unfortunately, this didn't work to resolve the issue either, because it made 1 dualistic, and Unity no longer had its single nature. With such a glaring inconsistency at the very foundation of Pythagorean ideas, it cast a long shadow of doubt over the rest.

Pythagoreanism thrived from about 550 B.C.E. to 400 B.C.E., when it was finally subsumed by the philosophy of Plato. Understanding of Greek number symbolism gradually dwindled over time and entirely disappeared somewhere around 500 C.E. The end came not so much because of the flawed system, but because ". . . the disciples of the great mystics hardly adhered to anything more than the single technique of combinations and permutations, without having the courage to follow the difficult way of rational mysticism."[14]

Considerable research and thought into this matter have persuaded me to believe that perhaps the fatal flaw in the Pythagorean system lay in the lack of the zero. Now, the zero, as will be established later in this book, is among other things the true number of origin. It is here that every manner of paradox, polarity, and the infinitely varied panorama of life spring forth undifferentiated. Moreover, the zero is abstract—a concept the Greeks did not have. Zero would have allowed 1 to be the first masculine number instead of 3, and 2 would have remained the first feminine number. Without zero, the Greeks had no choice but to combine the meanings of two numbers—the 0 and the 1—into the 1, causing 3 to be the masculine principle and the first masculine number. These contradictions were apparent even in the time of Pythagoras, although the reasons eluded them and the system did not hold up.

The centuries passed. In India, another numbering system began to develop around 200 B.C.E. By 600 C.E., a breakthrough occurred of the greatest significance for the world, producing the system of writing numbers we now use. It was the first truly abstract numbering system consisting of our present-day nine digits and zero. It used place-value as we do today, so that the same number—say, 3—could be 3, 30, 300, or 3000 simply by adding zeros to change its value. With the inclusion of zero as a number, virtually any number could be written and any computation calculated using just the ten single-digit numbers. It was this achievement in India that has made modern mathematics possible.

The Arabs picked up the new Indian numbers in the 700s. They had recently conquered all of North Africa and Spain right up to the Pyrenees Mountains just to the south of France. In the rest of Europe, the inhabitants continued to use Roman numerals, as they had done for a thousand years. The first introduction of Indian numbers into Europe came around 1000 C.E. A certain man named Gerbert, who was to become Pope Sylvester II, discovered the numbers that Arabs were using during his travels in Arab-held Spain. Unfortunately, Gerbert and the people associated with him had no knowledge of written computations. They did not understand the Indian system of writing numbers, and most especially the role the zero played. Gerbert's principal contribution to mathematics was the apices used on the

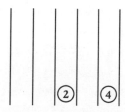

Figure 6. The number 204 represented on the counting board using Gerbert's apices.

counting boards. The apices were counters with the numbers carved or written on them. So, instead of having to use two counters for the number 2, for instance, it only required one counter with the number 2 written on it. There was no apice for zero, and the column was left empty, as before (see Figure 6).

Since the "foreign numbers" were not understood, they were not accepted at that time and Europe slumbered on for another two hundred years using Roman numerals and counting boards. The breakthrough came in 1202 C.E. with the publication of a book called *Liber Abaci: Book of Computations,* by the renowned mathematician Fibonacci, also known as Leonardo of Pisa. This book contained all the mathematical knowledge of the time. It was successful in introducing Arabic numbers to Europe because it showed how to use them to solve everyday problems. Nevertheless, it still required another three hundred years for these numbers to be fully used and accepted by Europeans. In France, even as late as the 1750s, Roman numerals were defended as the true numbers of the state. Europeans resisted the new system so doggedly because they found it very hard to grasp, especially the zero. How, they wondered, could there be a number for "nothing?" Further, if the zero had no value whatsoever, how could it and it alone multiply a number tenfold, a hundredfold, or a thousandfold simply by being placed to the right of that number? Impossible! Incomprehensible! Null as a name for zero first appeared in Italy in 1485. "It is the figure of nothing and thus no numeral, no figure at all, *nulla figura,* in Latin."[15] It was often looked on as a creation of the Devil. The great fear and confusion that surrounded the zero for centuries is most certainly the reason that number symbolism today, in particular Pythagorean numerology and Kabalistic numerology, does not include zero as one of the symbolic numbers. Further, alphabet numbers, which strongly influenced Pythagorean numerology and form the basis of Kabalistic numerology, have only positive, whole numbers.

In the centuries that followed the introduction of Fibonacci's arithmetic book, Europeans struggled with the use of Arabic numbers. During that period, there occurred some curious mixes of Arabic numbers and Roman numerals, such as: CC2 (for 202, with C equaling 100 in Roman numerals); 15X5 (meaning 1515, since X is 10 in Roman numerals); and 1·5·|||| (signifying 1504, written with the Roman numeral for 1 repeated four times).[16] In Florence, Italy, it was made illegal in 1229 to use Arabic numbers since Roman numerals couldn't be falsified. Many people felt reassured if they verified Arabic calculations by finger counting. Ultimately, it was merchants and the new use of paper that brought acceptance of Arabic numbers beginning around 1500. The increased need for record keeping combined with the greater efficiency of Arabic numbers forced the change.

Thus, approximately five hundred years ago, the stage was finally set for modern mathematics. Algebra had been invented in the early ninth century by Al-Khowarizmi, an Islamic philosopher in Persia. In the early seventeenth century, some eight hundred years later, René Descartes and Pierre de Fermat presented the concepts of analytic geometry. Soon after, differential calculus was developed, giving mathematical expression for the first time to the concept of the infinite. Statistics and probability theory evolved in the 1700s, followed by thermodynamics toward the end of the 1800s. . . . Mathematics had taken off.

Unfortunately, the same could not be said for number symbolism. For many centuries, the rapidly growing Christian Church had been working to eradicate non-Christian beliefs using methods that were extensive, extreme, and brutal. "As early as 300 A.D., the church officially declared that any opposition to its creed in favor of others must be punished by the death penalty."[17] The church sought energetically to eliminate its competition, the great myths and wisdom systems of the past, including number symbolism and virtually anyone, saint or sinner, who would stand against the church or who was perceived to do so.

Throughout much of this millennium, these kinds of efforts continued unabated. "The study of medicine was forbidden, on the ground that all diseases were caused by demons and could be cured only by exorcism."[18]

The devastating ignorance and superstition of the Dark Ages in Europe was caused at least partially because "Christians said one of the diabolic symptoms of the oncoming end of the world was the 'spread of knowledge,' which they endeavored to check with wholesale book-burnings, destruction of libraries and schools, and opposition to education for laymen."[19]

In the early seventeenth century, the scientific revolution became established and fired the imagination of the world. This was the era of Galileo Galilei and Isaac Newton, and the beginning of that period of rational thinking and optimism known as the Age of Enlightenment. Its special emphasis was the experimental method of science. In this atmosphere, number symbolism and many other forms of what might be called prescientific systems of knowledge were discredited and largely abandoned. Spirituality and wisdom were no longer values of prime importance in a world increasingly enthralled by the astounding discoveries of science and sobered by the necessity to establish proofs through carefully designed experimentation.

The tradition of number symbolism continued to persist despite persecution from the Christian Church and outright dismissal by a world that had turned its interest and attention to science. In the early 1500s, the mystic Heinrich Cornelius Agrippa invented the system of numbering the alphabets of Germanic and Romance languages according to the position and order of the letters. This is the basis on which Pythagorean numerology today functions. The great innovation of Pythagorean numerology has been the development of reducing numbers to single digits as a complete technique of numerological analysis. The term numerology, which today is used as a general reference to the entire field of number symbolism, was first coined in the late 1890s, just a little over a hundred years ago. Since then, considerable work has been done to expand and deepen the concepts and interpretations of Pythagorean numerology. However, mathematical structure, which is the real basis of the art, has for a good many centuries been dormant and inoperative in number symbolism. This has served to limit Pythagorean numerology to the most rudimentary level.

So the great mythic baton had passed from the pagan gnosis to science and mathematics. The industrial revolution, which began in England around 1760, fully matured in the course of the pragmatic, industrious 1800s. Concurrent with it, all areas of science and mathematics expanded prolifically. In the space of little more than a century, the world had shifted from an agrarian culture deeply attuned to the dynamics and cycles of nature to a mechanistic and technological society looking to science and mathematics to discover the objective truth about life and about reality. As the nineteenth century confidently drew to a close, there seemed no limit to what science and mathematics could accomplish.

Then, in the opening years of the twentieth century, a revolution of mind took place, a stunning intellectual awakening occurred; it was a transformation of perception so profound it changed everything . . . and still is changing everything.

In mathematics, that evolution of thinking is called nonlinearity.

Endnotes

1. Ernest G. McClain, *Myth of Invariance* (York Beach, Maine: Nicholas-Hays, Inc., 1984), 85.

2. Dion Fortune, *Sane Occultism* (London: Inner Light Publishing Company, 1938), 25.

3. Karl Meninger, *Number Words and Number Symbols: A Cultural History of Numbers* (Cambridge, Mass.: The M.I.T. Press, 1970), 35.

4. Ibid., 12.

5. Ibid., 16.

6. Ibid., 134.

7. Murry Hope, *The Sirius Connection* (Rockport, Maine: Element Books, 1996), 19.

8. *The I Ching or Book of Changes;* translated from the Chinese to the German by Richard Wilhelm; rendered into English by Cary F. Baynes (Princeton, N.J.: Princeton University Press, 1971), 71.

9. Ibid., 72.

10. Meninger, *Number Words and Number Symbols: A Cultural History of Numbers,* 400

11. Joseph Campbell, *The Masks of God* (New York: Penguin Books, 1976), 185.

12. Unity did not have the modern meaning of the seamless oneness and connectedness of all that makes up the universe. It referred rather to the universal primal unit, always the same, from which everything in the universe is made. In geometry, this was represented by the dot, from which all geometric forms are constructed.

13. J. E. Ravens, *Pythagoreans and Eleatics* (Chicago: Ares Publishers, 1966), 129.

14. Lucien Gérardin, *Le Mystère des Nombres* (St.-Jean-de-Braye, France: Editions Dangles, 1985), 190 (author's translation).

15. Meninger, *Number Words and Number Symbols: A Cultural History of Numbers,* 403.

16. Ibid., 30.

17. Barbara G. Walker, *The Woman's Encyclopedia of Myths and Secrets* (San Francisco: Harper and Row, 1983), 209.

18. Ibid., 210.

19. Ibid., 208.

chapter 2

The New Mathematical Thinking

Said of Carl Jung, Swiss psychologist, and Wolfgang Pauli, Nobel prize-winning physicist: If these men are correct, then physics is the study of the nature of consciousness.

—Gary Zukov, *The Dancing Wu Li Masters*

The twentieth century has witnessed the rise of a new mode of thinking that in previous centuries would have been labeled demented. The new perception was a non-rational way of seeing reality that emerged in the arts, the social sciences, and physics toward the beginning of the twentieth century. It took the form of concepts that went beyond common sense and logical reasoning, and ideas that made no sense to the mindset of the day. Even today, almost a hundred years later, many people still struggle to understand, or live their lives oblivious to, the new consciousness.

In psychology, the new concept was the idea of the unconscious. Today, acceptance of the subconscious mind is so commonplace in our civilization, it is difficult to imagine life without it. Yet when Sigmund Freud, the Austrian psychoanalyst, came up with the idea in 1893, it was a very bizarre thought: beyond everything we think and of which we are aware, an entire level of our being exists that is completely unknown to us. The unconscious represents the gut level of our being where instinct is king and two plus two does not necessarily equal four. Also, in 1913, Igor Stravinsky's symphony *The Sacred Rites of Spring* was first presented. He used harsh dissonances to express the awakening of spring from the long sleep of winter. These were strident and tuneless sounds that were irrational to ears accustomed to harmony and melody. Nowadays, when dissonances occur in music, we are far more prepared to appreciate them or even enjoy them than people living in the days preceding World War I.

In that same era, Spanish painter Pablo Picasso created the style of art known as *Cubism* that thrived between 1908 and 1914. Many of his paintings portray multiple perspectives of an object or diverse states of being of a person that in this reality cannot all be seen simultaneously. These kinds of "impossible" depictions defied conventional ways of seeing things or people one aspect at a time. Concurrent with Cubism, the Russian painter Vasily Kandinsky was developing a fully abstract art of ". . . forms moving in abstract spaces. . . ."[1] These were paintings inspired by some unknown reality or state of being that was unrelated to ordinary life and nature. Several decades later, the Surrealist painter Salvador Dali was painting subjects from the dream state or other reality. For example, *The Persistence of Memory,* painted in 1913, portrays clocks wilting in a dreamlike setting that is nonexistent in everyday life but accurately represents some realities described by physics!

Nowhere has this revolution in perception been more evident than in physics. Our fundamental understanding of life was completely reconceived in the twentieth century, and much of it proven scientifically. This new vision of reality is so totally different from the one that seems self-evident to our eyes and to our minds that it verges on being inconceivable to us. It began in 1905 when Albert Einstein formulated his Special Theory of Relativity, and continued in 1915 with his General Theory of Relativity. From these two watershed events has come the startling idea that space and time are connected elements of one thing: space-time. They go together, so if you have space you also have time. Space and time are so inseparably linked that if the state of one is changed, the other is changed also. This is in fact exactly what happens when the speed of an object is increased. As the speed increases, time slows and physical size diminishes. Although the greatest changes occur at speeds far beyond present human capability, physicists have nevertheless been able to prove this with speeds available to us. One way to understand this concept is to think of twins who are separated, one staying on earth, the other traveling through space at a speed close to that of light. After a few years, the traveling twin would return to find that hundreds of years had elapsed on earth! In different parts of the universe, space-time exhibits different conditions. In the most extreme cases—the so-called black holes—space and time do not even exist, as we know them. In fact, what we call the laws of nature do not apply there at all. Throughout the rest of the universe, space-time is a continuum much like a fabric that may be twisted, convoluted, bent, or otherwise altered. It is not the smooth and uninterrupted continuity it was once thought to be. Now it appears that objects like the sun and moon are concentrations of space-time, a state somewhat analogous to vaporous steam that congeals into ice under certain conditions. Gravity, rather than being a force of attraction between objects, seems to be a distortion of space-time, a distortion caused by matter.

This initial glimpse into the realm of physics clearly demonstrates the dramatic break with scientific thinking prior to the twentieth century. As we near completion of this briefest of mathematical histories, our purpose is twofold. It is first to see how mathematics, physics, and number symbolism all speak in the language of numbers. It is instructive to know the common history of the several dialects. Second, physics is reaching profound conclusions about the nature of reality that, in some cases, are nearly identical to beliefs mystics have been propounding for millennia. Like physics, I believe it is possible to discover spiritual principles in the concepts of number symbolism. This will be no easy task. The science of physics has been strongly in development since the work of Isaac Newton in the late 1600s. Since then, dozens of geniuses have gradually evolved physics to its current level of knowledge. I further believe it is possible to discern spiritual principles in the formulas and theories of physics by interpreting them according to the concepts of number symbolism. Full development of this knowledge is a process that will not be completed by any one individual or any single generation. The contributions of many will be required. This book proposes that such an effort is valid and worthy of the undertaking.

If the reader will allow for some speculative thinking, I will illustrate the potential of physics for spiritual insight by interpreting a formula of physics familiar to nearly everyone and understood by nearly no one: Einstein's $E = mc^2$. This formula expresses the idea that mass (meaning "matter") and energy are different states of the same thing. They are related. The formula spells out the relationship between energy and matter specifically. It says: energy is equivalent to mass that is multiplied by the speed of light squared. Fortunately, in order to understand this concept in terms of number symbolism, it is not necessary to grasp the mathematical concept of the formula. What is necessary is to relate this concept of physics to certain mechanics of living. Let us begin with E, which represents energy. In physics, this is a force and is measured by its capacity to do work. The nature of energy is opposite from the nature of matter in that it has no structured material form. In order to understand what "energy" is in terms of number symbolism, the question we must ask is: what do we call that part of our Being that is exclusively energy? In my estimation, this would be our life force, our spirit, or our soul that animates our physical form. Release from physical form usually comes about as a result of physical death. It can also occur (and this is my conjecture) as a result of applying Higher Knowledge, and that is precisely what this formula appears to be describing!

On the other side of the equal sign we find m, which represents mass. In physics, mass is the physical matter of an object. But to what could "mass" correspond on the spiritual level? In number symbolism, mass would be our physical body, which is, after all, the form that our Spirit Being assumes during its life on earth. So, what we have so far in our discussion is a formulary statement that the soul and the incarnation of the soul are in a certain way related. But how? In Einstein's formula, that relationship is established by multiplying the mass by c^2, the speed of light squared. In number symbolism, I am speculating, this explains exactly what our Being must do in order to go from one state to the other. In other words, this formula appears to explain how to pass into and out of the body!

Most people have opinions of some sort about the body and the soul. The only complication in this matter is the role that c^2 plays. What could the speed of light have to do with passage in one direction or the other? It is common knowledge that the speed of light is a constant 186,000 miles per second. Right off the bat we know we are in trouble with this part of the formula because of the supreme difficulty we have in imagining a photon of light moving that many hundreds of thousands of miles in a single second. That is about 6½ times around the earth in a heartbeat! In number symbolism, large numbers equate to deep meanings, which in this case is almost more than we can grasp. The speed of light squared is an exceedingly large number: 15,996,000,000. As I explain later, the more digits a number contains, the more profound the human experience it represents. As a number in the tens of billions, c^2 refers to a state of spiritual purification in which the self is liberated from the Wheel of Karma. The dual dilemma of fear and desire is resolved. So, in order to activate Einstein's formula on the spiritual level, it is necessary to apply an absolutely pure spiritual intent to one's life. The numbers that are present in 15,996,000,000 indicate the specific form that this pure spiritual intent must take.

A final word about the spiritual import of Einstein's famous formula. Although its meaning in number symbolism has been explained, no part of it has been interpreted into personal meaning. Until each and every part of the formula is fully understood in personal terms, it remains powerless to transform our lives. Everyone is familiar with the "personal meaning" of a variety of common life experiences such as happiness, fear, curiosity, hatred, the pleasure of beauty, and so on. But what exactly is the psycho-spiritual experience being symbolized by the speed of light squared? How might a person set out to apply an absolutely pure spiritual intent to his life? Until we know *that* to the same degree we know the taste of chocolate, we are like a person who has the combination to unlock a padlock, but not the ability to turn the knob and open the lock.

Later in this book we will discuss how to interpret numbers for personal meaning, an often-overlooked aspect of the study of number symbolism. For now, let us return to our synopsis of modern physics and explore some of the astonishing conclusions that physics has reached about the nature of matter. Quantum physics is the branch of physics that investigates the very smallest particles that make up matter, the so-called subatomic particles, or quanta. Quanta are the very tiny packets of energy that constitute atoms. In your average atom, the part that consists of quanta amounts to a mere one quadrillionth of the atom's total size. The rest is empty space. Nothingness. The void. This means that the book you now hold before you actually consists of almost no "matter" at all. You are holding a whole lot of nothing! This means that if your car were ingeniously designed to start one time every quadrillion tries, and if, out of understandable desperation, you tried once every second to start it until the motor turned over, it would take you over thirty million years!

As small as atoms are, subatomic particles are considerably tinier. Over 140 such particles have been identified. A key element in their study is the nature of light, because space (which includes matter) and time become totally transformed when the speed of light is reached. Since 1803 and the work of Thomas Young, it had been believed that light was composed of waves, meaning waves of energy that somewhat resemble waves in the ocean. However, this concept was confounded in 1900 when Max Planck, the founder of quantum physics, proved that light was instead composed of small packets of energy, not waves, which he called quanta. The result of this discovery produced a paradox that physicists to this day have not been able to understand. It is that light exists in both states—waves and particles—but never at the same time. Thus, if photons are being examined in their particle state, they cannot at the same time exist in wave-form, and vice versa. No one yet understands how light can exist in two mutually exclusive forms.

In 1905, Albert Einstein then expanded this line of thinking by proving that not only light exists in quanta, but energy of all types exists in the form of quanta, and these quanta consist of certain patterns of energy. Energy, as well as its nature and make-up, is vital to the understanding of matter, because atoms, once believed to be composed exclusively of solid particles, are now thought to be composed exclusively of energy. This was the theory put forth by Erwin Schrödinger, who believed that instead of being solid particles, protons and electrons and neutrons are comprised of what he called "standing waves" of energy. In other words, in the vastness of atomic and subatomic space, the rare bit of matter is in reality a piece of energy with structure. So the book you are holding in your hands, and your hands, too, are entirely space peppered with the tiniest imaginable fragments of energy; in other words, matter. But *what* matter?

As physicists continued to explore the nature of subatomic particles, they were in for another surprise: subatomic particles are changed when a human being observes them. We cannot avoid this: to observe them is to alter them. A jolting example of this concerns physicists' observations that there can exist two particles, and when they are subjected to human observation, one of the particles literally disappears. Where does it go? Scientists do not know. Now let's allow ourselves to be jolted a second time, this time by the behavior of photons. To simplify this illustration, imagine that you are observing a single photon of light that could travel to you along two different paths. "If you sit quietly waiting for the photon to arrive and only see it when it does arrive, the particle travels along both paths. I know this is impossible, but we're speaking in quantum terms."[2] That is an account of light traveling when a person does not observe it. But if you decide to observe this photon as it goes on its way in order to see the routes it took, "This creates an entirely different quantum situation. It means that the particles must . . . go down one path or the other. So, as soon as you decide to observe the particle, it only moves along one path."[3]

To the physicist working in the field or laboratory, the above conclusions are but straightforward facts about physical reality. Most physicists, in fact, would vehemently resist the suggestion that any of their findings have philosophical or mystical implications. Yet to anyone familiar with metaphysical teachings, it is quite evident that the concepts of subatomic particles discussed previously closely resemble meta-physical concepts. At the heart of wisdom traditions everywhere is the idea that the world is illusion, that what we perceive with our senses is not in fact real. In physics, the conclusion that only one quadrillionth of space contains matter would seem to be the same idea. Although the world (and everything in it) gives every appearance of being solid as a rock, physicists have proven that solid matter as such does not even exist because the subatomic world consists of nothing but energy patterns; and that those energy patterns are changed when human beings think about them. This, too, appears to confirm the spiritual teaching that we can create our reality by con-trolling or influencing primal energy. It would seem that the main difference between "subatomic particles" and "primal energy" (a metaphysical term) is one of semantics. They are different terms that refer to the same thing. If this is true, as I believe it is, then physics is setting forth the precise mechanics of spiritual principles one after another.

As we continue the discussion of subatomic particles, the case for metaphysical interpretation of physics becomes increasingly compelling. The notion that human observation invariably changes subatomic reality is a troubling one for the physi-cists. This quite naturally suggests that we humans create our own reality, which is a key concept in metaphysics. The spiritual premise is that each individual has a spark of the divine within whose prerogative it is to create the life and the reality it desires. Yet very few physicists indeed want this to be true: the science as a whole seeks objective truth, not the messy alternative that necessarily brings in elements of psychology, spirituality, the purpose and meaning of our lives, and other intangi-bles that lie outside the capabilities of scientific experimentation. For these kinds of reasons, physicists work around (sometimes *way* around) the creative impact humans have on subatomic particles. It is surprising that a physicist somewhere has not postulated the existence of *mental quanta* as the mechanism by which we humans alter reality. Mental quanta would be some type of hitherto unknown energy emitted from our minds that interacts with quanta we observe. The instance of a light photon traveling both paths until a human observer induces it to follow one path or the other is an indication of tremendous creative potency. As things stand now in physics, the effect of human observation is simply noted as a result of the experimentation process, no conclusions drawn and no meanings deduced. In metaphysics, however, its importance cannot be overlooked. Perhaps the fact that the unobserved photon that we have been discussing travels both paths simultaneously is a demonstration of the deeply held mystic belief that "all things are possible." Mystics also believe that when the observer causes the photon to follow one particular path, this is a choice on the part of the observer—a *choice*, a *creative act*, not merely an objective event that somehow accompanies human participation.

As we continue our discussion of subatomic particles, it will become increasingly clear how all this is a plausible interpretation of physics. Subatomic particles, or quanta, are the most fundamental level of physical reality to which physicists have penetrated to date. As previously stated, subatomic particles actually consist of energy patterns having a certain size and structure. Yet, they are even less substantial than size and structure suggest. Instead of being definitively formed, physicists describe a subatomic particle as being an *idea*. They are not firmly set, structured patterns of energy, but literally just tendencies. In 1924, Neils Bohr and two colleagues described subatomic particles as "probability waves." Probability waves ". . . referred to what somehow was already happening, but had not yet been actualized. It referred to a *tendency* to happen, a tendency that in an undefined way existed of itself, even if it never became an event. Probability waves were mathematical catalogues of these tendencies."[4] Concepts of physics can be very hard to grasp for those not accustomed to working with them. So consider that a metaphor for "tendency to happen" is a seed stirring to growth in the springtime. The seed represents a subatomic particle. As the weather warms, the seed is *likely* to sprout a plant. But not every seed succeeds in germinating. Therefore, we can say it is *probable* a plant will grow, but it is not a certainty.

In our daily lives, we do not view the things of earth in this speculative manner. The house, the car, the family, and the pets will be tomorrow much as they are today barring sudden, unexpected events. But if the family car fender were unexpectedly dented in the mall parking lot, it would be highly unrealistic to consider it a "probability dent" that will have a tendency to be there tomorrow, but which, on the other hand, may not be there after all. In today's world, it is axiomatic that if the dent is there now, it is going to be there tomorrow as well. On a subatomic level, however, the certainty of form is replaced by a tenuous, ethereal reality of possibilities, perhapses, and maybes.

This is a paradox, and a confusing one at that. What our senses tell us about physical matter is an interpretation of the stimuli that is not at all like what science has proven that stimuli to be. We are quite literally making something out of nothing. As incomprehensible as this thought is, it is possible at least to relate to this idea by comparing it to clouds. When we gaze up at clouds in the sky they appear to be large puffy forms. From afar, a given cloud has a clear, distinctive shape. As we near the cloud, however, its contours dissolve away altogether. Suddenly there is only mist, or, to be more accurate, *degrees* of mist. In the immediate vicinity, clear air indistinguishably hazes, thicker here, thinner there, present in some measure even in the "clear" air. It is all a matter of perception. *Mist* is the reality, like the empty vastness of subatomic space. *Cloud* is the interpretation we make of it, like our physical reality to which we are so well accustomed.

The conclusion we can draw from all this is that matter—the house, the car, and so on—is not permanent and immutable after all. It is not real. This is also the metaphysical view and the rationale of ritual and prayer, and the basis on which magic is worked.

Some physicists have further suggested that subatomic particles may have consciousness and the ability to make decisions. This is due to experiments in which photons are sent through a screen, first one at a time with two slits in the screen through which the photon can pass, then one at a time with only one slit in the screen. Different patterns of light are produced, depending on whether light is going through one or two slits. But, even though a single photon is being emitted at a time, it seems to know whether it is forming a pattern on the basis of one slit or two. How can a photon know this unless it has some sort of conscious, decision-making capacity?

Results of experiments also demonstrate that information can be transmitted instantaneously between particles no matter how great the distance between them, even a distance of light years. This was the conclusion in 1935, when Albert Einstein, in collaboration with Nathan Rosen and Boris Podolsky, worked with what is called a "twin particle system with no spin."[5] Almost all subatomic particles have a certain spin associated with them. It is one of their defining characteristics. Twin particles are two distinct particles that somehow exist with each other as a single unit. Each particle has a spin of its own, but over all there is no spin because the two spins together cancel themselves out. What Einstein and company did was to separate the twins, then change the spin of one of the particles. Startlingly, ". . . when you change the spin of one particle, the spin of the other changes instantaneously.

This happens however far you separate them. For the second particle to change at all, there must be an information exchange between them."[6] And this exchange of information occurs at rates faster than the speed of light or *any* speed—it is immediate. These kinds of considerations induced Gary Zukov to write: "We have little choice but to acknowledge that photons, which are energy, do appear to process information and to act accordingly, and that therefore, strange as it may sound, they seem to be organic."[7] In other words, photons may be alive!

Here again, a fundamental concept of physics coincides with a basic tenet of metaphysics: that all things of the physical plane have consciousness and life. The first lines of a poem by David Cloutier sum up this mystic perspective:

> Everything that is
> is alive.[8]

This includes all those things in our world that are generally thought of as being completely without life: stone, metal, wind, fire, water, and so on. Given sufficient spiritual evolvement, it is believed to be possible not only to see this living presence, but also to communicate with it and to even influence its behavior. Carlos Castaneda, the popular metaphysical writer, expresses the same idea from a different perspective by writing ". . . that in the universe there is an unmeasurable, indescribable force which sorcerers call *intent*, and that absolutely everything that exists in the entire cosmos is attached to intent by a connecting link."[9] Intent, like purpose, is a characteristic only of living beings that have consciousness and make decisions.

It would appear, then, that at the very basis of matter are conscious and organic subatomic particles making decisions. They are more substantial than a thought, but not yet fully in a "material" state, and when human beings observe them, they are changed. If this were the full extent of the theory of physics, we could state with confidence that human beings have a definite role in creating matter. But there is more, and this is the most bizarre part.

Physics experiments are set up in the "region of preparation," where the actual physical event is to take place, the one that physicists are interested in researching. The "region of measurement" is the means devised by physicists to assess the experiment. The "observed system" is the actual event they are attempting to understand.

. . . what happens to the observed system between the region of preparation and the region of measurement is expressed mathematically as a correlation between two observables (production and detection). Yet we know that the observed system is a particle. Said another way, a photon is a *relationship* between two observables . . . elementary particles don't have an existence of their own.[10]

This is because:

> Things are not "correlated" in nature. In nature, things are as they are. Period. "Correlation" is a concept that we perceive. There is no "correlation" apart from people. This is because only people use words and concepts.
>
> "Correlations" is a concept. Subatomic particles are correlations. If we weren't here to make them, there wouldn't be any concepts, including the concept of correlation. In short, if we weren't here, there wouldn't be any particles.[11]

Since it is subatomic particles that make physical reality what it is, that, too—the very world we live in—would not be here if we were not here to conceive of it!

This seeming contradiction is similar to the age-old question: if a tree fell in the forest and there were no one there to hear it, would there still be the sound of the falling tree? The answer is: no . . . there would be no sound because "sound" is an interpretation, or experience, the brain produces when certain types of stimuli impact the eardrum. Without the presence of a person to hear sound, the dynamics caused by the tree crashing to the ground remain nothing but vibrations of various types. Sound is a human and animal perception, not something inherently existing in nature.

It is highly significant to our discussion that subatomic particles equate to concepts. Subatomic particles are not, of course, the only concepts to be found in physics. Our entire system of mathematics, which physicists use exclusively to know and describe the subatomic realm, consists of a vast and complex system of concepts. Beyond the concept of the numbers themselves, there are the laws of mathematics and all the formulas and theorems. Concepts and symbols are nearly identical in function. Following is the definition of concept given in Webster's Dictionary: "an idea of something formed by mentally combining all its characteristics or particulars."[12] The same dictionary defines "symbol" as "something used for or regarded as representing something else."[13] Symbols are concepts of that to which they refer; and concepts symbolize, or represent, that to which they refer. The difference between the two terms is a subtle distinction. Concepts are generally considered objective ideas put together with conscious intent, whereas symbols tend to be thought of as subjective ideas concerned with philosophical or spiritual meaning. However, it is not so generally realized that true spiritual symbols are concepts that are scrupulously created with what may best be described as scientific precision. It should, then, be entirely accurate to say that the concepts of physics, and in fact physics itself, are symbols of reality. While science and mathematics are usually enshrined in an aura of objectivity untainted by attitudes of "what they mean," nonetheless, what could have more meaning than the nature of physical reality?

This is an important point in our discussion. It consists of both physics and mathematics symbol systems and thereby places them on an equal footing with a wide variety of spiritual symbol systems whose purview is the Truth of Life. These include the great mythologies of the ancient world, the major religions, and the profound spiritual sciences of mystery schools. For the past four hundred years or so, science, physics, and mathematics have established themselves as perhaps the dominant symbol systems of this age that deal with reality. As symbol systems go, however, science is young and still very much in the initial stages of development; but despite its youthfulness, science has engaged the imagination of humankind. It has generated breathtaking ideas and theories and profoundly stimulated the creativity of geniuses. It has gifted humankind with a vast assortment of nearly miraculous inventions and technologies.

Yet for all its undisputed greatness, science lacks one fundamental element common to all other venerable symbol systems that have matured and persisted through time. That is the element of *meaning*,[14] without which science can never speak to the human spirit. Therefore, science is, as an interpreter of reality, an incomplete symbol system at the present time.

Endnotes

1. Joseph Loffan Morse, Editor in Chief, *Funk and Wagnals Standard Reference Encyclopedia* (New York: Funk and Wagnals, 1962), vol. 1, 120.

2. J. H. Brennan, *Time Travel: A New Perspective* (St. Paul, Minn.: Llewellyn Publications, 1997), 160.

3. Ibid., 161.

4. Gary Zukov, *The Dancing Wu Li Masters* (New York: Bantam Books, 1986), 66.

5. Brennan, *Time Travel: A New Perspective*, 158.

6. Ibid., 159.

7. Zukov, *The Dancing Wu Li Masters*, 63–4.

8. The poem "Things a Shaman Sees" is quoted in its entirety on pages 55–6 in *The Way of the Shaman,* by Michael Horner (San Francisco, Calif.: Harper and Row, Publishers, 1980).

9. Carlos Castaneda, *The Power of Silence: Further Lessons from Don Juan* (New York: Pocket Books, 1987), xii.

10. Zukov, *The Dancing Wu Li Masters*, 70.

11. Ibid., 71.

12. *Webster's Encyclopedic Unabridged Dictionary of the English Language* (New York: Gramercy Press, 1994), 304.

13. Ibid., 1440.

14. By use of the single word "meaning," I refer to and include the following: purpose, truth, ethics, morality, spirituality, character, metaphysics, conscience, values, beliefs, heart and soul, and the true origin and nature of human beings.

chapter 3

The Eternal Quest

We can never really understand something until we can create a model or metaphor derived from our unique personal world.

—Eric Jensen, *Brain-Based Learning and Teaching*

We live immersed in a sea of symbols. They are far more pervasive and fundamental to our lives than is generally recognized. This is why it is important in our examination of mathematical symbolism to take a look at the nature of symbols and how they work. We tend to think of symbols in rather formal terms, as special objects or pictographs with potent meanings. Certain spiritual and religious symbols come quickly to mind as examples, such as the *yin yang* symbol, the *Star of David*, the *AUM*, the *Cross*, *rosary beads*, and *tarot cards*. Symbologists, scholars who make a study of the nature of symbols, go further and identify five broad categories: language, science, art, myth, and religion, to which I add culture. Again, given these six classifications, it is easy to name a wide variety of symbols, from *light* and *dark* (symbols of good and evil), to *advertising icons* (symbols of products and culture), to *computer icons* (symbols of computer functions), to *wine* (symbol of fine dining), to *iron* (symbol of a long period of human development), to *Wall Street* (symbol of financial power), to the *dove* (symbol of peace). Innumerable additional examples could be cited.

These kinds of symbols are what might be called *conscious symbols*. When they are used, there is always some degree of awareness that a mundane object is being utilized as a vehicle to express a meaning unrelated to it. The added significance is not a natural attribute of the object itself; instead, meaning is a value artificially grafted onto the symbol-vehicle through a complex process of development. Light and dark, for example, are neither good nor evil; they are degrees of luminescence, that's all. When we speak of light as a symbol of good, there is generally a self-conscious mindfulness that we are "using light" for symbolic purposes. We know full well that there is no real or literal aspect of light whose essential nature is goodness. Nevertheless, light has become a way of expressing the quality of virtue that is natural, familiar, and widely accepted.

Conscious symbols are those that are formally designated as symbols. They constitute only a very small portion of all the symbols in our lives. The great preponderance of them are *unconscious symbols*. We do not even realize they are symbols because their meanings so thoroughly permeate the symbol-vehicles that they become one and the same. The "simple object" and its "meaning" are synonymous, so that the act of seeing or even thinking of the object is to experience the meaning. Words are a good example of this. We all know that written words are composed of letters (which are symbols of sounds) and that words are symbols of thoughts. Yet, when our eyes read words such as the ones on this page, we do so without any cognizance of the symbolic dynamics at work. Rather, as we physically read the printed letters and words, the letter-symbols per se are forgotten as our minds focus entirely on the meanings. We make instantaneous associations between the words and their significance—*Bam!* Word symbols are actually only partially unconscious because we can be reminded at any moment that words are symbols and, for a few moments while we are thinking about it, we are able to mentally disassemble the symbol from its meaning.

There are myriad symbols that are entirely unconscious. They are not even considered to be symbols by the world at large, or by those who specialize in their study. No one looking at the ordinary things of life—things like paper, grass, porch steps, cucumbers, a bowl of water, a cloud—would say they are symbols of anything. *They just are.* Paper, most people would say, is only paper and grass only grass. What is not realized is that the things of daily life *are* the meanings, the symbolic representations. What is being symbolized is *reality*. We think we experience reality as we go through the days of our lives, but we do not. It is really our *interpretation* of reality that we experience. This is so because human beings do not see—indeed, we are not capable of seeing—Ultimate Reality. We exist within this limitation as best we can by creating ideas about life through our limited understanding. In other words, we put together our own version of reality, and this is what we understand

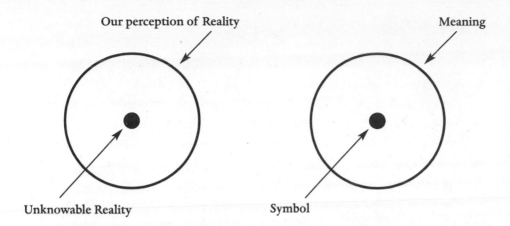

Figure 7. Our perception of Unknowable Reality is a limited knowing by which we live and understand life. This is functionally the same relationship as that between formally-designated symbols and the meanings attributed to them.

reality to be. Our world is a symbolic world (see Figure 7). It is a shock to gaze upon whatever is around you and realize that all of it, including the thoughts running through your head, is symbolic!

It is a metaphysical teaching that we humans do not see Ultimate Reality, although it is possible to do so if we undergo sufficient spiritual training. Subatomic physics also bears out the concept of an Unknowable Reality. At the subatomic level, the familiar physical universe is no more. Matter consists of immense expanses of space filled with rare bits of energy patterns. At that level, tiny fragments of firm matter do not exist. Physicists agree that we have no idea what this bizarre, subrealistic domain looks like. The best description of it is abstruse mathematical relationships. In other words, what physics teaches us is that physical reality is neither physical nor real.

I have used the term "meaning" many times to refer to the importance attributed to symbols. Meaning is not passive understanding or intellectual interest. Rather, meaning is potent, creative force. In some mysterious way, our conviction of what reality is actually brings that reality into being. This is the idea behind the spiritual principle that we humans create—literally create—our own reality. Somehow, Ultimate Reality allows us this leeway. This principle is supported, and even clarified, by physics. It is an established fact that when experiments in subatomic physics are observed by physicists, the simple act of observation changes the event from what would have happened had it not been observed in the first place. That act of observation is customarily viewed as an entirely passive one. It involves no interaction at all with what is being looked upon. Yet, mysteriously, it exerts a potent physical effect on the focus of attention. This is more than the power of consciousness. It is far greater than any will to achieve this or that goal. The generator of creation is an automatic reflex of our total nature—*who we are*. The creation occurs when we give *form* to the meanings inherent to our Beings. As those meanings reach their potential according to the Way of Things, they become so-called Objective Reality. It is through *observation,* then, that physicists add meaning to their experiments, thereby creating their version of reality, as we all do.

Let us take a look, now, at how all this works in practice using symbols of American national lore as examples. We have many symbols that signify America in one way or other: the Statue of Liberty, the flag, the eagle, Uncle Sam, the Declaration of Independence, the Boston Tea Party, democracy, the free enterprise system, baseball (the national pastime), Main Street U.S.A., the Vietnam era, the Civil Rights Act, the Alamo, leader of the free world, the Constitution, the Bill of Rights, the founding fathers, Pearl Harbor, D-Day, public education, small town America, American ingenuity, Hollywood, Thanksgiving Day, life in the suburbs, the Grand Canyon, Johnny Appleseed, and the Unknown Soldier, to name only some, in no particular order. Each of these national symbols contributes bit by significant bit to what it means to be an American.

The full complement of symbols that together make up America represent and define the American spirit. Not one of the symbols is by itself the spirit of America. At the same time, in touching on any one of them with heart and mind, we succeed in touching that intangible energy we call America. Without all the national symbols, without concrete concepts on which to focus and ground our thoughts, this "spirit of America" (the phrase itself is a national symbol) would exist only in fleeting, illusionary, and formless moments. It is only through those defining forms we call symbols that the mind is able to perceive and grasp (and hold on to!) what is otherwise elusive and unknowable.

This conglomerate group of national symbols that articulates the American spirit is one example of what is called a *symbol system.* A symbol system is an organized body of concepts that makes it possible to have a particular type of experience. Every symbol system consists of key components, and without all components, the experience is significantly modified or limited. This principle can be clearly seen in any number of technical symbol systems. In mathematics, removal of the number 4 from the system, or eliminating the process of addition, would be devastating. In music, the banishing of a key or whole notes would gravely impair the ability to create music as we know it. The principle is the same for cultural symbol systems, but also more difficult to perceive. This is so because they tend to compensate when parts are lost or gained, and then become whole again; and the same happens in nature. This process of restoration-after-change is routine in nature, and we know it by the name *evolution*. All types of symbol systems adapt to change, whether due to loss or gain, and the process is gradual indeed. It will be recalled from chapter 1 that centuries were required in Europe before the zero gained full acceptance, and for counting boards to be rendered obsolete and fall into disuse.

Only the symbol system as a whole—all the symbols that are part of it   can produce the experience it represents. In the case of the American experience, no single symbol, or sampling of national symbols, can replace or function as the whole of the system. Apple pie and Niagara Falls are important threads in the symbolic fabric of American life, but they are fragments of Americana only. In this manner we depend on all our national symbols to bring into solid focus our ineffable and ethereal national character. All together, they form a working model of the American spirit or character. This working model provides an encompassing context for our lives, establishing structure, and even endowing purpose, meaning, and values that are perhaps summed up in the symbolic concept of the American dream.

Each component of our symbolic landscape is so imbued with meaning that it can be difficult to segregate the plain object from its significance. That meaning, often deep and passionate, leaps to our conscious mind upon mere mention of, or mere sight of, the object or idea. In other words, the thing itself and the meaning we give to it become synonymous. The Statue of Liberty, for example, stripped of its cultural patina, is nothing more than a large, old-fashioned sculpture of a lady prominently situated on an island in New York Harbor. It is only metal molded out of the artist's imagination. Even the individual words—statue, of, liberty—when considered separately do not evoke anywhere near the depth of meaning that is immediately present upon hearing about or seeing the Statue of Liberty. It is as though the meaning entirely covers the physical statue, almost literally altering its appearance. It might even be said that our concept of the Statue of Liberty is everything while the actual object itself is meaningless by comparison, merely a triggering mechanism for a particular mental and emotional experience. Thus, the statue in the harbor is incidental to the wealth of meaning we associate with it.

The impact of overlaying everyday objects with symbolic meaning can be observed easily in symbolism of whose meaning we are entirely ignorant. If you have ever attended a meeting of a secret society, encountered an unknown inner city gang, or been to a sporting event with which you are not familiar, it becomes immediately apparent that a lot is happening and you understand nothing. Minor gestures, special body positions, key words, certain colors, particular designs, portentous pauses, the evoking of strange names, and a wide variety of apparently momentous moments—all these symbols, pregnant with intense meaning to informed participants, are virtually lost on the uninitiated. The colors, the gestures, and all the other elements of significance are perceived literally for what they are physically and many go unnoticed and uninterpreted, a dizzying succession of undifferentiated patterns viewed without understanding or appreciation.

Imagine an uninstructed foreigner sailing into New York Harbor for the first time, unfamiliar with nineteenth-century sculpture, long flowing robes, and American lore. . . . What would be his associations upon espying the Statue of Liberty? He would "see" through eyes accustomed to viewing another symbolic landscape. Perhaps he would think America honors her all-powerful queen or maybe a magnificent water goddess.

Symbols are extremely powerful elements of living. If they are touched on or violated in some way, they can be the source of enormous passion and conviction, strong opinion and unrestrained action.

> From the stream of human experience at any given moment, one can identify incidents or acts that manifest the fact of almost irrepressible power. For example: In Kashmir in late 1963, there was stolen from a Mohammedan mosque a relic of the prophet in the form of a single strand of hair. The incident caused a riot. More than 100,000 Muslims took part in it. Fires were set, shots were fired, and many died in the melee. What power to be channeled through a single, slender thread of hair![1]

Symbols are deep wells of meaning. They guide, inform, and form our attitudes and actions, often in conventional, ready-made ways. Symbols are themselves conventions of thought, general agreements throughout society of what certain concepts mean. When issues surrounding a particular symbol arise, reactions are generally of a predictable nature, almost as though they popped out of a mold. The freedom symbol is like that. It requires a great effort of mind and emotion in order to reach profound and insightful personal conclusions about freedom. It is far less trouble (and often the only practical course to take) simply to draw on accepted interpretations to use as one's own: "It's my life, I'll do as I please," "I have my rights," "You can't tell me what to do," "This is a free country," "I can say anything I want to," "Give me liberty or give me death."[2]

The freedom symbol makes the concept of freedom a known quantity, spells it out for us point by point. The comprehensive definition of this symbol is indispensable in helping us to sort through the complexities of a situation, enabling us to figure out the next move and decision to make.

Acting on a freedom issue is often seen as a defense of a standard American value, and the patriotic thing to do. To act in any other way is, as they say, un-American. But this is not strictly true, curiously enough. From an objective perspective, opposition to freedom is simply the other side of the coin. Every symbol has its reverse expression that is unique to it. When Americans stand up for freedom, it expresses our national character. When Americans abuse freedom (through suppression of certain groups or police excesses, for two examples) this also expresses our national character because both negative and positive use the same point of reference. It is another form of the metaphysical principle that states that "without evil, good cannot exist." We are speaking here of the dark side of American life. The truth is that disowning it, while at the same time idealizing the bright side, only acknowledges half of the symbol's activity. Both aspects are not only necessary to the proper functioning of a symbol but are literally a fact of nature. This is the teaching of the great Chinese yin yang symbol, which expresses not only the unity of good and evil, but also the seed-presence of each force in its opposite (see Figure 8). So that in the American symbol of freedom, even a heroic act in the defense of freedom (or an abject abuse of it) somehow contains the beginnings of the opposite behavior. Positive and negative are bound together tightly. It takes both for a symbol to be active. The act of standing up for freedom is not in and of itself "freedom." Repression of

Figure 8. The yin yang symbol.

freedom is not in and of itself "absence of freedom." Both are situational tensions. When they strain against each other—then and only then—there occurs that experience we call freedom.

This is an important point in symbol work. If a symbol is split against itself, if good and evil battle each other, then the symbol itself remains in perpetual turmoil, each part effectively consumed by the other without hope of resolution, like a dog endlessly spinning about in pursuit of its own tail. It is an approach of weakness. Such a divided symbol can never be a point of power. This is why "In the East, a virtuous person is therefore not one who undertakes the impossible task of striving for the good and eliminating evil, but rather one who is able to maintain a dynamic balance between good and bad." [3]

The battling of good against evil is a type of spiritual misperception. It is *maya,* as the Buddhists call it, meaning illusion, or what is not real. It is ignorance that lacks a clear, functional understanding of how life works. The consequence of it is disharmony. This is a tricky concept to grasp, for when "our good" is threatened by "our evil," our instinctive reaction is to eliminate the bad so we can get back to the good, the way we feel it should be.

This attitude is so ingrained in Western thinking, the point bears repeating: good and evil form an inseparable team. Just imagine any baseball or football game being played with one side only. There would *be* no game. The game requires both (opposing) teams. The study of a spiritual symbol system, such as number symbolism, develops correct spiritual perception over time. It is akin to a mental corrective lens through which the Real may be seen and experienced. Such perception is a finely honed skill that enables the practitioner to "use the images as a mathematician uses algebraic symbols."[4] It begins with learning a system of interrelated principles of reality on a purely abstract level on which ego—the lower self of desire and fear—has no participation. When the symbol system has been fully grasped by the mind, and when one is fluent with all the concepts and their diverse connections, then gradually applications of these learnings develop at other levels of one's life, at the levels now regarded as the "real" ones. It is a process of transformation of the deepest and most meaningful kind. "To acquire mystical knowledge means to undergo a transformation; one could even say that the knowledge *is* the transformation."[5]

As we live our lives day by day, symbols of America serve as landmarks of the national landscape as we negotiate our way through the vicissitudes of life. All of them together constitute a mental framework. In any situation, the relevant landmarks/symbols come into play. They represent established, timeworn values and standards. Our thoughts fly between them in a near instantaneous analysis and sorting out process as we try to figure out what to think and how to act. The symbols involved are givens—but *objective* givens—because they are shared understandings throughout society, not axioms of, or limited to, an individual. The way we interpret a situation and subsequently act is our own subjective approach. In this way, each of us makes a unique, individual statement of the American spirit. No two people can, or should, be expected to make exactly the same interpretation of symbols or their applications. There will be differences of every type. This is human nature.

Consider now the following three American symbols: military service; my country right or wrong; rugged individualism. The military, which is charged with the defense of the nation, is a very big symbol in America. It represents, among other things, strength and the willingness to stand up for who we are and what we believe. It relies on the ready compliance of those called to serve in it. The symbol "my country right or wrong" requires unquestioning compliance with whatever is asked of the individual. The symbol "rugged individualism" empowers each American to think and act on his own convictions without regard to the opinions or deeds of others. Now, every American knows about putting country first, as well as the opposing imperative to do as he sees fit. When called to military service, as could happen in a time of national crisis, many variables would come into play in addition to these two of obedience or noncompliance. There is a wide variety of interpretations possible. One approach, a fully American one, is to decide that no government shall have authority over the individual, and the rugged individualist therefore will not accept military service regardless of what authorities try to do to him. He may feel that those who conform to governmental authority fail to think for themselves or, worse, are incapable of making their own decisions. The majority of people who accept the need for military service will disagree strongly with the nonconformist's position, but in many cases will have respect for someone who follows his principles so strongly. Those with the attitude "my country right or wrong" will likely resent those who flaunt the law and even view them as traitors. Both of these symbols—the one you like and the one you do not like—are necessary for either one to exist.

No situation in life is ever limited to two simple, straightforward elements. With each symbol we add to our consideration of "military service or not," the process that leads to action greatly increases in complexity. There is so much more to think about when, for example, we add the symbol of *federal law,* which makes military service a legal requirement, the symbol of *conscientious objector,* which is a legal exemption, and finally the fear and pressure caused by the symbol of *the long arm of the law.* It would be possible to spend many pages discussing the ramifications of these symbols working and jostling amongst each other as they transpire in real life situations.

In symbol work, such "working and jostling" of symbols—the weighing and competing of factors in order to arrive at a conclusion and a course of action—is called *interpretation.* In all symbol work, it is the key skill because it is the quality of our interpretation that determines how well we navigate through the waters of life. Initially, it is an abstract process involving the comparison of mental constructs, or concepts. It works the same with any symbol system because all symbols are sculpted chunks of thought. With symbol systems like the American national lore, the sorting out process occurs in a flash, and subconsciously, for the most part. After all, these symbols have been an intimate part of our lives since the earliest moments of childhood. We know them thoroughly. Their use is virtually second nature and as automatic as awakening to the day.

This is not the case, however, with a symbol system learned as an adult. It must be thoroughly learned to do any good. The acquisition of fluency is profoundly personal and requires extensive reflection and practice in order to be able to recognize the many complex interactions. It is in the linking of connected ideas in the right way that the proper conclusions can be reached. Interpretation of a spiritual symbol system is a technical method of assessment requiring great understanding and wisdom. It involves a union of one's individuality with objective symbols that each person uses in order to function in life. The effectiveness of a symbol system, *any* symbol system, occurs because the group of symbols as a whole, when correctly used, empowers the individual to create certain experiences. There is widespread belief that the symbol itself—whether talisman, chalice, sacred rite, number symbol, astrological sign, and so on—is the source of power. But it is not: the power is in the meaning we give to the symbol. ". . . the initiated know that the material object is not employed to enable the power to come down, but to enable the mind . . . to go up along a particular line of consciousness."[6] In a symbol system, all the parts fit together in particular ways, each performing its appointed task like parts of the proverbial well-oiled machine. If any single part is removed, the engine sputters or fails entirely. Each symbol of a system has certain functions with regard to every other symbol in the system. If this is so, how do the symbols of "rugged individualism" and "my country right or wrong" connect with each other? They appear to be two extreme and mutually exclusive attitudes that seem only to be at odds with each other. Yet is it not so that every American who enters military service struggles with this same conflict in milder form? That back-and-forth tug shows the de facto connection of the two forces. Their resolution determines in part the individual's experience in the military, American style.

This same issue has repercussions on the level of society as a whole. If complete submission to military authority were not balanced out with an equally extreme form of individual autonomy, America would be quite a different place. We would be a passive and conformist people. On the other hand, we might not even have a nation if there were no cooperation symbol to balance out the anarchy of absolute freedom. Despite their outward differences, these two symbols are indeed intimately connected in their functioning. A similar analysis of any other two or more symbols of the American national symbol system will equally disclose their intrinsic and connected inner workings.

In science, this unity of function is called self-consistency, which Fritjof Capra refers to as ". . . the essence of all laws of nature."[7] Without this homogeneity, no symbol system can hold together. Inconsistency between symbols occurs when there is no relationship that can be established between them and no compatible associations to link them together. This is immediately self-evident in technical symbol systems, and less so in cultural symbol systems. The chemical symbol *H* for the element hydrogen cannot, by definition, be used in mathematics to function as a number. There is no basis on which to attempt it. A clear example of a cultural symbol, which cannot be made part of our national symbol system (a cultural symbol system), is the sacred cow of India, one of their national and spiritual symbols. Cows in India—common cattle—are very highly regarded and are never interfered with or harmed as they wander freely through town and countryside, even when they block roads or trample gardens. Such an ideal could never be part of the American national symbol system. Cows in the United States hold no such status. They are raised for their meat. There are no elements whatsoever common to both; consequently, there is simply no way to include the Indian sacred cow. The American expression of scorn that such and such a belief or activity is a sacred cow further illustrates the point. Another good example of symbol inconsistency is the ancient Mayan custom of preserving and caring for their dead leaders as though they were fully alive. Once a year, the dead were all paraded about for a ceremonial review of their realm as a way to honor them. In our society, this practice is considered extremely grotesque and unacceptable for modern civilization. Once again, there is no possible rapport between the Mayan symbol and the American national symbol system.

These two examples of inconsistency between symbols are conclusive. The American mindset recognizes their foreign nature immediately and instinctively. On the same basis, though a much subtler one, the fact is that no national symbols of other countries can be substituted into our system without some degree of disruption even though they may appear on the surface to be quite similar or even highly compatible. When the proposed new symbol is examined in full, it will be evident that the compatibility that seemed indisputable at first does not really exist after all. Consider a national symbol present in nearly every country on earth: a standing army. At first glance, a standing army might be taken for a universal symbol whose purpose and key elements are the same everywhere. Such parallelism is a true thing in armies the world over, but only as an abstraction. In everyday life, as we shall see, it is not true that an army is an army. That overly broad generalization proves nearly meaningless when the armies of any two countries are examined and compared. It quickly becomes apparent that there is no real fit in the sense of substituting one army (one symbol, in other words) for another. For an illustration of this, let us take a look at the armies of the United States and Russia. As soon as you get into the details, it is obvious that we could never replace the American army with its Russian counterpart for many reasons. It goes way beyond the obvious political reasons. There is nothing of their military culture, military mission, military law, or even their self-image that corresponds to ours in the least detail. The "feel" of it is altogether different. The loyalties, the heroes, the defining victories and defeats, what is traditionally defended and who is protected, the physical well-being and expectations of individual soldiers, the type of typical young person entering service, the military subculture, the different music and language—all these and myriad other organizational, cultural, and societal factors result in an astonishingly different army from our own.

The example above illustrates the point that symbols from different symbol systems are not interchangeable even though they may appear to be comparable or nearly identical on the surface. A symbol artificially introduced into a different symbol system does have power or influence, but only as a confusion, disturbance, or disruption. It remains a virtual foreign body that will never be at home in the new system unless, over a long period of time, it becomes extensively modified. If America and Russia violated the substitution law by exchanging armies, it would be a tumultuous disaster on many levels. Given enough time, perhaps five hundred years, a process of adaption would occur through which the Russian army would be gradually refashioned to suit the American spirit, eventually to be absorbed into the American system. Over the same course of time, the American spirit would also become altered as a consequence of interacting with the foreign symbol. In time, the "Russian" character of the army would be utterly lost, and the American spirit would have evolved as well.

All this is not to say, however, that there is no rapport at all between symbols of different systems. An army, after all, is an army in some basic ways. At the risk of discussing ideas that may require a broader understanding of these matters than can be developed here, I will say this: it is possible to correlate the meanings of symbols from different systems, but if, and only if, they are understood in purely abstract terms. Truth is to be found in every valid symbol system. Consequently, there does exist a subtle comparability between like-symbols of different systems. The elusive connecting links can only be ferreted out if we honor what is true, and therefore comparable, in like-symbols wherever they are to be found. This is not a process of comparative symbology that consists of compiling lists of common characteristics. That effort builds up knowledge without gain of insight because the essential connections and related meanings cannot be derived from external qualities. The driving dynamic, or principle, of each symbol must be ascertained by using the imagination to give form to perceptions of the intuition. By thus probing deeply into the nature and causes of things and events, it is possible to understand beneath the surface to the level at which All Is One.

The ill-conceived tendency in spiritual and metaphysical circles to equate, and often to incorporate, symbols from different symbol systems has caused untold confusion and ignorance. In many books, symbols from a variety of systems are linked as though there is a precise connection they share. A certain stone is purported to be comparable to a certain color, and to a particular tarot card, and to a specific astrological sign, and to a particular god of mythology, and to a ritual of one group or another, and to a number, and so on, endlessly. Many people have told me, and I have read this also, that there is a one-to-one correspondence between the numbers of Pythagorean numerology—1 through 9—and the twelve signs of the zodiac. This is careless thinking. A major indicator that this is not correct is the differing number of basic elements: nine and twelve. If there were an exact correlation of these two systems, it would logically only apply to the first nine signs. After that, there would be no more of numerology's basic elements to apply to the last three astrological signs. It is symbolically dysfunctional to rework numerology in order to cause it to fit astrological counterparts (see Figure 9).

Aries	Taurus	Gemini	Cancer	Leo	Virgo
1	2	3	4	5	6

Libra	Scorpio	Sagittarius	Capricorn	Aquarius	Pisces
7	8	9			

Figure 9. Matching the numbers of Pythagorean numerology with the signs of astrology.

It is more telling still to compare the attributes of these signs and numbers to see what they have in common. The astrological-sign attributes given are the attributes agreed on by most astrologers. Characteristics found in both are italicized.

Aries: *Ego, self-assertion, leadership, action,* adventurer, explorer, *motivated, impulsive, pioneer, innovation,* quick

1 *Individuation, self, belief in self, inner strength, strong personal needs and desires, self-centered, independence, leadership, courage to go own way, attainment*

Taurus: Dependable, conservative, stable, clings to past, stubborn, *passive,* practical, productive, creative, sensual, appreciation of art and need for beauty, faithful, loyal

2 Relationships, cooperation, diplomatic, friendly, soft, good listener, helper, ability to compromise, patient, considerate, *passive,* indecisive, sensitivity and vulnerability, detail oriented, follower

Gemini: Quick thinker, quick learner, communicator, salesmanship, freedom-loving, inconsistent and waffling, separation of thoughts and feelings, mental nervousness, restless, mood swings, many projects going on at once, versatile

3 Easygoing, charming, living in the moment, scattered, unpressured, avoids self-discipline, unmotivated in matters of duty and hard work, avoids confrontations, needs approval of others, good intellect, good conversationalist

Cancer: Deep, powerful emotions, sensitivity, *hides emotions,* softness, caring, compassion, home-loving, stable domestic partner, fierce protector of family, self-assertion

4 Practical, organized, systematic, conscientious, patient with details, serious, responsible, honest, purposeful, hard working, good with hands, strong likes and dislikes, stubborn, inflexible, *hides emotions,* literal, grounded in reality, realistic, strong, persevering

Leo: Egotistical, prideful, ostentatious, obstinate, vain, selfish, extravagant, generous, warm-hearted, flamboyant, expects to be chosen as leader, needs an audience, *creative, needs space and freedom to thrive*

5   *Freedom,* versatile, resourceful, quick thinking, takes risks, opportunity, loves change, survivor, wheeler-dealer, bold, adventurous, *creative,* restless, needs variety, impatient, fun, enthusiastic, irrepressible, irresponsible, difficulty with commitment

Virgo: Martyr, service, self-sacrificing, analyst, fussy, perfectionist, orderly, preoccupied with cleanliness, pure, potent, practical, productive, responds to flattery, easily exploited, robust, resistant to change, social climber, lack of self-confidence

6   Responsibility, commitment, involved in others' lives, pillar of the community, gossip, generous, helpful, ability to balance and heal others, manipulative, artistic, emotional, puts others' needs first

Libra: Need for harmony and beauty, diplomatic, seeks to resolve conflict, overlooks own needs, puts others first, mental balance, aware of many possibilities, indecisive, sticks blindly to commitments, charming, artistic qualities, need for justice and balance

7   Inward, introspective, meditative, thinking and analysis, good mind, intelligent, intellectual, awkward in relationships, incommunicative of real thoughts and feelings, aloof, reserved, deep, sees below the surface, good intuition, insightful

Scorpio: Deep, interested in dark and hidden things, gossip, obsessive, intense emotions, *rigid,* strong instinctive sense of right and wrong, interest in occult, psychic, commitment, devotion to causes, inflexibility, anarchist, vengeful

8 Power, empowerment, achievement, competitive, ambitious, materialistic, status conscious, serious, sober, realistic, purposeful, hard working, energetic, good judge of character, strong, commanding, authoritative, dictatorial, *stubborn,* deals with problems and issues

Sagittarius: Sensual, parties and fun are mportant, driven by both instinct and reason, values both body and spirit, deep need to search for truth, experiments with drugs, experiments with religion and philosophy and the arts, idealistic, reconciles opposites, enthusiastic, optimistic, rapidly changing enthusiasms, instability, wanderlust, uncompleted plans

9 Unconditional love, selfless giving, humanitarian, philosophical, understanding of the human condition, interested in spiritual and idealistic issues, total involvement in commitments, impractical in the real world, passionate, dramatic, deep change and loss, impersonal in intimate relationships

Apart from strong similarities between Aries and the number 1, there is clearly no likeness shared by the remaining eight signs, Taurus through Sagittarius. This same type of symbol commingling has long plagued number symbolism itself, resulting in a general degradation of its symbolic meanings. The error frequently lies in the belief that a particular number shares everywhere and in all eras a common meaning regardless of the culture or number symbol system of origin. Number meanings from Sumeria, Greece and Pythagoras, the Maya, the Kabalah, China, the so-called Pyramid numbers, and a variety of other sources are often indiscriminately mixed with disastrous results.

An example of such tampering involves the number 5 in modern Pythagorean numerology and in the number philosophy of Pythagoras in sixth century B.C.E. Greece. The meanings of the two 5s are entirely different. Today, 5 is associated with freedom and opportunity. In ancient Greece, 5 was the number of marriage. This illustrates the point that number symbols can never be severed from their original system and grafted onto another. Symbol substitution is contrary to the laws of symbols.

A further look at the number 5, ancient and modern, will serve to clarify the above differences. Freedom and opportunity chiefly characterize the modern 5. Since present-day Pythagorean numerology centers on psychological interpretation, we can ask, "What basic human drive causes a very strong need for freedom and opportunity to dominate in a person's life?" It is the inner imperative to prove one's individuality. This is because, in order to fulfill that inner directive, one must exercise the maximum amount of freedom and be free to seize upon the opportunities that present themselves. This, then, is the guiding principle of the modern 5. The ancient Greek 5 was a philosophical principle not readily applicable to personal psychology. That principle was marriage. This included the union of a man and a woman in matrimony, but only as a specialized aspect of that principle. The larger concept was that of union of opposites in life. To the Greeks, two numbers represented the most fundamental pair of opposites: the 2 and the 3. Two was feminine, dark, negative, unlimited. Three was masculine, light, positive, limited. They considered 2 and 3 to exemplify *all* opposites in life of whatever type. Five, then, was the universal principle by which any opposites could be united and reconciled, because $2 + 3 = 5$.

Having determined the essence of both the modern and the ancient concepts of 5, we may now consider the connection they share. Our purpose will not be to discover a way to make substitutions. Rather, by understanding both 5s in purely abstract terms, we will determine the meaning the ancient 5 can add to the current concept of 5. Five has, of course, been the same five-count throughout history, so it is logical to think the earliest interpretations drew from the same well of truth from which we ourselves draw today. It is, therefore, probable that the earlier understanding will have some bearing on today's interpretation.

As stated earlier, the modern 5 has a profound need to establish individuality. It sallies forth in life in a confidant, adventurous manner that can only be managed by someone who is secure within himself. Such a basic confidence of self occurs (and here is where the ancient Greek 5 sheds light) when there has been a general resolution of debilitating inner conflict. Every form of inner conflict involves a pair of opposites, "a 2 and a 3," as it were. Five is the state of mind in which all 2–3 dilemmas are overcome, freeing up the individual to experience his inner nature as a whole. In this manner, the ancient 5 enriches the meaning of the modern 5.

Symbols change over time. All symbols evolve . . . symbols of every type: scientific, artistic, language, cultural, even spiritual and religious systems. An informed glance back to any aspect of the past bears this out. Nothing of human culture or beliefs is the same today as it was before. This is why it is said that symbol systems must adapt to the changed conditions of different eras. The truth that certain symbol systems currently make available to us comes embodied in set forms. Those symbolic forms themselves must evolve or they will cease to be effective. "Your mythology, your imagery, has to keep up with what you know of the universe, because what it has to do is put you in accord with the universe as known, not as it was known in 2000 B.C. in the Near East."[8]

The American national symbols of "military service," "rugged individualism," and "my country right or wrong" have changed perceptively over the last fifty years. Further examination of each symbol shows they are not the same as they were during the tumultuous Vietnam era of the 1960s and 1970s. Prior to and through the war, military service was compulsory in the United States and was based on conscription through the Selective Service Board. Subsequent to that time, participation in the military has been voluntary. So, while "military service" has continued to be an extremely important national symbol, it now has a different connotation: men are no longer required to do it. "My country right or wrong" was a common response to the war effort amongst those who favored the governmental policy. After the terrible trauma of Vietnam, and the many revelations about the real reasons for our involvement in the war, the attitude of unquestioning obedience to country was diluted with the awareness that hindsight has brought: America fought the war for narrow economic and political reasons, not for the stated and idealistic goal of liberation of another country from Communism. Today, consequently, many Americans are fiercely patriotic, but with limitations. Governmental policy is no longer accepted without a second thought. The third national symbol discussed earlier, "rugged individualism," has a long tradition in the United States. It remains a cherished American ideal. However, the increasing need in our modern, crowded world for cooperation and the acceptance of authority has gradually and imperceptibly eroded the basis for this symbol. It is still a value many hold dear, but more often as a romantic notion of what America should be like rather than as a realistic way to behave in our demanding, hectic lives. The present generation looks on the 1960s version of these symbols as "old-fashioned." These changes have occurred in less than fifty years. As we look further back into the past—to the Middle Ages or just to the past century—it becomes increasingly difficult to relate to earlier interpretations of symbols, even those we consider to be constant values.

Today, the universe is known and understood through scientific research and experimentation. There is no question that science is at the leading edge of today's knowledge. Its theories and insights into physical reality dazzle the imagination. Its achievements are convincing proof that if science is not now in possession of the truth, it has the capability of discovering it given sufficient time and funding. This strong belief in science is backed up by the unparalleled progress of the past four hundred years, with the result that the scientific concept of reality is, at present, universally accepted and virtually unchallenged in the world.

And yet, history teaches us that all this is about to change. As surely as autumn leaves change color, the same process that has brought us this far will continue to evolve monumentally. Ten years from now, there will no doubt be a few fundamental differences of scientific knowledge that will modify or negate some of today's cherished beliefs and concepts. A thousand years from now, it is virtually certain that our entire scientific cosmogony will be little more that a historical curiosity, a quaint reminder of one of humanity's primitive stages of development.

Given the transitory nature of scientific thought, we may well wonder why it is that people the world over have such a profound belief in science and the scientific method. A big part of it is that science produces results: computers, space stations, laser beams, electron microscopes, and much more. But the passionate faith in science goes far beyond its ability to invent products; it goes to a near mystic awe of the process. Science, it is believed, is going to solve all the mysteries of life! Underneath it all is a wondrous hopeful enthusiasm that we are on to something. And we are, but we know nothing of where it will lead us or what it will ultimately mean to humanity. Now consider this: rosy predictions are often made of the form scientific knowledge and achievements will take in the future. Prognostications are made on the basis of the direction research appears to be heading. In writing about the scientific progress he expects for the next century, physicist Michio Kaku interviewed 150 scientists and concluded:

> The fact is there *is* a rough consensus emerging among those engaged in research about how the future will evolve. Because the laws behind the quantum theory, computers, and molecular biology are now well established, it is possible for scientists to generally predict the paths of scientific progress in the future. *This is the central reason why the predictions made here, I feel, are more accurate than those of the past.*[9]

No doubt they are. However, I believe even predictions as well considered as these must inevitably fall short. However farseeing, all envisioned future developments can be no more than a function of the present moment. Every last detail of projections of the future is based on no more than knowledge and beliefs as they exist at the present time.

What science does have, which accounts for its extraordinary role in this day and age, is *movement*. It is a happening thing. It is evolving. It is progressing. It is going somewhere. But the fact is that *every* great belief system of the past also had movement and was going somewhere at one time. In its time, each fulfilled humankind's destiny 100 percent, just as science fully engages so many minds today. There is a curious equality among major symbol systems past and present. Each made sense of the universe to one people or another during the time of its ascendancy. There has always been amongst people throughout history a strong need to believe that the explanation of their symbol system is superior to all others. The universality of this conviction demonstrates a human need to choose one interpretation of truth over all others. Almost every imaginable type of belief has been raised up somewhere, sometime, as the true belief. It appears we can only conclude that the truth is always bigger than the ability of an individual or people to fully conceptualize it.

There are many to whom this is heretical thinking. To the scientist, nonscientific methods of searching for the truth are suspect. They see the past as littered with bizarre myths and superstitious religions that have added little substance to humanity's efforts toward real progress and real knowledge. Today, in light of unprecedented progress and achievements, scientists feel it is absolutely baseless and incomprehensible to compare the merits of early culture to those of science: science is real and proven, after all, while other conceptual models were failed attempts to deal with reality. The renowned science scholar and philosopher Edward O. Wilson puts it this way:

> I mean no disrespect when I say that prescientific people, regardless of their innate genius, could never guess the nature of physical reality beyond the tiny sphere attainable by unaided commonsense. Nothing else ever worked, no exercise from myth, revelation, art, trance, or any other conceivable means; and notwithstanding the emotional satisfaction it gives, mysticism, the strongest prescientific probe into the unknown, has yielded zero.[10]

These are strong and uncompromising words. He continues:

> The uncomfortable truth is that the two beliefs (science and religion) are not factually compatible. As a result, those who hunger for both intellectual and religious truth will never acquire both in full measure.[11]

He concludes with:

> Some (cultural anthropologists) have even gone so far as to adopt the extreme postmodernist view that science is just another way of thinking, one respectable intellectual subculture in the company of many.[12]

It is my position that the cultural anthropologists are in fact correct. The above stated opinion that the metaphysical model has produced nothing is an inaccurate assessment that is entirely lacking in respect and appreciation for its many significant contributions. Ultimately, metaphysical knowledge/wisdom systems have as their goal the development of human and spiritual potential of individuals and civilizations. Science does not count character building as an achievement because this is not a purpose or value of the scientific philosophy. To set forth knowledge of physical reality as the litmus test of validity, as Professor Wilson asserts, is a limited standard indeed. It presupposes that the final answers to the eternal mysteries are all to be found in physical reality. That is an untenable assumption and an unscientific approach because it is selective in the factors it considers.

It is telling to note that science is attempting to do what humanity has always striven to do: to understand life through the use of symbols. This is the eternal quest. There have been many knowledge/wisdom systems throughout human evolution. "An estimated one hundred thousand belief systems have existed in history . . ."[13] in the estimation of Professor Wilson, each with its unique perception of reality. The important point about all of them, as the eminent philosopher Ernst Cassirer has observed, is:

> They are image-worlds whose principle and origin are to be sought in an autonomous creation of the spirit. Through them alone we see what we call "reality" and in them alone we possess it: for the highest objective truth that is accessible the spirit is ultimately the form of its own activity.[14]

There is, then, this common link between science, mythology, and religion: they all operate through the use of symbol systems. Not one of them deal directly with reality. Hence," wrote Cassirer, "there is no privileged status for science over art or any other symbolic formation that constitutes some kind of interpretation of experience."[15] It is fundamental to all spiritual, metaphysical, mythological, and religious symbol systems that meaning, ". . . making sense of our experience . . . ,"[16] is an indispensable part of the formula. "The search for meaning is innate . . . ,"[17] and to eliminate it arbitrarily from a search for truth is to take the heart out of the matter. As Fritjof Capra states, this has even been partially demonstrated scientifically: ". . . neuroscientists have discovered strong evidence that human intelligence, human memory, and human decisions are never completely rational but are always colored by emotions."[18] This is consistent with the view of the renowned eighteenth-century German philosopher Immanuel Kant, of whom it has been written: "In his idealistic view, mathematics and physics do not exhaust all reality, because they are far from encompassing all the workings of the human spirit in its creative spontaneity."[19]

If, as I believe, science excludes certain of the primal elements pertaining to the search for truth, then science is limited to a partial, or inadequate, determination of truth. At the same time, it is my estimation that in the course of its evolution, science will inevitably come to embrace the cultural, moral, humanistic, and even spiritual aspects that are at present absent. This must inevitably occur because a point will be reached beyond which progress is no longer possible without considering all the elements necessary to a complete search for truth.

Science will likely exist for some time to come as only a partial quest for reality. Until the time that science reckons with all the basic elements, scientific theory is forever consigned to continue evolving without ever having the luxury of achieving stability. Such an enduring theory of science, currently expressed in physics as the aspiration for a Unified Field Theory, will have the capacity to explain all new phenomena and yet remain intact, rendering unnecessary any further modification in order to give a full accounting of reality. In that far-off time, science will barely resemble its present-day form. Still, even in that advanced state of knowledge and understanding, there will always remain a degree of enigma that precludes complete resolution of life's mysteries.

So it is. So it ever has been.

Endnotes

1. Everett M. Stowe, *Communicating Reality through Symbols* (Philadelphia: The Westminster Press, 1966), 24.

2. Most of these statements on freedom have been repeated so long their original author is no longer known, with the sole exception of the last, which was made by Patrick Henry in a speech to the First Continental Congress in 1774.

3. Fritjof Capra, *The Tao of Physics* (Boston: Shambhala Publications, 1991), 146.

4. Dion Fortune, *The Mystical Qabalah* (York Beach, Maine: Samuel Weiser, Inc., 1989), 165.

5. Capra, *The Tao of Physics*, 307.

6. Dion Fortune, *Sane Occultism* (London: Inner Light Publishing Society, 1938), 73.

7. Capra, *The Tao of Physics*, 45.

8. Joseph Campbell, *Transformations of Myth through Time* (New York: Harper and Row Publishers, 1990), 22.

9. Michio Kaku, *Visions: How Science Will Revolutionize the 21st Century* (New York: Anchor Books, 1997), 6–7.

10. Edward O. Wilson, *Consilience: The Unity of Knowledge* (New York: Alfred A. Knopf, 1991), 46.

11. Ibid., 262. It is curious that Professor Wilson here refers to science as a belief rather than as an objective form of knowledge. Equating both science and religion to beliefs puts them on an equal footing in an important way because it infers that both disciplines rely on the faculty of human understanding.

12. Ibid., 186.

13. Ibid., 244.

14. Ernst Cassirer, *The Philosophy of Symbolic Forms, Vol 1: Language,* trans. by Ralph Manheim (New Haven, Connecticut: Yale University Press, 1953), 111.

15. Ibid., 58.

16. Renate Nummela Caine and Geoffrey Caine, *Making Connections: Teaching and the Human Brain* (Menlo Park, Calif.: Innovative Learning Publications, 1994), 89.

17. Ibid., 89.

18. Fritjof Capra, *The Web of Life* (Boston: Shambhala Publications, 1991), 68.

19. Cassirer, *The Philosophy of Symbolic Forms, Vol 1: Language,* 79.

chapter 4

What Life is All About

All our sensory perceptions of things in this world are subjective—within ourselves. They are nothing but energy patterns upon the vacuum surface linked inward to the structure of the human mind. We are all co-creators and shareholders in the universe. We have collectively created our circumstances through the medium of our own minds and under the dominion of the Universal mind.

—John Davidson, *The Secret of the Creative Vacuum: Man and the Energy Dance*

There are, of course, many symbol systems operating in our lives beyond the national system. They form a nearly endless group of interconnected and overlaid systems that covers our entire existence, extending from matters of no personal concern to the most intimate areas of our lives. Some systems common to the life of every American are politics, jobs, the economy, the stock market, education, advertising, power status, age, male and female, relationships, love and romance, values, etiquette, proper conduct, laws, the justice system, time, past and future, heroes and villains and celebrities, movies, fashion, societal problems, health and medicine, diet and exercise, healing, spirituality, television, computers, even the traffic system. You get the idea. For each person, the total of symbol systems is extensive and an individual mix, unique to him. These systems-upon systems are profoundly internalized within our being. Despite the extreme complexity of all the interrelated dynamics, we are able almost automatically to process them effortlessly with the kind of ease and familiarity that comes from a thoroughly learned habit.

As we go through life day-by-day, events tumble into our lives evoking a kaleidoscope of thoughts and feelings, reactions and actions. These experiences and how we handle them are symbolic activities because the events originate from our symbol systems and play out according to their rules. Each symbol system functions on the basis of a particular line of thinking, toward which every symbol in that system contributes. Through each moment of living, we continuously interpret and process great quantities of symbolic input. We use this raw data to steer our lives by determining patterns with which to associate meanings and outcomes. To this objective process we also bring our subjective needs and desires. The role of symbols in our lives involves the whole person inside and out, conscious and unconscious.

It is important not only to comprehend symbolic principles on the abstract level, as we have been discussing, but also to use them in life. Anything less and they remain only ideas that have yet to become functioning symbols. They become real on the physical plane, and complete in our understanding, when they are grounded in reality. Consequently, it is necessary here to show how the above ideas about symbols play out in the real world. Any symbol system could be used to illustrate the grounding of the principles we are discussing because symbol systems all function on essentially the same basis. I decided to use the traffic regulation system for this purpose because it is unambiguous and straightforward. The overall objective of this system is the safe management of traffic. The traffic signs and regulations (the symbols) are designed to ensure safe driving in a variety of situations. They all contribute toward the same goal. So, although a stop light, a "Watch for Deer" sign, a pedestrian crosswalk, a left turn only lane, and a "One Way" sign all require very different behaviors, at the same time they (the diverse symbols) all play a coordinated role in realizing the prime goal of the proper management of traffic. As with any symbol system, one traffic symbol follows another in the course of driving. This continuously necessitates modifying how we think and act, which, in symbol work, is called *interpretation*. Judgment and quick decisions are required: a stop sign followed by a 35 mph speed limit sign followed by a passing ambulance followed by a yield sign all necessitate changes of behavior. The various traffic control mechanisms (the symbols) are all in dynamic interplay; they are not in the least static or set. There is no one, single way to react to them (no single interpretation of the symbols) because so much depends on the traffic conditions and the state of the driver. A 35 mph speed limit, for example, only represents a general condition. In that speed zone, some drivers, having arrived at their destination, pull to a stop; others creep along at 5 mph as the result of a traffic jam; and a police car races toward a crime scene at 55 mph. To any driver, none of the signs or regulations governing driving (none of the symbols) seem puzzling, out of place, or randomly chosen.

Every licensed driver is thoroughly familiar with the entire system. Long before anyone is issued a license to drive a car (in other words, long before he becomes a bona fide user of the symbol system), he must have demonstrated understanding of how all the signs and regulations (all the symbols) work together *and* that he is competent to handle them in traffic (and that he is qualified to interpret). The idea of driving only becomes a physical reality when the learned principles are actually used on the road. Prior to demonstrated mastery and licensing, the closest he can get to the act of driving is to think about it (until a symbol system is sufficiently mastered, the learner is unprepared to use it for his own purposes). Another factor affecting driving is the driver himself. Every driver knows what needs to be done in order to make this system work successfully (everyone who has mastered a symbol system understands how it works), yet each also has a personal understanding of it (each person interprets the symbols uniquely). Traffic signs and regulations are about as cut-and-dried as those of any symbol system. Nonetheless, there is still room for individual approaches: the teenager for whom driving restrictions are a challenge to be defied; the mature driver who calculatedly drives exactly 1 mph over the posted speed limit; and the overly cautious octogenarian who drives 20 mph in a 30 mph zone. Another major influence on driving (on symbol interpretation) is the current state of the driver's personal life. Attitudes, moods, problems, and crises of the moment are fully capable of greatly altering someone's driving style (significantly changing how he interprets and acts on the symbols). He may feel rushed or seriously distracted by an argument he just had, physically ill, full of road rage, sleepy, overwhelmed by too many things happening at once, or any number of other preoccupations of the moment. Thus, a person's typical manner of driving (his characteristic approach to interpreting and handling the symbols) is highly individual and always in flux, generally evolving over time to a higher and more successful ability to handle a car on the road (learning to achieve the primary purpose of the symbol system with greater skill and judgment). There is also a moral to all of this. If the driver consciously decides to cooperate fully with the spirit of the traffic laws (if he aims for the highest, most ideal experience the symbol system has to offer), he is most likely to avoid a variety of penalties and traumas (negative experiences), such as car wrecks, personal injury, fines and arrests, a reputation as a bad driver, or the resentment and legal battles of those he has hurt. Plus he will successfully reach the goal of this symbol system: safe driving.

Symbolism, then, is humanity's Tool for Living. It is how we deal with reality. Not directly with *the* Reality, although it usually feels that way, but with daily life through the use of complex perception mechanisms that I have been calling symbol systems. But above and beyond the fray of day-to-day existence, there also exists a higher, more fundamental Reality with which we reckon at all times and under all circumstances. With regard to *the* Reality, truly we are like the blind men who felt different parts of an elephant's body and came to radically different and incomplete conclusions of what an elephant is like. None of them see or can conceive the whole animal. Like the blind men, we call Reality by the names of the several symbol systems we know, while other equally meaningful symbol systems lie fallow in our imagination. Our personal, subjective take on Reality constitutes *our* reality. It is the interpretative mental lens through which we understand life and live out our days.

Our quality of life is dependent on how we handle our symbolism: how we see it; how we interpret it; how we act on it. No matter how marvelous our selection of symbol systems is, like any tool, its effectiveness is contingent upon the skill and care with which it is used. Any symbol system tends to organize order out of chaos, and to bring purpose to that organization. The lack of such order and purpose defeats our ability to succeed, regardless of how pure or strong the intent to achieve. Consider again the commonplace symbol system of traffic laws and regulations found everywhere there are roads to carry cars. If there were no common understanding of driving protocol, if we had no limitations on speed and other behaviors behind the wheel, if there were no regulations or signs with which to represent correct driving, it would no doubt be so dangerous to operate a motor vehicle that it is even questionable whether cars would be manufactured. Who would wish to invest serious money—not to mention personal safety—in a product that could be ruined within hours of purchase? Thus, our traffic system not only organizes traffic conditions, but it also imbues an attitude of safe driving in almost every driver.

The American national symbol system, the ones mentioned at the beginning of this chapter in addition to myriad others, all bring organization to their purview.

Taken together, the total symbol systems of each individual organize and stabilize his life, making it possible to function and to live on earth. Actually, symbol systems only perform this marvelous function for us because it is human nature to find patterns in the stuff of life. No structure is inherent. Rather, it is our genius to create patterns (concepts) of our own making in the surrounding environment, and to decide what it all means to us. First, we see meaning in individual symbols, then we go on to conclude how certain symbols function together (that is, we become aware of the pattern).

The power to symbolize begins and ends within. When the meaning of a particular symbol is so strong it nearly overwhelms us, it needs to be recognized that the *symbol itself* has no inherent force to bring this about. It merely serves as a triggering mechanism for our consciousness, which then supplies all the intensity of thought and emotion. When we turn an electrical switch on, starting up a large engine, there is no thought that the switch itself is the source of power. It is the same with symbols: they suggest, remind, or in some way stimulate us (they switch on our consciousness), and our mind supplies all the rest, including whether or not to power up the symbol. For each of us, there are many symbols pregnant with meaning that we choose not to empower. For me, symbols having to do with bodybuilding, special breeds of dogs, fashion, car racing, country and western music, and baseball cards have no interest or personal meaning, no judgment against them intended. When I run across symbols from any of these six areas (such as this year's popular colors, the characteristics to look for in a champion dog, the ten things fans most want to know about their favorite country and western singer, the technical innovations in this year's Indianapolis 500 fastest car, and so on), I recognize them for the symbols they are. I may acknowledge the particular significance they have for others, yet I am unmoved and completely oblivious to the power other people attribute to them.

The experiences—or meanings—we associate with a given symbol, and the symbol itself, are entirely independent of each other. They are unrelated. Yet, they seem to be one and the same, inextricably wedded together, virtually inseparable, especially when we are in the middle of things. It does not even seem possible to disassociate life's doings from the meanings we link to them, even for an instant, even on a strictly theoretical basis. Yet, in fact, we frequently have the experience of working with them separately, either grafting new meaning on to a symbol or retaining established meaning following the loss of a symbol. In the first instance, the addition of something special to our lives—a spouse, a pet, a keepsake, a hobby, a hero—brings about the creation of a new symbol. Here, the new symbol is like an empty vessel into which we pour meaning. In the second instance, the loss of a symbol (spouse or pet, for example) leaves us with just the memories (that is, just the meaning) we associated with it. More often than not, those memories continue to have a great impact on us, if only in our thoughts. This suggests as well as anything that the symbol proper does not, and cannot, house the meaning itself. *That* capability lies in our consciousness and, in truth, is entirely independent of the symbol with which we habitually associate it.

The difficulty of extricating the experiences we create (separating the meaning . . .) from the events (. . . from the symbols) that unfold before us in life lies in the fact that everything is connected with who we are. When we invest meaning into a symbol, we extend a bit of ourselves into that symbol: we are *that*. We forge our symbols from the depths of our being, which in turn causes a deep bond between ourselves and that with which we identify. Most of ourselves that we project into symbols comes from the subconscious levels over which we exercise little or no conscious awareness, judgment, or control. When we reflect on ourselves and the life we are living, we are only prepared to own the symbols we have consciously chosen. The rest, the vast majority of symbols, arise out of our being without conscious participation. Consequently, we do not remember creating them and, further, often do not feel we should have to take responsibility for them. Then, when they do not fit our self-image or when we see them as negative to our well-being, we do not want to admit we made them. Consequently, we see ourselves as separate from the world at large. We call it "objective reality."

It is important to grasp that symbol systems do not in and of themselves bring meaning and order to our lives. Until we see meaning in each part and until we understand each aspect and put it all together, symbols are void of significance and undifferentiated. Even the most marvelous, revelatory symbol system is without interest or value if no personal, relevant meaning is associated with it. This point has been abundantly clear in modern times to people confronted with trying to understand modern abstract art. The artists themselves undoubtedly worked passionately with meanings and symbols. They expressed their ideas as best they knew with paint on canvas. But for the most part, the public has simply been unable to relate to it. Many people, when gazing at an abstract work of art—even one that is clear and articulate in the statement it is making—can only wonder, *What is it?*

I personally had the "incomprehension" experience for many years with regard to the Cubist paintings of Pablo Picasso. Through the course of my high school and university years, his work was discussed in a number of art and humanities classes, several times at great length. Picasso was praised and hailed as a pioneering genius time after time. Yet through it all and into my late forties, I had no clue as to what was so well appreciated. Nor did I know how to take that first step toward understanding. His paintings did not speak to me. They meant nothing to me. Then one day while watching a television biography of Picasso, the commentator made an offhand observation about his Cubist period and something awoke me to the meaning of it all. Suddenly I saw it. I made the connection. The effect of the painting being shown at that moment was so powerful to me, so electric, that I nearly fell to the floor in amazement! Symbols in and of themselves do not originate meaning or experience. We infuse meaning into the symbolic form, and we reap experience back from it.

Readers unfamiliar with number symbolism or numerology will keenly appreciate this "incomprehension" point with regard to the many intricate meanings of the symbolic numbers 0 through 9. These simple, unadorned ciphers . . .

$$0 \quad 1 \quad 2 \quad 3 \quad 4 \quad 5 \quad 6 \quad 7 \quad 8 \quad 9$$

. . . are of themselves suggestive of nothing beyond digits for counting. Yet their metaphysical significances, when learned, can open the way to profound spiritual experiences.

We, individually and personally, then, breathe life into symbol systems. At first, it may be difficult to see that this is the case because of our own personal symbol systems to which we have long since given life. Their reality is, well, so *real*. People often forget, or, more commonly, are unaware of, ever having breathed life into any symbol system of any kind. They are generally unaware, as well, of the lengthy gestation period that led up to the appearance of the "real symbols" and "real world experiences" they now find in their lives. Nor is there usually any appreciation of the extent to which "real things" are partly *subjective*, meaning they are to some extent the result of personal conclusions they have reached.

When a symbol system first comes to our conscious awareness, it represents a potential new experience in life. Although at first we may not know all the details and how they fit together, if we are sufficiently attracted to the symbol system, there forms within our being a purpose and a yearning for it. Whether the new realm of experience is specific and describable or elusive and instinctive, the symbol system is now part of our lives. The act of recognition begins a process in which we gradually build up and cement together the experiential components that become part of reality—our reality. To help further this course of development, there exists a wealth of information and guidance—such as this book—from a variety of sources about every imaginable symbol system. All of those sources, however, are limited in their ability to contribute understanding. They can only help indirectly in our efforts to formulate the necessary inner concepts of the symbol system. The understanding of others, no matter how inspired, cannot bestow strength and courage, nor can it labor and learn on our behalf. The building material of symbol systems is always our own personal experience. Upon making a symbol system our own, we enjoy the fullness of its experience. We may or may not like what we find there. We may (or, more likely, may not) understand all of it. Either way, we are at home with it.

With the above in mind, it will be clear why a person's intent, or purpose, in symbol work is so crucial. The intent, which acts to fertilize development of a symbol system, contains in latent potential every last aspect of what will become the "real symbol system" in its maturity. For this reason, the teaching of every spiritual symbol system begins with a discussion of Proper Intent: that which we invest into our symbol system in the formative stages returns to us as the reality with which we subsequently deal. The same principle applies as well to mundane symbol systems. The present make-up of the symbolism in your life—"the way things are"—is the direct consequence of an earlier symbolic process. That earlier process is a kind of planning stage in which philosophical ideas and attitudes are given specific form. The stresses and strains being set up between the various symbols are as yet tentative and untested. It is only in the crucible of time and space that the consequences become apparent and play out, consequences that are often unanticipated and unintended.

You may now be thinking of a number of situations in your life, situations that you feel certain you never intended. And you may go on to conclude that someone or something other than your own intent must be coming into the process to cause the trouble, something beyond your control that you would like very much to eradicate from your life if only you could. But, in fact, this line of thinking goes directly back to your original intent, where almost imperceptible and unrecognized flaws were included in the primal conceptual mix. Choices that are initially a matter of inclination and preference later become, as it were, set in stone. The mischief of early on, which seems insignificant when all things are malleable and fanciful, invariably develops into a disability or dysfunction when the concept fully comes into its own. At that endpoint it becomes clear, if one cares to know, that the end result is due to such and such a cause; and the happy outcome of this whole process is wisdom—knowing a better way to handle things.

Once symbolic concepts have fully gelled, we do well to handle adverse circumstances in a spiritual manner. Spiritual symbol systems *are* expressions of wisdom, and to apply them to life *is* to apply wisdom. Even though this approach does not cure the ill of negative or destructive symbolism, it will cause no further harm. It will also develop important attributes of character like strength, discipline, concentration, discernment, humility, selflessness, and so on. This is, of course, a necessary part of living a spiritual life. It should also be recognized that confronting negativity with spiritual principle is, in a sense, a maintenance effort rather than a deep transformation of self. Once a symbol system becomes real for us, the die is cast and we have to live with the dynamics such as we have created them.

It is an altogether different matter to cast a spiritual symbol system—or any symbol system, for that matter—from the very beginning, or to recreate an existent one, according to spiritual principle. Certain impurities can be resolved or eliminated right at the outset. As a result, entire categories of disease and discomfort never arise in the first place to form a part of our lives.

On this basis, it is the most idealistic, the most pure, and the most holy of intent that proves to be the most practical.

Of the vast array of symbol systems in the world, spiritual symbol systems are unique in one respect: like all symbol systems, they are a mode of perception, but their essence, or basis, is *nothing*. This curious phraseology defines the distinction to be made between spirit and things of form. "Nothing" is the technically correct term, because Spirit is unmanifest, without form and void. It does not originate from the physical, mental, emotional, or ethereal planes of existence. It has no qualities, characteristics, or attributes. Spirit is quite literally *nothing*, having no appearance, structure, or organization of any kind. Nothingness occupies a singular place in a world of profound form. The concept of form encompasses far more than is generally supposed. It includes the physical world, of course, but also anything that is characterized by any sort of quality, pattern, concept, or organizing principle. Under this definition, all thoughts, feelings, ideas, ideals, and aspirations are instances of form, just as surely as rocks, trees, and matter itself are examples of form.

The concept of "nothing" is as close as we can get in word and in thought to the literal and absolute *nothingness* of Spirit. In our language, even the word "nothing" is a concept full of connotations and implications. Despite this difference between spiritual symbol systems and their mundane counterparts, they function the same because all symbol systems are conceptual forms whose components serve to produce certain experiences, or certain states of being. While it is true that Spirit is *nothing* that is *unmanifest* and is *not an element of physical life,* at the same time it is paradoxically all of these things. Spirit is nothing and everything. It has no influence and it determines all that occurs. It cannot be represented symbolically *and* it is the cause and substance of all symbol systems. It is accurate to say that a spiritual symbol system represents creative potency. This is so because when a spiritual symbol system is learned in every respect, it allows Spirit to permeate mundane symbology as a transforming elixir. Having said that, it should be remembered that Spirit transforms symbols and it changes nothing.

The purpose of spiritual symbol systems is transcendence of form in order to experience union with Spirit. There are many spiritual symbol systems in addition to mathematical symbolism, such as the I Ching, Buddhism, Tarot, Kabalah, a wide variety of religions, paganism, nature worship, yoga, the discipline of breath, plus numerous others.[1] All other symbol systems are mundane and serve to expand our opportunities for experience on this physical plane and other planes of form.

The latter might be called *form symbol systems.* They are by nature limited in purpose and in scope of activity. They are of this world. Spiritual symbol systems are in this world but not of it. They use the words and ideas and images of earth, but they are not physical or literal, *especially* not literal. The only way symbols of the ineffable can successfully represent spiritual subject matter is through unconventional combinations of qualities and characteristics. In fact, they often appear to defy reason, logic, and common sense. The Hindu pantheon, for example, is filled with figures that combine human and animal parts in addition to other improbable characteristics. Ganesha, the Hindu elephant god, has a human torso and the head and trunk of an elephant, which his father, Shiva, gave him to replace his human head that was lost when he was beheaded. Clearly, the goal of Ganesha is not to symbolize any physical reality. Rather, the Intent is to give expression to what we call a spiritual idea. There is, in fact, no literal, one-to-one correspondence between a spiritual symbol and the mundane image that gives it form.

This is profoundly perplexing to those unfamiliar with spiritual symbolism. They wonder, *What can this be: a dead person resuscitated with an elephant head!?* This kind of mundane thinking can only conclude that Ganesha is somewhere between preposterous and insane. The image just makes no sense. In Hinduism, however, Ganesha is the God of Wisdom, Prosperity, and Remover of Obstacles. Such a lofty idea can only be expressed in the Hindu symbol system with a being having the history, character, and make-up of Ganesha. In spiritual symbol systems, the breach between meanings and the images that represent them is crucial to the integrity of the symbolism. For otherwise, spiritual symbol systems would be mundane and subject to all the limitations and restrictions that bind *anything* of form. Many a spiritual symbol system has crashed to earth because the mundane images were taken literally for what they resemble rather than as empty, albeit suggestive, vessels of meaning. Spiritual belief systems that are seen exclusively as the embodiment of good and used to combat evil in the world, or that are believed to be Absolute Truth and used to condemn opposing concepts, fall into this fallen category. Such spiritual systems are fallen because their transcendent purpose has been supplanted by a down-to-earth, conceptual content. Good versus evil and truth versus ignorance are both dualities, divisions of the One Reality into mutually exclusive forces. That is the world of form. In Spirit, pairs of opposites dissolve together, disappear, and are no more. That is transcendence.

In order to understand spiritual symbolism, then, it is necessary to set aside the known meanings of the images being used so that new metaphysical meaning may emerge. The new meaning is freeing to the individual, releasing him from being held tight to the line of thinking that governs the world.

The total of all our assorted personal symbol systems is what we call Reality. For each individual, it is a unique and personal conceptualization. It is through this composite medium that we cope with Reality, *the* Reality that we cannot otherwise know or understand. Whatever that personal symbolism consists of, however limited or expanded it is, it is our personal Way of Being. Our personal Way of Being is the most we can know of Reality. Understandably, the symbolism that serves us day in and day out tends to assume the role of the Reality in our minds instead of our knowing it for what it is: ephemeral, impermanent conditions. Those personal, mundane symbols are, after all, what we see, hear, feel, taste, and smell. They are what we use and depend on to live every day. In the absence of tangible Knowledge of Reality, and out of a deep need to be grounded in Reality, we take the next best alternative—our own symbolism—as the Real Thing. It is for this reason that the Reality of this world, along with its multitudinous quantity of symbol systems, is called *illusion*.

Despite the abundance of symbolism to help us manage in every area of our lives, there comes a time when it is no longer enough. We desire something deeper, something more meaningful. Perhaps we simply yearn for what-we-know-not or we envision a clear aspiration. This brings on a crisis, since the current symbolism is no longer adequate for all our needs, and, in turn, a willingness to develop new experience. This might mean seeking out new symbolism or it might mean discovering new interpretations of known symbolism. One way or another, our outlook and the environment around us are set to change.

It is always this way in the realm of form. All things change. Knowledge and understanding evolve. Using our symbol systems, we are forever organizing and reorganizing our lives into scenarios of reality. Always it is with the implicit hope that *this* form of reality will be the one to endure. We want it to be permanent. Although we recognize that our ideas and beliefs may be imperfect, we at least want them to be basically true and essentially real. However, form is by nature incomplete. It is inherently limited. In form symbol systems, the truth of today gives way to a different validity tomorrow. Everyone observes these kinds of changes large and small in his own life. But instead of realizing that all form invariably evolves through time, most people attribute the evolutions to being the direct result of specific processes such as aging, the march of history, revolutionary ideas, progress, education, or the vision of genius, for several examples. It is a universal assumption, for instance, that as a person becomes older, his ideas will change and mature accordingly. The belief is, I think, that the successive stages of our lives *cause* the changes of form, and in a way they do. The predictable pattern of change associated with growing older is a function of the age symbol system. Changes of form occur in all symbol systems (including the spiritual ones) according to the dynamics of the particular symbol system.

Yet at any given age, there are few individuals who view their current set of beliefs as temporary. Almost no one sees his concepts of things as being in flux and part of a continuously regenerating continuum. Rather, most of us share a profound conviction in each moment of our lives that our lives at this time, along with our knowledge and understanding, are *real,* and that we are experiencing our lives in the only way possible for us. After all, events unfold inexorably in their appointed order despite our best efforts to the contrary. Those events are definitive. We must deal with them just as they are or suffer the consequences. Period. We cannot modify them in the light of our future truth because we do not yet hold those views, nor can we use the convictions and certainties of the past from when we were younger and did not understand as much as we do now. The truth of the present moment, however fleeting or enduring that might be, is *always* the truth, and it is always compelling.

Which is the period of true perception in a person's life? Is it the innocence and trust of childhood? The radical experimentation of adolescence? The family-raising years? The wisdom of old age? It is tempting to say a person attains the highest truth in his maturity when he has a lifetime of learning and experience on which to draw. But on what basis are we to say the perceived truth of one period is superior to another? The idea of truth is a concept just like the many other concepts we have been discussing throughout this book. Truth is not universal, however. No form of truth is applicable everywhere and at all times. Nonetheless, we commonly speak of this or that being true, as though there were an underlying and absolute standard to which we all refer. Actually, truth is relative because it is symbol system-based. It is an inseparable part of the system in which the truth-assessment is made, and it varies from system to system. All realities of a symbol system result from the nature of the component symbols and their interactions. Truth is a conclusion we reach about the functioning of key patterns of a particular symbol system, making truth a function of the system from which it derives.

It is always vital to our self-interest (and, in fact, it is an inherent need) to determine what makes our symbol systems "really work." This is one of the archetypal lifelong struggles of every human being: how best to live. It is accomplished to the degree that we ascertain the basic truth patterns of our symbol systems. As we mature, it is not solely the skill of perceiving truth that brings success in living. There is also the ability to employ wisdom. Wisdom is defined as a combination of knowing what is true or right *and* exercising sound judgment in taking action. Truth is what works and wisdom is how to make it work best *within a particular symbol system.*

We are accustomed to think of truth and wisdom as powerful forces that cut through to the essence of all situations and circumstances. The Bible states, "The truth shall set you free." For many committed to a spiritual or religious path, determining the *absolute* truth is a goal of fundamental importance—this would be truth whose reality transcends time and space to portray the Real. It also suggests a human ability to identify ultimate principles and to apply them to our lives on the physical plane. However, the term "absolute," when applied to truth, or to wisdom, for that matter, is a misnomer. Neither truth nor wisdom can be absolute because they are both concepts, and, therefore, are limited, born out of the web of dynamics of this or that symbol system. Far from absolute, both principles are dualities: truth and ignorance, wisdom and folly. Duality involves a co-dependent relationship of two opposite dynamics, which stimulate and define each other. Both forces are necessary for either one to exist. Without the darkness of ignorance there would be no light of truth.

The symbol system-specific nature of truth/wisdom becomes clear from the following examples: winning strategies of basketball; effective courtroom tactics; successful sales techniques; winning at poker; speculating profitably on the stock market; time-tested farming methods; the art of diplomacy; sound banking procedures; proven communication skills. All the above exemplify the skillful use (wisdom) of practical methods (truth). In each case, the particular form that truth and wisdom take is unique to the symbol system of which they are part. Also, they do not readily transfer for use in different symbol systems. For example, it is not possible to make literal use of "effective courtroom tactics" in order to "speculate profitably on the stock market." The stock market does not consist of a decision-making process in which advocates argue for and against an accused whose fate will then be decided by twelve citizens. The character and make-up of the courtroom that spawned its winning tactics are nothing like what goes on in the stock market. That notwithstanding, some people do seem able to transfer truth/wisdom from one system to another. Consider the master stockbroker who uses the drama and maneuvering of courtroom tactics to show how to be successful in the "adversarial" stock market. Utilizing an astute comparison of courtroom principles with those of the stock market, he is able to explain the intricacies of maximizing the market in a striking and effective manner. This is not, however, the literal transfer of truth/wisdom it appears to be. Courtroom truth/wisdom is not actually standing in for that of the stock market. This use of such foreign principles is based entirely on the stockbroker's expert grasp (that is, his truth and wisdom) of how to work the stock market. Without that comprehensive understanding, he would not be capable of designing a courtroom metaphor to illustrate the workings of the stock market. It is no more than a clever analogy.

In addition to the limitation inherent in all mundane symbolism, which we have been discussing, there is another subtler and more complex aspect of symbolism to consider: how spiritual principles figure into mundane symbol systems.

As we have seen, all symbol systems organize meanings so as to make certain experiences possible. They all function on the basis of their own internal logic and self-consistency. This inner connectedness is a result of the underlying purpose that unites all parts of the system so they contribute toward the same goal. The basic principles (or modes of living) of a given symbol system can be used to reach a desired goal if they are properly handled. Consequently, within the context of the particular symbol system, principles that aid in the achievement of goals are considered "good" because they provide the means to succeed. Conversely, the principles that undermine our efforts to achieve goals are considered "bad" because they cause us to fail.

The success principles of mundane symbol systems very often conflict with common spiritual principles. Yet at the same time, it is a spiritual axiom that the earth and all that is upon it is an expression of Spirit. Why, then, do many parts of life (the mundane) seemingly undermine or oppose other parts (the spiritual)? The answer, I believe, is that each part of earth life serves a particular spiritual purpose, that purpose generally being a lesson or experience of some sort. From One Spirit there spring infinite parts—spiritual fragments, as it were. The apparently chaotic array of these fragments (that is, mundane symbol systems) in actuality has an ordered, a progressive, even a mathematical organization to them when viewed from a spiritual perspective. Accordingly, each mundane symbol system takes its place in life as one of many spiritual learnings that ultimately lead to transcendence of earth plane limitations. It is the job of the mysterious spiritual symbol systems to provide the means to understand . . . , no, not just to understand, but to *live,* spiritually. That includes every symbol, every symbol system, every obstacle, every achievement, and every experience. This is a high calling where the line between thinking and alchemy blurs. . . .

A great many people do not see the spiritual connectedness and metaphysical purposiveness of all the assorted symbol systems in their lives. Those systems often seem unconcerned with spiritual matters and sometimes downright immoral, being preoccupied primarily with worldly affairs, materiality, or self-advancement. Often, we simply don't consider the lower end of life as bona fide spiritual—yet it is.

The confusion is due to the division of the One into the Many. We are familiar with this division on a metaphysical and abstract basis. We all accept the component parts as spiritual even though they are different or in direct opposition to each other. For example, the twofold division of the One—called duality—is widely accepted. The most well known representation of duality is the yin yang symbol, which shows two opposite forces forever entwined, each force containing the potential of the other (see Figure 8 on page 42). This symbol represents such pairs of opposites as good and evil, light and dark, male and female, odd and even, plus a near infinite number of other polarities. Although any of the resulting two forces are very unlike the state of Oneness, as well as being opposite to each other, duality is still considered spiritual. In many religions, the godhead is conceived in three parts, known as the Trinity. Enigmatically, this represents three-in-one and one-in-three, which symbolizes, for example, the Creator, the Preserver, and the Destroyer, or the common Father-Mother-Son/Father-Son-Holy Ghost conceptualizations. Here again, the three parts of the Trinity are both different from the godhead and from each other. Yet nobody considers any of the three parts unspiritual, even though one of them is the Destroyer. Likewise, a fourfold division of Reality has been extremely common throughout history, almost invariably concerned with the elements of physical reality. A few examples include the four elements (air, fire, earth, and water), the four directions, the four winds, the four seasons, and the four cardinal virtues. In fourfold division, once again, the parts are unlike each other and unlike the One Reality. Yet the differences and negativities (fire and water are "negative" to each other) do not cause some parts to be praised as spiritual and other parts to be spurned as worldly and ungodly.

In modern Pythagorean numerology, the complete set of basic elements is 9 in number. In the ancient number symbolism of Pythagoras, in the Kabalistic Tree of

Life as well as in this book, 10 represents all the basic elements of the universe. There are other basic numbers in the symbolic realm, of course: the 12 of astrology; the 22 of the Hebrew alphabet and of the tarot; and the 64 of the I Ching, to cite four prominent examples. Despite the multitudinous variations and contrasts possible with 9, 10, 12, 22, and even 64 constituent parts, every last part is fully accepted and included as necessary to the functioning of reality.

In all the above cases, the various quotient numbers show how the One operates when divided into this or that many parts. Although the parts may be many and varied, they still work together as a single, organic, *spiritual unit*. Every part, whether positive or negative, is accepted and honored as fulfilling a necessary role.

This is not, however, the case with mundane symbol systems. In form symbol systems, the holistic approach does not apply. They are divided *from* the One and, in their isolation, live in their own little worlds, complete unto themselves. All symbol systems—mundane and spiritual—have a unified self-consistency. This is what holds them together and enables them to operate. But whereas spiritual symbol systems are universal and encompass the whole of life, mundane systems are linked to time and place, and they specialize in one aspect or another of the One. Mundane symbol systems are, therefore, fragments of the whole. This is another way of saying that each mundane symbol system is dominated by certain spiritual principles (that is, types of experience) while they are unaffected by other spiritual principles, leaving a void. Each fragment develops according to the predominating energies of the spiritual principles involved. However, without all the principles necessary to life, mundane symbol systems are inherently unbalanced. Indeed, the extremes of mundane symbol systems keep them eternally tumultuous and ceaselessly changing. Like wheels unbalanced by weights on their rims, they never achieve an enduring state of equilibrium.

On the surface, many mundane systems seem to be the antithesis of what we ordinarily consider to be spiritual. This is because they frequently include such elements as greed, avarice, deceit, cruelty, recklessness, alienation, killing, warfare, lust for power and glory, selfishness, anxiety, hopelessness, despair, egotism—all conventional evils, fears, and desires. When these kinds of negativities occur in a spiritual symbol system, there are remedies (that is, spiritual principles) available to right the wrongs. Mundane symbol systems, on the other hand, have no such self-regulating mechanism for negativities inherent to them. Excesses are natural to mundane systems. In fact, within the context of the mundane symbol system itself, a spiritual negative is sometimes deemed necessary for success and is, therefore, considered to be good!

Since mundane symbol systems have no inner resolution mechanism for what might be called their spiritual ills, the solution lies outside them. The very idea that a symbol system itself is a problem is a concept of spiritual symbol systems. I do not speak here of individual belief systems being singled out by other belief systems as being inherently wrong or evil. Rather, I refer to *all* mundane symbol systems as being incomplete in their representation of All Life. As it is the nature of life to restore wholeness, mundane symbol systems ceaselessly evolve toward wholeness without ever reaching it. When things in our lives change, there is always work and effort to be done. The evolution of a given symbol system involves the same kind of struggle, meaning that certain characteristic difficulties are uninterruptedly present. It is for these reasons that, from the spiritual perspective, mundane symbol systems are essentially lessons to be learned with issues through which to work.

What, then, is the spiritual nature of mundane symbol systems? They are lessons or stages of growth. This is their purpose. Once one has puzzled over and struggled through the issues of a particular symbol system to a true spiritual resolution, those concerns are permanently brought to stasis. They have been transcended. The individual has advanced.

It is a tribute to the genius of our spiritual forerunners that they conceived such profound yet simple metaphysical symbols that can be used in any situation to rise above it and to grow spiritually.

Let's see how this works in practice, using the concept of the ego as an example. In all spiritual symbol systems, the ego is a crucial issue through which to work. The ego is the lower self, an individual's self-concept of his "I." It is the part of our nature that is "attached" to the world and its problems through the dual impulses of desire and fear. It is the ego that is trapped on the wheel of karma and is thereby consigned to reincarnate life after life until its lessons are learned and the slate of misdeeds is cleansed. Thus, in spiritual symbol systems, it is a universal goal to purify the ego and to let go of it.

Ego issues are present in many mundane symbol systems, but generally in ways that ignore or negate the spiritual goal of transcendence. As a consequence, many religious and metaphysical groups respond by instructing their adherents simply to reject "the ways of the world" and to rise above personal faults without addressing those issues or working them through. At the same time, we know the world is Spirit, and the ways of the world are Spirit, too.

But in what way?

We will examine this question in terms of two mundane symbol systems: the military and the American. Both are tremendously vast and multifaceted. No simple or brief interpretation can encompass the full scope of ego in either system. However, if the reader will bear with one well-known ego perspective from each of these systems, they will fully serve to illustrate the spiritual nature of our mundane reality.

The ego has a prominent role in the military symbol system. In a sense, the military requires a resolute ego. The ideal is for people in the military to be strong, courageous, able to demonstrate unwavering purpose, and willing to put their lives at risk when required to do so. A prerequisite to this strong-mindedness, beginning with the recruits' first moment of training, is to accept the external authority of the military over their own lives by sublimating their individualities. They learn to follow regulations and to obey orders unquestioningly, regardless of personal preference or belief. Every recruit who enters military service brings his own unresolved issues of ego. During military service, life inevitably causes him to address some of his personal issues one way or another, but not as part of the military symbol system. Its purpose is to maintain an organized and disciplined fighting force. This can only be accomplished if the individual's personal ego is repressed, to be superseded by the military imperative. Consequently, nothing of the personal ego is resolved, healed, or transcended. Apart from a particular type of issue concerning strength, perseverance, and the like, which are necessary to perform well in the military, no flaw or weakness is questioned or faced. If anything, some of the baser instincts are reinforced, and some shortcomings of the lower self are strengthened.

A very different approach to the ego occurs in the American national symbol system. Here the emphasis is on fulfilling personal wants and needs. The American dream promises every American that wealth, well-being, achievement, and happiness are within reach if the proper effort is made to attain them. Freedom and opportunity are the bywords of this culture. The pursuit of all these attainments has a bit of the "Wild West" in it, along with the added proviso "may the best man win." "Best man" here does not mean the one who is the most just, the most worthy, the most generous, or the wisest, but the man or woman who is the most tenacious and competitive, and who, in fact, is willing to sacrifice "impractical ideals" in order to reach the top. Instead of being concerned with such values as self-discipline, sacrifice, patience, and moderation, we are encouraged to follow our whims and desires as far as they take us. And we admire things done on a grand scale: bigger, faster, richer, newer, better, and so on.

This portrait of the American ego is essentially opposite to a spiritualized ego. The entire emphasis is on chasing after external things with no heed at all paid to the inner self. The values and aspirations are all decidedly worldly and materialistic with no regard for character development. American ego specializes in ease, comfort, and the good life.

At first glance, the military ego and the American ego seem unrelated to what is required in spiritual life. The goal in spiritual symbol systems is to attain a balanced, disciplined, and moderated ego that is attuned to higher principles. In contrast to this, the military ego is essentially fear-based, while the American ego is desire-based. On one level, both ego concepts cited here are legitimate and equal inasmuch as each is valid within its own symbol system. But from the spiritual vantage point, the military and American versions are stages of development through which the individual self must pass before he can achieve full selfhood and rise to a higher plane of being. With regard to the military, the emphasis is on the dominance of its system and organization, and the submission of the individual to its purpose and authority. Spiritually, people in the military are at a certain stage of growth of their soul. In number symbolism, these learnings are right at the heart of the kinds of experiences represented by four digit numbers, 1,000 to 9,999. On the positive side, these numbers concern what it takes to establish, and to follow through on, purposeful activity. On the negative side of four digit numbers, the lessons have to do with experiencing servitude.

The American emphasis on freedom, individuality, and the fulfillment of personal desires finds its place in the kinds of experiences represented by five digit numbers, 10,000 to 99,999. On the positive side, this stage of growth has to do with having the adventurousness and resourcefulness to experience the world as opportunity, and to make the most of it. The negative polarity of five digit numbers is fearing to be who and what one is in the world. Thus, although the American national symbol system cannot be considered to be anything like a spiritual symbol system, it nonetheless has a distinct spiritual role to play. (Much more will be presented concerning the meanings of polydigit numbers—ten through one billion—in later chapters of this book.)

In this manner, all mundane symbol systems can be shown to work out certain aspects of spiritual principles. Using this approach, it becomes possible to understand each of our symbol systems as part of a spiritual continuum that is our uninterrupted journey as spiritual beings.

Every human being lives according to the precepts of the symbol systems to which he adheres. All of the systems together constitute a *personal operating method* for living. They are eminently pragmatic because they cover exactly how to handle all aspects of a person's life. All concepts of being must, by definition, also be spiritual, because they arise out of Spirit. Consequently, those symbol systems are also collectively what might be called a *personal spiritual symbol system,* in contrast to a *universal spiritual symbol system* such as number symbolism. This body of personal symbolism is not an arbitrary selection. It exactly mirrors the needs and the level of evolution of the incarnated soul.

Now, there are innumerable people in the world whose symbol systems do not appear to be "of spirit" by any stretch of the imagination. Furthermore, they do not consider, or even desire, their worldly symbol systems to be spiritual. This amounts to differences in the definition of *Spirit.* Many people have a form-based concept of Spirit. Their understanding is based on their personal set of symbol systems. Their concept of Spirit is therefore limited and evolves as their symbolic understanding grows and matures. Stated another way, understanding of Spirit advances as the lessons of mundane symbol systems are learned and mastered.

If this point can be grasped—that all symbol systems are spiritual in that they are workings of aspects of Spirit—it helps greatly with learning the deeper meanings of spiritual symbol systems. This way, the "bits and pieces of life" can be correctly connected, organized, and eventually absorbed into the spiritual symbol system with which one works.

The personal set of symbol systems you have accumulated up to this point in your life represent reality to you. Those concepts give form to your Deep Purpose, and also represent a kind of strategy for how to achieve it. In other words, if you take a close look at your personal symbolism, it will tell you *what life is all about* for you. This approach will no doubt come as a shock to the person who has decided that the answer to the question "Why am I here?" is too deep a mystery to know, or who has concluded there is no ultimate purpose. It would not occur to such a person that the Present Moment is a concise statement of his life's purpose and how he is striving to achieve it. To a great extent, this is because he does not view the events and challenges of his life as being on the level of spiritual activity. He generally passes off his daily existence as too ordinary, too common, too flawed, even too mundane to qualify as being "spiritual." He may feel that in the course of his life he occasionally encounters spiritual issues, but that his life as a whole falls through the metaphysical cracks and fails to meet the high standard of things spiritual. People with these kinds of attitudes are arbitrarily choosing which elements of life to view as spiritual and which to reject as unworthy of being spiritual. Needless to say, it does not work that way.

What, then, are symbols? In essence, they are abstract concepts that represent the intangible substance of inner self. In order to build up a body of symbolism, we create mental constructs that give form to meanings of personal significance. These concepts overlay everything—*everything*—in our lives, with the result that all things of which we are aware have a symbolic meaning and function. This includes not only formally designated symbols like those of religion, science, and art, but the entirety of daily life—home, career, family, friends, entertainment, travel—all the typical fare of life, in other words, and even intangibles like thoughts, feelings, attitudes, problems and challenges, goals and achievements, and so on. All things are symbolic.

It is of enormous value to learn the nature and workings of the symbols we have in our lives through the study of spiritual symbol systems. Such reflection teaches values and priorities. Our daily life and all that is in it is a metaphor of our spirit, a living image of who we are. Symbol knowledge and understanding help us to live better. There is additionally a far deeper potential of spiritual symbolism hidden from the prying eyes of mundane consciousness. I refer to the enigmatic creative potency of spiritual symbol systems to modify, or to bring into being, what we call the conditions of reality. Ultimately, the value of spiritual symbol systems is union with Spirit.

In order to be real and to function fully, symbols must carry through to the physical level and be grounded in daily existence. Symbols that are conceived only on theoretical, intellectual, or emotional levels do impact our lives to one degree or another, but they do not take root in reality. Their full blossoming can only occur when they live where we ourselves live: in the heart and mind.

Symbols do not exist when they are in isolation, just as "shadows" have no independent existence from "light" or from "something that blocks" the light. A pattern of "light and shadow" comes about only as the result of all three of these symbols operating together. This is a difficult point of understanding because we live in a world where everything is in combination. We have never known of any symbols that were not combined with, well, *everything else*. Although we talk of what a symbol becomes when it is in a state of isolation, that can be no more than a hypothetical discussion. We can only transcend symbols in our imagination while in deep meditation. Even though we might contemplate a particular symbol alone and by itself, in fact it is not in true isolation. It is only being emphasized to the exclusion of any other symbols. All the other symbols are still there, still fully "combined" with the one being examined. Consider another example, the characteristic of tall and short people. If every person on earth—newborns, children, and adults—were exactly six feet tall, the concept of tall and short people would cease to exist. If it were pointed out that those people who were six foot people would be taller than, say, dogs, and shorter than houses, this would resuscitate the concept of tall and short. But it would do so only by putting the *height of people* symbol in relation to other symbols. It is the *combination* of symbols plus their *interrelationships* that enable us to ascribe people with the characteristics of tall or short.

In the same way, the reality of our lives exists as a result of the interactions of many symbols. We gain the ability to function in life by ascertaining useful patterns for living from amongst the multitudes of symbols we have created. We instinctively group related patterns into basic "areas of experience" called symbol systems. These are *artificial* organisms because they are not inherent in Spirit, but instead are devices of perception created by human beings. Once a symbol system becomes established in our consciousness, we are then able to create and sustain the forms of thinking, feeling, and acting that derive from the matrix of that symbol system. Every individual has many hundreds of such symbol systems in his life.

Although symbol systems encompass within them every manner of opposite and contradiction, they are in actuality wholly unified, integrated, and self-consistent. Inner differences—polarities—do not cause symbol systems to combat themselves and thereby to self-destruct. Rather, oppositions breathe life into them much as free market competition brings vitality to commerce.

All but a few symbol systems (those we call spiritual) have their basis in form. Form symbol systems (or mundane symbol systems, as I have been calling them) are by nature limited and are not, therefore, universal. Form, as the reader will recall, refers to anything having structure, pattern, organization, or an essential nature. A moment's reflection on this point will demonstrate that virtually everything we know in life has form, even those elements we might characterize as being chaotic, undefined, abstract, spiritual, ineffable, or inexpressible. Each form symbol system has its own characteristic nature unique to it, which differentiates it from any other symbol system. This can sometimes appear to be not entirely true. When an individual adapts different symbol systems so they work together in his life, those systems can appear to blend together and to function as one comprehensive, homogeneous symbol system. The fact that they are in relationship does not, however, change the fact of their different natures.

Each individual chooses and is responsible for the symbol systems that make up his life. It is a person's Deep Purpose that determines which symbol systems he adopts. That Deep Purpose, in other words, develops into a "Philosophy of Life." That Philosophy of Life is not exclusively the result of intellectual endeavor through book learning, discussion, or thought. It is, rather, the nuts and bolts principles (that is, the symbol systems) by which we live and breathe every day. It is through use of his own philosophy that an individual interprets and manages his conglomerate of symbol systems. All of a person's symbol systems work in tandem under the direction of his Deep Purpose / Philosophy of Life.

Spiritual symbol systems, the main subject of this book, are an exception to the limitation of form. This is because ultimately they have no form and are consequently unlimited and universal. They *appear* to have form (and thereby seem to be limited) because Spirit uses mundane form to express and manifest itself. Spiritual symbol systems are but portals through which Spirit may flow without being diminished or fragmented.

For our part, we humans rely on spiritual symbol systems to reach out to Spirit. When we devote ourselves to a spiritual symbol system, it becomes for us a state of readiness in which to receive Spirit. This Tool of Being comes as close as we can get to Spirit on our own devices.

The term "symbol" is commonly thought to be an object, pictograph, or idea that represents something else. In my thinking, this is misleading. It leads us to believe that symbols are something outside ourselves that we experience externally. It gives the impression that symbols are naturally imbued with their own significance.

As we have previously discussed at length, however, it is the individual, and the individual alone, who creates symbols and finds meaning in them. "To symbolize" is an ability we have. It is an innate aptitude deep within our being very much akin to that of *thinking.* Think about it. Webster's Dictionary gives as its first definition of the verb *to think:* "to form or conceive in the mind; have in the mind as an idea, image, conception, etc."[2] I suggest that the faculty of thinking is synonymous with the capacity to symbolize. Every thought we generate is a symbolic act. Every time we think something through, we are processing symbolic matter.

The essence of symbolism, therefore, is not to be found in objects or concepts outside us. Those things we recognize as symbols are but instances of an inner process of conceptualization that works at every level of our being, conscious and unconscious.

In the remaining chapters of this book, we will discuss how to learn and use number symbolism, a spiritual symbol system. The material presented on these pages should not be considered strictly informatory. This work is in actuality a manual for the training of the mind. *If* we are able to penetrate deeply enough into our inner process of symbol-making in the proper way, *if* we fully integrate these learnings into our living, and *if* we apply this knowledge perseveringly day-by-day until it becomes automatic to our nature, then we will achieve what every spiritual system promises.

Endnotes

1. Neither the examples cited nor the order in which they are given are intended to express an opinion as to their relative merit. It is the author's conviction that there are many valid spiritual symbol systems whose only criterion for use is personal preference.

2. *Webster's Encyclopedic Unabridged Dictionary of the English Language* (New York: Gramercy Books, 1994), 1475.

chapter 5

Toward a Science of Meaning and Relationship

We are, in effect, metaphors for the Spirit.

—Sarah Voss, *What Number is God?*

Mathematics is the symbol system of symbol systems. This is not because mathematics is the best of all symbol systems, but rather because it is universally applicable. It is literally all system without any meaning of its own inherent to it. There is, in other words, no scientific, religious, cultural, artistic, mythic, or any other type of subject matter intrinsic to mathematics. Its vast structure consists entirely of highly elaborated sets of relationships. Those relationships, of course, are those shared by the numbers where the potential for meaning lies.

Numbers are the most abstract of concepts. Beyond this, it is difficult to say what numbers are because they fulfill so many functions. They have an astonishing array of uses, from ordinary counting to the representation of numbers that defy mathematical principle, called *imaginary numbers*,[1] with measurements, proportions, averages, probabilities, variables, functions, and much more in between. We are fully accustomed to the use of numbers to represent concrete qualities (6 oranges or 5 houses, for example), as well as less tangible amounts (sixty miles per hour, seventeen degrees Fahrenheit, sixteen days, twenty dollars, and so on), and even some purely mathematical constructs (such as algebraic formulas, number sets, and formulas of fractal geometry that represent the shapes of nature).

If we base our definition of numbers on their use in daily life, it is tempting to say that numbers quantify. But this is simply not adequate as a definition. Consider the numbers 5 and 10, with the x representing an unknown in the formula $5x = 10$. In this case, 5 and 10 are not quantities of anything. What this formula expresses is a *relationship* between 5 and 10. More than that, it is a relationship *in the abstract,* with no application to anything specific yet established. The x plays an interesting role here: it is a symbol of a symbol (numbers are symbols) whose numeric value is yet to be determined. And what of imaginary numbers that cannot exist, but do? Again, they express relationships in an esoteric corner of mathematical thinking. It is clear that numbers do much more than count.

A key element in the understanding of what numbers are lies in the function they serve. Plainly stated, they are nothing if they are not used for something. They must have a purpose for them to be valued. Numbers in pure mathematics are considered pointless and irrelevant until it can be shown they have a use. The bottom line is: "What are they good for?" The answer in innumerable guises is always the same: they must have meaning for us. Meaning is what gives mathematics and all other symbol systems their significance. The marvel is that mathematics, more so than any other symbol system, can be applied to any area of human activity or experience that has some sort of order or organization.

With this in mind, I was fascinated recently to learn of efforts to apply mathematics to human mental activity as part of the research into artificial intelligence. Of this, James Gleick wrote:

> Many other scientists began to apply the formalisms of chaos to research in artificial intelligence. The dynamics of systems wandering between basins of attraction, for example, appealed to those looking for a way to model symbols and memories. A physicist thinking of *ideas* as regions with fuzzy boundaries, separate but overlapping, pulling like magnets and yet letting go, would naturally turn to the image of a phase space with "basins of attraction"! Such models seemed to have the right features: points of stability mixed with instability, and regions of changeable boundaries. Their fractal structures offered the kind of infinitely self-referential quality that seems so central to the mind's ability to bloom with ideas, decisions, emotions and all the other artifacts of consciousness.[2]

The above quoted passage is packed with mathematical images and concepts: chaos (theory), basins of attraction, ideas as regions with fuzzy boundaries, phase space, fractal structure, infinitely self-referential quality, and so on. All this demonstrates an imaginative effort to make mathematics work in a new way: to represent the underlying nature of mental activity and intelligence. I have no doubt that these elusive and complex processes will eventually be shown to have an inner structure that can be expressed with numbers and formulas.

What then, can we say, is the definition of numbers? They are a set of abstract symbols, without built-in meaning, that share precise relationships with each other from which they cannot be separated. Numbers and mathematical principles are inextricable, in the same way members of a family cannot be separated from who they are to each other. Each individual—wife, husband, daughter, son, aunt, uncle, grandmother, grandfather—is fully her or his own person. Yet it is not possible to mention two or more of them without evoking their relationship to each other at the same time. In a similar manner, numbers and mathematical principles have no existence apart from each other. Consequently, any concept of numbers (including symbolic numbers) that does not include the mathematical system cannot be considered complete.

Almost every last symbol system in existence is known first and foremost by its subject matter. That is to say, it is the surface meaning and experience that catch the eye and engage the interest. For many people, that is all there is to any symbol system. Think about it. At the mention of such symbol systems as space exploration, the ancient culture of Egypt, coin collecting, the plight of endangered species, global warming, and the value of a university education, most peoples' attention focuses on the external images and facts, and the feelings they have about them. Few people seek to know the underlying causal essence of the symbol system that determines the outward effects and appearance. Ironically, the very concepts and experiences by which a symbol system is known also curiously tend to distract attention from the fundamental mechanisms of its real inner nature.

Such is not the case with mathematics, and this is the significant point. Its components (the numbers) and their interrelationships (the mathematical principles) *are* the symbol system. Although its complexities can be exceedingly difficult for the intellect to grasp, at the same time, they are what they are: straightforward, clear, and unobscured. However, that clarity tends to become clouded and subject to differences of understanding as soon as mathematics is applied to something; when, that is, some form of meaning or human experience becomes the subject matter of mathematical thinking.

Despite what we generally think of mathematics, the system is not actually made up of numbers and the principles that express relationships between numbers. Rather, the mathematical system consists of the *idea* of numbers and the *idea* of principles. This is no hairsplitting distinction. Mathematics has no physical existence. The entire system is a mental concept—a tool of the mind—that we express with written symbols in order to make it easier to use. Its use can apply to anything having form. The term "form" is employed here in its broad philosophical meaning, which encompasses all that makes up the physical, manifested level of existence. Here, all aspects of life are characterized by having "structure, pattern, organization or an essential nature."[3] This is what mathematics is all about in the final analysis. It is a grand metaphor of this inclusive concept of form. All the diverse uses of mathematics are but specific applications of this archetypal symbolism of form. For these reasons, it can be said of mathematics that it symbolizes the nature of form itself. Form is the true subject matter, the real meaning, of mathematics. Thus, mathematics is more than a technical form of knowledge. It is a philosophy because it is an interpreter of this plane of existence, the archetypal level of form.

Mathematics does, of course, have structure, so it does itself have form. But this is an elastic, elusive, ethereal kind of form. It can assume any shape, so to speak, from the most concrete to the most abstract levels of earthly existence. Said another way, mathematics is capable of representing, or modeling, the inner and outer natures of anything. A striking example of this is the strange, super minuscule world of subatomic particles. This surrealistic realm forms the basis of our physical universe. Yet, no one knows what it looks like, how it functions, or even what it really is, despite the many verbal descriptions and illustrations widely available. It is described as consisting solely of nodules of energy (no hard matter) all spinning and traveling at inconceivable rates of speed. Although the subatomic level is nearly unimaginable in ordinary human terms, it does have form, and this has enabled physicists to express that form mathematically.

Among the fields amenable to mathematical representation is the spiritual path. Although this way of life is far removed from the hustle and bustle of daily life, as well as being eternally enshrouded in mystery, it has form nonetheless, with an identifiable structure to it. Part of its mystique arises from the belief that the spiritual path is profoundly not-of-this-world, and that it originates in Realms of Spirit, giving it an unfathomable and impenetrable quality. The initial inspiration of spiritual belief systems may well be from a transcendent source, but the concepts and symbols developed to represent the Way of Spirit are human conclusions. Thus, while the ultimate goal of the spiritual quest is unpredictable and unknowable, the path that leads toward it is quite well known. That path can definitely be represented mathematically.

In earlier chapters, we discussed how number symbolism has been used all over the world to signify spiritual principles and ideals ever since the initial development of mathematics thousands of years ago. Over time, many different forms of number symbolism have been developed. Today, "numerology" is the best known term for this type of symbolism, but "number symbolism" is a more accurate reference. Yet both terms are truly inadequate to describe that to which they refer. Numerology is described as the study of numbers in order to determine their influence on our lives. Number symbolism, equally, emphasizes the role of numbers. Almost nowhere is mention made of mathematical principles as being part of the symbolic meaning, neither the necessity of their inclusion nor the wealth of information they contain.

This omission is certainly the case with Pythagorean numerology. The meanings of the numbers 1 through 9 have been extensively developed, but the mathematical principles, symbolizing the many ways to use those numbers, are virtually ignored. This is a most bizarre situation. Without addition, subtraction, multiplication, division, and all the many other functions, principles, and formulas that are part of mathematics today, symbolic numbers are inert and nearly useless. Consequently, in my view, the correct and proper term for symbolism consisting of numbers is mathematical symbolism. Henceforth in this book, the term mathematical symbolism will be used to refer to any symbolism whose basis is numbers.

It is a given that the technological level of today's world could not exist in its present form if we had no means to add 6 to 8 or to divide 11 by 4. Spiritual mathematical symbolism is equally limited when deprived of the mathematical system. If symbolic numbers have no mechanism governing their interactions, they do no more than lay fallow. On their own devices, *nothing happens*. They do not *become* anything. Pythagorean numerology does, of course, use addition and subtraction to calculate many numbers of the numerology chart. But they are only considered to be procedural techniques, no more. There is no recognition that those procedures have symbolic significance. For example, when two symbolic numbers are added together, their respective meanings are synthesized, producing a new number and a new meaning. We are accustomed to think of addition quite differently, simply as a mechanical method for combining separate units into one, larger group of units; for example, 8 pears + 7 bananas + 4 strawberries = 19 fruits. It is entirely another matter to add symbolic numbers; this process is more like chemistry when chemicals are combined. When hydrogen and oxygen are combined (or added, as we say in mathematical symbolism) to form water, the chemical properties (meanings) of each chemical (number) are synthesized (added) to form a new chemical (number) with an entirely new group of chemical properties (meanings). In numerology and mathematical symbolism, there is no part or aspect that is strictly objective. All of it has meaning, *subjective* meaning.

In all of mathematical symbolism in use today, the role of mathematics has yet to be discovered and understood. This was not the case in Pythagoras' time, when all known mathematical principles were part of the system. But Greek mathematical symbolism, fraught as it was with weakness and controversy, faded from use in the fifth century C.E. During the ensuing eight centuries, there was no culture of mathematics in the West to foster development of a new mathematical symbolism. Then, in the 1200s, Europe began to experience a renaissance of mathematics with the adoption of Arabic numbers. Numbers themselves could now be used for calculations. No longer was it necessary to add and subtract on the abacus-like counting board, then record the result with Roman numerals in a second and separate step.

Mathematical symbolism was set for a rebirth along with the rest of European culture. Unfortunately, its development was stymied for most of the twentieth century by a two-pronged assault. First, the heresiologists (papal authorities who studied and identified heresy) of the Catholic Church worked tirelessly to distort and discredit all non-Christian beliefs. The best known part of this centuries-long vendetta was the infamous Inquisition. Even the celebrated artist Michelangelo was forced to beg for his life in a church-sanctioned trial because he had placed the figure of a human being higher than that of Jesus Christ in one of his paintings. Second, metaphysical and religious beliefs of all kinds began to be spurned by large segments of society with the advent of science in the 1600s. As a result, various forms of the gnosis—the direct experience of Spirit—were forced underground into secret societies. Occult knowledge became profoundly camouflaged behind perplexing symbolic images.

Although mathematical symbolism is no longer actively persecuted in the present age, it has not yet recovered from the prolonged repressions of the twentieth century. So it is today that Pythagorean numerology's principles are all based on no more than the characteristics of the numbers 1 through 9. There can be no doubt that 0 would universally comprise the tenth number if the zero had been present in the mathematics of ancient Greece. All the above notwithstanding, an analysis of the nine numbers as they appear in a modern numerology chart offers a fascinating spiritual and psychological profile of an individual. Such an analysis includes insights into a person's basic nature, personality, motivations, perceived purpose, approaches to work, relationships, and making decisions, traits, characteristics, strengths and weaknesses, imbalances, inner conflicts, cycles that focus on challenges and on ways of coping with people and situations, and much more.

As marvelous and penetrating as a Pythagorean numerology analysis is, it is perhaps insignificant when compared to the full potential of mathematical symbolism. This is because numerology, which uses numbers without mathematical principles, lacks any interpretative mechanism in two decisive areas. First, there is no way to determine how a life is being lived; in other words, whether an individual is living to his full potential or simply existing in a low, even depraved, state of being. The way a life is lived is symbolized by mathematical principles and formulas, beginning with the four basic functions of addition, subtraction, multiplication, and division, and continuing all the way up to the specialized operations of geometry, algebra, trigonometry, calculus, and even the profundities of physics. Every last function of every branch of mathematics represents some mode of living, behavior, action, skill, or spiritual power.

The debilitating limitations of number-only symbolism become abundantly clear when considered from the perspective of other fields of endeavor. Take music, for example. Someone who is expert in playing the scales—the basic elements of music—but who produces no songs, symphonies, or other kinds of compositions, cannot be said to make music, no matter how exquisitely he plays the scales. Now consider chemistry. People who are proficient in their knowledge of chemical elements, but who go no further to combine them into compounds or products, or even to experiment with different combinations of elements, cannot be said to be chemists. Finally, think about language. Anyone whose expertise in language is his mastery of the sounds and letters of the alphabet, but who forms no words or sentences, who never gives verbal expression to thoughts or converses with others, would never be said to speak language. In each one of these three cases—music, chemistry, and language—use of no more than the basic elements is insufficient for them to exist as disciplines of skill and expression in the first place!

On this basis, a person who has a thorough understanding of symbolic numbers and knows how to compare their characteristics, but who makes no use of the mathematical system, has no means to bring those numbers to life. He cannot be called a mathematician.

The second void of interpretation in present-day Pythagorean numerology is that it is unequipped to reveal the spiritual level at which a person is living. The single digit numbers (which are its mainstay, along with an occasional use of two digit numbers) cannot be more than the most general of indicators. Each of the numbers 1 through 9 has a tremendous range of levels at which a person could be functioning: from positive to negative, and from nascent soul to highly-evolved being. The same combination of single-digit numbers in a numerology chart could be those of a Ghandi or an Einstein, a Picasso, a Shakespeare, a President Kennedy, or it could be those of a hobo, a criminal, a mentally retarded individual, or someone suffering from psychosis. In Pythagorean numerology, there is simply no way to distinguish one extreme from the other. Both of these interpretative voids will be extensively explored and developed throughout much of the remainder of this book.

We now turn to a consideration of Pythagorean numerology as it is presently practiced, complete with the numerology chart on which the numbers are displayed. The chart location of each number, called the *position*, identifies a particular aspect of human nature. Numerology charts vary tremendously as to the number and selection of positions. As a general rule, they contain at least a dozen. Here, we will discuss only four of the positions found in most charts—those that represent the four key aspects of a person's nature. This approach will necessarily exclude a wealth of information and modifying details that individualize a chart and provide subtlety of insight. The benefit of studying a foreshortened chart is that it enables the reader to grasp the basic principles of numerology without having to grapple with making sense of its full complexity. This approach also provides the means to gain a personal concept of, and a rapport with, the numbers as universal principles. This is accomplished by recognizing the universal elements as they are present in our own nature, which results in knowing the universal in subjective, or personal, terms. In this manner, the abstract nature of numbers can be linked with personal experience, helping to make the numbers real and dynamic in the mind of the learner.

In today's numerological literature, numbers are usually defined by their effects, which are described in detail in extensive lists of characteristics. Those attributes, however, are secondary to the essential nature of numbers, that which *causes* the effects. Effects cannot define what symbolic numbers are; they only give evidence of the numeric activity. In mathematical symbolism, numbers are energies or forces. Each of the ten numbers, 0 through 9, relates to a major area of human experience. On the philosophical level, numbers are spiritual principles, the most basic elements of life.

It is self-evident that with just ten numbers, the applications and consequences of each number are extremely broad and comprehensive in their implications. They are, in fact, infinite. Consequently, an individual's understanding of each number progresses indefinitely, and he can never attain a final and complete grasp. Work with symbolic numbers is ever in process, a living and personal evolution. The goal of these efforts might be thought to be a perfect realization of the potential of each number. There is great beauty and dignity that comes with mastery of a high degree. But this is akin to striving for the never-never state of infinity: infinite mastery over infinite changes. An alternative goal, and one that is fully attainable, is to reach a state of balance and harmony with each number, regardless of the form of its expression. Numbers are quite literally *forces of experience,* which compel us irresistibly through a course of development. Certain numbers are present in the life of each individual, in particular combinations. The individual lives them at a particular level of spiritual development. The challenge facing each person is to maximize the potential of his combination of numbers at the level of his ability. The full realization of that is an achievement indeed! This road might be called the *personal spiritual path.* For a deeper spiritual experience that transcends the personal (or lower) self, it is necessary to extend one's involvement equally to all the numbers in all their combinations. This is the *universal spiritual path.*

There are nine basic numbers in Pythagorean numerology, 1 through 9, to which I now add the tenth: 0. Zero is, of course, a prominent number in today's mathematics. It has been so for hundreds of years. Yet most numerologists do not accept 0 as a symbolic number. This is due to the fact that mathematical symbolism reached a peak of development in early Greece during the time of Pythagoras before 0 existed in mathematics. At that time, ten numbers were the basis of their mathematical symbol system, 1 through 10, reflecting the same base ten numbering system we use today. Of course, in today's mathematics, 10 is a two digit number, which was not the case in ancient Greece. In our time, however, 10 begins a new class of numbers, that class being numbers consisting of two digits: 10 through 99. Some of these two-digit numbers are used as symbolic numbers, including 10, 20, and 30. Consider, now, that these two-digit symbolic numbers are no more than combinations of single digit numbers that include 0. If 0 were not fully a symbolic number, it could not be used to make composite symbolic numbers.

When 0 did finally enter mathematics in Europe, beginning around 1200 C.E., it was highly controversial for centuries and actually feared as evil. Few could understand (or accept!) a number that stood for *nothing.* Lodged deep within the cultural mind was the concept that a number stands for *something,* a quantity that could be counted. The nothingness of 0, along with the reverence for sacred tradition, ensured that 0 would have no place in mathematical symbolism for many centuries to come. Therefore, even though 0 has no current role in Pythagorean numerology,[4] I include it here. It is one of the ten elemental, single-digit numbers of mathematical symbolism that can no longer be ignored.

The meanings of the ten basic numbers are as follows:

0 Nothingness. Nonexistence. Formlessness. The unmanifest. The void, beyond Time and Space. Realm of Spirit. The Eternal Force. The basis of all that exists. The potential of infinite possibility.

Types of experience associated with this Force: bliss, serenity. Alternatively: annihilation.

1 *The Force:* the will to be.

Types of experience associated with this Force: belief in self, self-confidence, going one's own way, strength of will, independence, self-assertion, taking initiative, taking action, leadership (with others or oneself), starting anew, creativity. Alternatively: egotism, bossiness, unwillingness to cooperate, stubbornness, aggression, being a loner, fear of being, dependence.

2 *The Force:* to differentiate all things infinitely.

Types of experience associated with this Force: being a follower, sensitivity to others, attentiveness to others, depth of feeling, helpfulness, deference to others, gentleness, modesty, willingness to listen, willingness to cooperate, diplomacy, having a sense of timing, skillfulness in relationships. Alternatively: indecisiveness, emotional confusion, inability to act, helplessness, apathy, passivity, vulnerability, lacking a sense of self, instability, being easily hurt, timidity, fearfulness.

3   *The Force:* to develop a concept of the "I."

Types of experience associated with this Force: enjoyment of being in the moment, happiness, optimism, friendliness, graciousness, charm, popularity, playfulness, fancifulness, being imaginative, verbal ability, self-expression, sociability, self-fulfillment, personal creativity. Alternatively: self-centeredness, selfishness, hedonism, scatteredness, superficiality, indolence, neediness of appreciation, escapism, living in a fantasy world.

4   *The Force:* to be purposeful in living.

Types of experience associated with this Force: rationality, being systematic, being organized, groundedness, seriousness, practicality, honesty, responsibility, stability, diligence, working hard, strength, patience, perseverance, endurance, building a foundation. Alternatively: dullness, dryness of feeling, literality, intolerance, unforgiveness, limitation, frustration, inflexibility, resistance to change, stubbornness, bossiness, dogmatism.

5   *The Force:* to live according to one's individuality.

Types of experience associated with this Force: being free, enthusiasm, sensuality, adventurousness, seeking and searching in the world, expansiveness, eagerness to learn, love of exploration, flexibility, resourcefulness, gutsiness, taking risks, showmanship, quick thinking, wittiness, wheeling and dealing, maximizing opportunities, prospering on the earth plane. Alternatively: fearfulness of taking chances, impatience, restlessness, rebelliousness, flightiness, sensationalism, being consumed by sensual needs, needing to be entertained, unwillingness to make commitments, opportunism.

6   *The Force:* to live by spiritual values.

Types of experience associated with this Force: being there for others, meeting others' needs, being responsible, making commitments, love, marriage, strength of feeling, involvement in others' lives, being a pillar of the community, balance, harmony, beauty, artistry, teaching and healing others. Alternatively: repression of individuality, having unmet personal needs, sacrificing personal interest, being overly emotional, distorted idealism, interference in others' lives, needing to gossip, control and manipulation.

7   *The Force:* to live the truth of one's self.

Types of experience associated with this Force: needing to be alone, introspection, depth of thought, searching for insight and understanding, resolution of inner negative karma, intelligence, analysis, studiousness, professionalism, reflection, being philosophical, meditativeness, individualism, pureness of heart, being intuitive, spiritual seeking. Alternatively: being withdrawn, mysteriousness, difficulty dealing with feelings, reluctance to share feelings, aloofness, unwillingness to trust, being critical, social awkwardness, preference to work alone, eccentrism, fear of the unknown.

8   *The Force:* to be empowered in living.

Types of experience associated with this Force: self-confidence, being highly energetic, seriousness, purposefulness, competitiveness, self-sufficiency, forcefulness, powerfulness, discernment, having good judgment, decisiveness, authoritativeness, doing what needs to be done, resolution of negative karma, productivity, bringing about justice, attaining achievement. Alternatively: weakness, being a victim, coldness of feeling, inconsideration, contentiousness, ruthlessness, being overly demanding, materialism, stubbornness, dictatoriality.

9   *The Force:* to be one with life.

Types of experience associated with this Force: giving unconditional love, humanitarianism, universality, having charisma, romance, theatricality, having intuition, artistic creation, humility, compassion, selflessness, idealism, spiritual growth, inspiration, freedom from egoism, pure knowingness, living spiritually, divine love, transcendence. Alternatively: profound egotism, fanaticism, grandiosity, being melodramatic, impracticality, selfishness, experiencing pain and loss.

Numerology charts are calculated by first converting the letters of the birth month and birth name into the numbers that correspond to them. The idea of assigning single-digit numbers to the letters of the alphabet originated with Cornelius Agrippa (1486–1535), German astrologer and Kabalistic philosopher. Prior to his time, letter-number alphabets like the Hebrew alphabet and the Greek alphabet served both as alphabets and as numbering systems, establishing a tradition of associating numbers with letters. To this end, the first nine letters of the Hebrew alphabet also stood for the numbers 1 through 9. The second group of nine letters was also the tens, 10 through 90, and the third group of nine letters also signified the hundreds, 100 through 900. These letter-number associations still exist today, but only for use in mathematical symbolism. Since the letters of the English alphabet have never served as numbers for mathematical purposes, all our letters are assigned a value between 1 and 9. This requires J through Z, the tenth through the twenty-sixth letters, to be reduced to a single-digit number. L, for example, is letter number 12. Its single-digit value becomes 3 when 12 is reduced by adding the 1 and 2.

The numerical values of the letters of the English alphabet are as follows:

1	2	3	4	5	6	7	8	9
A	B	C	D	E	F	G	H	I
J	K	L	M	N	O	P	Q	R
S	T	U	V	W	X	Y	Z	

The first position of the numerology chart with which we will be concerned is the Participation position. The number in this position indicates the way we relate to the world, and how we function in situations and relationships. It is, as it were, the role we play on the stage of life. This is the force, or energy, we mainly explore throughout our lives and with which we are most strongly involved in the world outside ourselves. It is a major area of learning and challenge in life because there is always more to learn about a number.

The Participation number is developed from the full birth date: month, day, and year. Pythagorean numerologists universally assign numbers to the month according to their position in the year. Thereby, January is 1, February is 2, and so on. A suggestion from my wife, Eve, prompted me to experiment with a different approach, that of converting the letters of each month into numbers and totaling them. She felt that the months, being primarily identified by name, should be handled the same way as personal names. I was open to considering this alternative because nowhere in the literature of Pythagorean numerology is the basis for traditional principles or techniques proven, justified, or even explained. Most everything is simply presented as though its truth were self-evident. I have found there are even some well-accepted techniques in numerology that are incorrect, a claim I do not make lightly. Consequently, there is no assurance that a given concept or technique is correct without carefully researching and testing it. My approach to decide the matter was to calculate the Participation number both ways, then to contrast the salient differences between the two numbers. When presented with this choice, I found people consistently identify with the characteristics of numbers developed from the names of months. The numbers of the month, day, and year (use all four digits) are then added together. To reduce the total, add its numbers until a single-digit number is obtained.

Example: figure the Participation number for the birth date of April 16, 1951.

First step: convert the letters of "April" to the numbers that correspond to them, then add the digits together.

$$1 + 7 + 9 + 9 + 3 = 29$$
A   P   R   I   L

Second step: total the numbers of the month, day and year. Use all four digits of the year.

```
   29
   16
+1951
 1996
```

Third step: reduce the total to a single digit by adding the numbers of the sum together, generally requiring several steps, until a single digit is obtained.

$$1 + 9 + 9 + 6 = 25, \text{ then } 2 + 5 = 7$$

The Participation number is **7.**

The practice of reducing numbers to a single digit has a long tradition in mathematical symbolism. It has been variously called the *conventional sum,* the *internal sum, diagonal addition,* and *mystical addition* at different times.[5] Its purpose is to determine the fundamental value of polydigit numbers— numbers consisting of two or more digits. This concept of reducing numbers to a single-digit number originates from ancient Greece, where they considered 10 to be the highest symbolic number. With 11 they started back again with 1, while 12 was 2, and so on. Although today 11 reduces to 2 (1 + 1 = 2) and 12 reduces to 3 (1 + 2 = 3), a difference due to the respective systems of mathematics, the underlying principle was that all numbers, no matter how large, are in essence one of the elemental, single-digit numbers. On this basis, 351, for example, has a reduced value of 9, because 3 + 5 + 1 = 9.

While there is clearly merit in determining the primary value of polydigit numbers, it should be evident that numbers consisting of two or more numbers contain additional information. With 382, for a random example, we have three numbers in fixed order that share a structured and meaningful relationship. Three is the lead number, which establishes the theme of this 382. The 3 is modified, first by the 8, then to a lesser degree by the 2. It is also of significance that 382 consists of three digits, indicating that this number expresses an aspect of "threeness"—3 energy. The full scope of 3 energy is expressed comprehensively in the set of numbers composed of three digits: 100 through 999. The overall meaning of numbers in the 300s—300 through 399—is concerned with formulating and expressing a concept of who

Numbers of the Months	
January	.27
February	.42
March	.25
April	.29
May	.12
June	.14
July	.14
August	.17
September	.40
October	.33
November	.40
December	.37

and what "I am" is. The overall meaning of numbers in the 80s—80 through 89—relates to developing techniques of achievement. The meaning of the final 2 is potential for discernment.

Based on the above, an interpretation of 382 is as follows: as part of the process leading toward development of a full concept of oneself—who I am—the self develops techniques on which to act by determining what will and will not work. This is a lot of information. Were 382 to be reduced to a single-digit 4 ($3 + 8 + 2 = 13$, then $1 + 3 = 4$), all the above meaning would be abandoned. Instead we would have a broad generalization: to be purposeful in living. The scope and specific character of 382 would be entirely lost. After all, every ninth number, from 13 to infinity, reduces to a 4!

The example of 382 is given here to demonstrate the rich meanings of polydigit numbers as compared with the relatively vague meanings of single-digit numbers. Later in this book, I will present an extensive discussion and interpretations of numbers from 0 to 1,000,000,000. These numbers concern the dynamics of living and how to progress spiritually. They are far beyond the scope of Pythagorean numerology, which is a symbolic mathematical practice based exclusively on the identification and comparison of reduced numbers—1 through 9. Its specialty is to provide insight into the lower self—the ego—that lives and functions on the earth plane. For this purpose, it is adequate in some ways, though not ideal, to use the broad generalizations of single-digit numbers.

Numerology books generally instruct readers to reduce numbers prior to totaling them. Mathematically, however, this is not correct. Reducing is always the last step after all the full numbers have been added. Unreduced numbers retain the greatest, most specific meanings. Reducing numbers prematurely can distort the result. In the case of the birth date we are using for an example—April 16, 1951—the total of the unreduced numbers is 1996:

29 (month)
16 (day)
+1951 (year)
——————
1996

The number 1996, then, is the most comprehensive and most precise meaning of this birth date. But if, on the other hand, each part of the birth date were first reduced, the sum would fall far short of representing the full scope of the meaning:

$$2 + 9 = 11, \text{ then } 1 + 1 = 2 \quad \text{(month)}$$
$$1 + 6 = 7 \quad \text{(day)}$$
$$1 + 9 + 5 + 1 = 16, \text{ then } 1 + 6 = \underline{7} \quad \text{(year)}$$
$$16, \text{ then } 1 + 6 = 7$$

The latter answer of 16/7 is also inaccurate; 1996 reduces to 25, then to 7; 16 also reduces to 7. There is, however, a big difference between a 1996/25/7 and a 16/7.

Do not think that this and other discussions of correct mathematical procedure are unimportant. For far too long, mathematical symbolism has ignored mathematical principle. The result has been a devastating inaccuracy and limitation of the art. If Pythagorean numerology is ever to progress beyond what it now is, it must be rigorously correct from a mathematical perspective. This is the same standard all branches of mathematics must meet.

The issue of whether or not to reduce numbers crops up in Pythagorean numerology with regard to the so-called "spiritual numbers," also commonly known as Master Numbers. These are two-digit numbers in which both digits are the same: 11, 22, 33, and so on, through 99. Of these nine numbers, numerologists recognize only some of them as spiritual numbers: most often 11 and 22, sometimes 33 and 44, and occasionally 55 and 66. Most interpretations correctly attribute special qualities and challenges to this set of numbers. Nevertheless, they have no place in Pythagorean numerology. Numerology is a discipline based entirely on the meanings of reduced numbers. As we shall discuss at great length in later chapters, *every number* consisting of two or more digits has special meaning. There is no mathematical basis for selecting certain two-digit numbers for interpretation while reducing, and thereby generalizing, all the rest.

When, then, is it mathematically correct to reduce numbers? Not very often. It is a technique applicable almost exclusively to symbolic numbers. It is used when one wishes to determine the broadest possible meaning of a polydigit number ("1992 was a 3 year"). Reduction is also a mathematical method to make sense of two or more numbers grouped together—say, 2, 3, 8, and 7—by adding them (2 + 3 + 8 +

7 = 20, then 2 + 0 = 2). This makes the meanings of a group of numbers manageable by summarizing them into one single-digit number.

The second position of the numerology chart we will consider is the Character position.[6] This position refers to a person's basic, overall nature—who he is, in essence. It is also an indicator of abilities. Whereas the Participation number indicates the role we play on the stage of life, the Character position denotes who is playing that role.

To figure this position, the complete name at birth (and *only* the complete name at birth) is used, even if that name was changed days or even hours after birth due to adoption or another reason. The original name contains the full blueprint of a person's nature, much as a seed contains in potential the exact likeness of the plant it will become. The conditions in which a plant matures may change, of course, affecting its size, rate of growth, or general well-being. Such influences alter the plant, but they never change the type of plant it is. In a similar way, every subsequent name of a person is a name change. Some names—like nicknames, stage names, or names changed due to marriage or adoption—are very important in the life of an individual. However significant, a name change represents no more than a modification of the original name. A surprising number of people do not know their full or correct name at birth. This may be due to uncertainty about one name or another, minor differences in spelling, a mistake on the birth certificate, and the like. If the discrepancy is due to any of the above, I invariably opt for the name intended by the parents. Surely carelessness in completing the birth documents or other circumstances that alter the birth name are insignificant when compared with the parents' choice of name, especially that of the mother. Still, when making a determination of the correct name, utmost care should be taken to ensure that the matter is decided on a sound basis. A careful contrasting of the qualities of the different numbers in question will readily reveal which is name is correct.

To calculate the Character number, convert all the letters of the complete name at birth into numbers. Add up all the numbers and reduce the total to a single digit.

Example: figure the Character number for **Wilma Dawn Thomas.**

First step: convert all the letters of **Wilma Dawn Thomas** into the numbers that correspond to them, and add the numbers.

$$5 + 9 + 3 + 4 + 1 \quad 4 + 1 + 5 + 5 \quad 2 + 8 + 6 + 4 + 1 + 1 = 59$$

W I L M A   D A W N   T H O M A S

Third step: reduce the total.

$$5 + 9 = 14, \text{ then } 1 + 4 = 5$$

The Character number is **5.**

In addition to a person's overall character, numerology identifies two other parts of human nature: the Heart's Desire and the Personality. The Heart's Desire number indicates a person's inner drive and motivation, hopes and aspirations. This position is figured by adding up the numbers of the vowels in the birth name. There is controversy among numerologists as to which letters are properly considered vowels. In addition to the standard five that everyone accepts—A, E, I, O, U—some numerologists include Y (as in Larry) and W (as in Matthew). My research into this matter has proven to me that Y and W are never vowels for numerological purposes because they do not have the quality of *pure aspiration* that characterizes the five standard vowels. My research method, again, was to calculate the number both ways, with and without Y and W. I then highlighted the major differences of the numbers for a particular individual and asked questions like, "Are you happier this way or that way?" The answer every time has reflected use of the five standard vowels only.

Example: figure the Heart's Desire number for **Wilma Dawn Thomas.**

First step: convert all the vowels into the numbers that correspond to them, and add the numbers.

$$9 + 1 + 1 \quad + \quad 6 + 1 \quad = \quad 18$$

W I L M A   D A W N   T H O M A S

Second step: reduce the total.

$$1 + 8 = 9$$

The Heart's Desire number is **9.**

The final of the four positions we will consider in this chapter is that of the Personality. This position represents a person's style of presenting himself to the world. It is his public persona, and how he feels comfortable coming across to others. To figure this number, convert all the consonants of the birth name into the numbers that correspond to them, add them up, and reduce the total to a single digit.

Example: figure the Personality number for **Wilma Dawn Thomas.**

First step: convert all the consonants into the numbers that correspond to them, and add them up.

$$5 + 3+4 + 4 + 5+5+2+8 + 4 + 1 = 41$$
W I L M A   D A W N   T H O M A S

Second step: reduce the total.

$$4 + 1 = 5$$

The Personality number is **5.**

Viewed together, the four positions of this numerology chart are as follows:

9		1	1				6		1						= 9 Heart's Desire
W	I	L	M	A	D	A	W	N	T	H	O	M	A	S	
5		3	4		4		5	5	2	8		4		1	= 5 Personality
5	9	3	4	1	4	1	5	5	2	8	6	4	1	1	= 5 Character

April 16, 1951   = 7 Participation

A numerology chart is literally a portrait of a person's inner nature painted in numbers. A chart consisting of only four positions, like the one above, outlines only the most basic of features, representing the core of the self. Most numerologists have their own personalized version of the chart that generally includes considerably more than four positions. My chart, for example, has 28 positions and 155 numbers. Most basically, a numerology chart is a form that identifies and organizes the various positions. Numerologists have never been in possession of a truly complete chart—complete, that is, in that it includes all spiritual and psychological elements of human nature. This is because we humans do not see the full picture. As human beings, we are aware of the dynamics and elements of life that engage our attention or imagination, or that we come to understand based on research or meditation. The set of elements we recognize in the present era is a definite reflection of our culture at this particular time and place in history. But our current concepts will not remain forever the same. What is perceived to be true by a people, an era, or a civilization will surely metamorphose in time as surely as the day turns to night, then to day once again. Consciousness evolves, always changing, never finished. The numerology chart that appears "complete" to today's eyes will inevitably appear less so to tomorrow's gaze. For the time being, a chart may be considered adequately complete when it meets the needs of our present state of consciousness.

Although the numerology chart is divided into different dynamics of character—its positions—this is a synthetic division for the purpose of understanding how and why the self functions as it does. In reality, the self functions all together, a seamless whole. The goal in understanding a chart is to know the unity of all the diverse numbers and positions. In this sense, the chart is a formula for how to live purposefully and successfully. It shows exactly how to harmonize with, and to coordinate, all the numbers for optimal fulfillment and meaning in being alive.

When examining an individual's chart, an experienced numerologist sees an astonishing likeness of a person's inner nature complete with many subtle attributes and dynamics. On the basis of a thorough knowledge of the numbers, it is possible to reach deep and enlightening insights into a person's fundamental functions of being: why he is the way he is and what he can do to improve his life. It is my belief that we determine the numbers of our life prior to birth while we are still in the Spirit State. For these reasons, the analysis of a numerology chart is akin to a spiritual report, an assessment of the state of the soul in this incarnation.

Thus, the most immediate benefit of studying the numbers of a numerology chart is insight into the workings of the self. A deeper study reveals the thought processes by which we live our lives. The complex numbers unique to a person denotes a strictly individual mode of perceiving and acting. It may thus be said that the complete numerology chart represents the earth-brain of the incarnating soul.

There are still deeper ways to work with numbers. We can go beyond a personal perspective to experience directly the energies of the numbers and their interrelations. Mathematical symbolism is a spiritual discipline for those who persevere in the study of it. At its base are ten spiritual forces represented by ten numbers and the mathematical principles that govern their use. If we approach these forces from our own individual viewpoint, we will only see what our ego allows us. It is only possible to penetrate through to the spiritual meaning of numbers by seeking on *their* level, in an impersonal or universal manner:

> So long as we live in a personal relationship with the world . . . things yield to our knowledge only those ephemeral and superficial aspects of themselves which link them to what is ephemeral and superficial in us. We are thus enslaved to the sense-perceptible. . . . But it is not necessary for us . . . to remain in the ignoble situation. We can overcome the personal. We can live in the imperishable at the centre of being. This True and Good and Beautiful will then relate itself to the Good and True and Beautiful in the world about us. Things then yield us their secrets. Dr. Steiner urges us to depersonalize our thinking: "If we approach a fact with a mental attitude arising out of our own past experience, we thereby prevent the fact from having its complete effect on us. We have to learn at each moment to make of ourselves an entirely empty vessel into which a new world can flow. Only in these moments in which all personal pre-judgments are silenced does real knowledge enter us."[7]

With an examination of the contents of the numerology chart, we begin our quest for the meaning of numbers.

Perhaps as you read through the preceding pages and learned how to calculate the numbers of the four positions, you figured your own. If so, then you most likely reread the meanings of your numbers and tried to apply them to their respective positions. Finally, especially if you are new to the study of numerology, you found yourself quite puzzled and confused. Where, you wondered, is all that promised deep insight and spiritual meaning . . . ?

This is the challenge of interpretation. It is the art and skill of understanding the meanings of two or more numbers together. Interpretation is the key skill in numerology, as well as in mathematical symbolism as a whole. Yet the teaching of it is virtually absent from the entire body of numerological literature.[8] There, interpretations are simply presented without explanation of the process by which the reader, too, may develop his own interpretations using his own understanding and wisdom.

In the following chapter, we will discuss the interpretation process—what it is and how it works.

Endnotes

1. Imaginary numbers are numbers that, by definition, cannot exist. An example is the square root of −4. The solution cannot be −2 because −2 x −2 = 4. It cannot be 2 because 2 x 2 = 4. The answer is 2i. The "i" signifies that 2 is imaginary.

2. James Gleick, *Chaos: Making a New Science* (New York: Viking Press, 1987), 299.

3. This is definition number 11 of "form," as given in *Webster's Unabridged Dictionary of the English Language* (New York: Gramercy Books, 1994), 556.

4. Strictly speaking, 0 is occasionally included in numerology books. However, this number is not well understood, and confusion and misconception frequently mark its use. An interesting instance of this comes from an otherwise excellent work, *Numerology: Key to Your Inner Self*, by Hans Decoz with Tom Monte (Garden City Park, New York: Avery Publishing Group, 1994). The following quotation, taken from page 59, illustrates the difficulty numerologists in general have in working with 0: "The Challenge numbers are one of the few places in the chart where a 0 can appear. This occurs in the case when two of the digits are the same (for example, the First Challenge for a person born on May 5 is 5 − 5 = 0). Also, the number 9 cannot appear in the Challenges. The largest difference possible between two single digit numbers is 8 (9 − 1 = 8). Therefore, with the Challenges, the 0 takes on the characteristics of the 9. *The 0 Challenge is actually the 9 Challenge.*" (Italics mine.)

5. I have even come across an additional term for reducing numbers in a discussion of modern mathematics with regard to perfect numbers. These are numbers that are equal to all of their divisors. Six, for example, is a perfect number because it can be divided by 1, 2, and 3, which in turn add up to 6: 1 + 2 + 3 = 6. The author goes on to write: "*The single-digit cross sum* (italics mine) of every perfect number, except 6, is 1: 28 ⟹ 2 + 8 = 10 ⟹ 1 + 0 = 1; 496 ⟹ 4 + 9 + 6 = 19 ⟹ 1 + 9 = 10 ⟹ 1 + 0 = 1." This quote is from Jan Gullberg, *Mathematics from the Birth of Numbers* (New York: W. W. Norton and Company, 1997), 82.

6. I should point out that there is a variety of names in use for each of the positions we are discussing. What I call the Character position is also known as the Expression, the Destiny, and the Integrated Self, to name three. In the same vein, the Participation position is commonly called the Life Path, the Life number, the Destiny number, and the Fate number. Within the field of Pythagorean numerology, there is little that may be considered universal practice among its practitioners. This is all right. There is no one approach that is *the only* correct way. Every numerologist uses a combination of names, positions, and interpretations unique to him. For the serious student, it becomes necessary sooner or later to decide for himself which is correct for him.

7. Arnold Freeman, *Meditation Under the Guidance of Rudolf Steiner* (Sheffield, England: Sheffield Education Settlement), 51.

8. The single exception to this, of which I am aware, is a long and convoluted discussion that is particularly difficult to follow and to apply. The sample analysis appears throughout nearly 700 pages of both volumes of *Numerology: the Complete Guide*, by Matthew Oliver Goodwin (North Hollywood, Calif.: Newcastle Publishing Company, Inc., 1981). Overall, the work is surpassingly organized, thorough, and excellent for use as a reference.

chapter 6

The Interpretation Process

Ultimately, you will learn symbolic sight, the ability to interpret the power symbols in your life . . . . But you need an internal method of absorbing this information to make it real for you.

—Carolyn Myss, *Anatomy of the Spirit*

The wonderful mystic writer Dion Fortune once wrote, ". . . all [terms of the Kabalistic Sephiroth] are as precise as scientific terms, which, in fact, is what they are."[1] And later, "He can use the images as a mathematician uses algebraic symbols."[2] He is capable of ". . . using them as the beads on the abacus of our calculations. . . ."[3] Although the above was written with the Kabalistic Tree of Life in mind, it equally applies to any true spiritual symbol system. What is being "mathematically manipulated," of course, are symbols. The management of symbols is what interpretation is all about.

In the beginning stages of learning interpretation, the focus is on understanding the assortment of numbers and positions of a numerology chart. Each chart consists of a particular combination of numbers that can provide extensive insights into the life and nature of an individual. Although such an interpretation may be highly accurate and complete, it is basically no more than an explanation of information. Its power is to clarify understanding, but it lacks the capability to foster spiritual growth. Pythagorean numerology operates at the level of describing and contrasting the characteristics of numbers. If this level of interpretation were to be compared with a discussion of gardening, it would be a theoretical description without hands-on application. For example, the varying need to water one plant or another in different and changing conditions is helpful and informative to know. But it is not the same as working with living plants and having dirt under the fingernails. Learning interpretation begins with book study. Wisdom and understanding come only from living through experience with heart, mind, body, and soul.

The laws, principles, and functions of mathematics represent the mechanics of living. Each of these (addition, subtraction, and so on) governs the form and evolution that numbers take. It is through the agency of these mathematical laws that all aspects of life as we know it are created and maintained: who we are, what we do, the decisions we make, our family, friends, work, education, hopes and fears, personal growth, nature, the universe, and everything else. Look around you. Reflect on what reality is for you—physical, mental, emotional, as well as spiritual—and the sum total of all that makes up your world. Ponder the state of your life right at this moment and how you feel about it. All these things are the symbols that compose your life; thousands upon thousands of them. They are living symbols, symbols that we have envisioned and activated, which thereby created our reality. It is a law of symbolism that once we commit to symbols and own them as our own, they take root in reality. They become our life. This is all to say that long ago, you Evoked the Symbolic Process. Its beginnings were in Spirit, in nonexistence, which in symbolic mathematics is called "zero." As the Process took hold, zero evolved first the one, then the two, which combined to produce three, stabilizing in four, individualizing as five, and so on through nine. The primal elements then locked together, synthesizing into endless combinations and permutations. Once the Symbolic Process began, everything changed. What had previously been the stuff of dreams and changeable at a shift of mood or preference became set. The symbols are real, or *appear* to be real at any rate. They are the things of earth that are hard and unyielding, both in the world around us as well as within each individual.

The Symbolic Process that produced the external world also brought into being the inner nature of the incarnating spirit. Both inner persona and outer reality are bonded together, a perfect fit with one another because they were both cut from the same swatch of cosmic cloth at the same time with a single pass of the scissors. All is One. This is your life. These are the symbols to be interpreted.

The act of interpretation is generally considered to consist of determining the meaning of something. This is just what occurs in a numerological analysis called a "reading." In a reading, the numbers are identified and compared as a method of building a body of understanding (a *concept*, in other words) of what the numbers mean all together as a group. The insight offered by such an analysis is a valuable benefit. It puts life into perspective. It does not, however, begin to approach the potential of mathematical symbolism. This is because symbolic numbers are usually thought to be static states of being, with set characteristics and qualities. They do have an enduring stability that holds against all efforts to alter them. But it is the formless Force that has stability, not the characteristics that routinely result from the activities of each Force. This is a shifting and changing kind of stability, capable of manifesting entirely different sets of characteristics. In this way, they are like the shape a cloud assumes. I have seen magnificent cloud formations that riveted my gaze as I drank in the beauty. Ten minutes later, though still striking, they were different. Only twenty minutes later, they were fully transformed. Life is like that. Although in each moment of time our thoughts, feelings, and experiences are sharp, clear, and in perfect focus, it all evolves. Those changes occur as a result of the inter-action of cosmic principles. In this book, those cosmic principles are called numbers. Far from being static, stagnant, or set states of being, they are irresistibly compelling forces that encompass our lives. They are a white water rapid's rush of power; they are awe inspiring, heart pounding beauty, they are soaring-or-plummeting frenzy; they have us in a grip that allows no independent movement. The power of numbers is denied when they are viewed simply as static states. Numbers are vitality—always new, ever becoming events and experiences in our lives that are frequently unantici-pated, unpredicted, and unavoidable.

The ceaseless mixing and reconfiguring of number forces swoon the individual into the belief that the Numeric Dream is Reality, causing him to forget momentar-ily (that is, during each incarnation) that he is Director of his Numbers and Captain of his Soul. This dreamy preoccupation is called Illusion, but it appears very, very real to the enrapt gaze of mundane consciousness. It is a cosmic case of the divine dog chasing after its own eternal tail: the dog cannot be made to realize that it is rushing its own tail away from its own eagerly onrushing mouth. This is a paradox to the dog, whose cause and inevitable effect are perfectly clear to humans, just as our own cosmic conundrums are obvious as self-induced traps to the Eyes of Cos-mic Consciousness.

For numerology as it is practiced today, earth consciousness is considered to be a given, unchangeable reality. This is a limitation that need not be. If numbers are viewed as Divine Forces, and if our physical reality is understood to be made up of combinations of those forces, that limitation cannot be valid because the Divine is not limited. We do not need to be held back by the "ignoble situation" dealt us in our earthly experience. At a deeper level of interpretation, it becomes possible to work with numbers so as to produce certain results, thereby evolving our "given, unchangeable reality." Those results arise directly from our purpose in working with the numbers. That is to say, with a spiritual goal underlying our efforts, we can remix and rework the primal energies in such a way as to realize Higher Purpose. To the extent that ego is involved—the lower self that harbors fears and desires—is the extent to which the purity of the numbers is distorted, producing undesirable effects. Use of the numbers involves mathematical principles, of course, because it is through our mathematical system that we know how to handle numbers. A great deal can be accomplished with mathematical symbolism that is presently not possible in Pythagorean numerology. When spiritual forces are experienced directly, we enter into that Stream of Power that heals, informs, and lifts us up.

The full definition of interpretation, then, is this: a creative spiritual initiative whose purpose it is to transmute energies to higher levels. Further, it is a postulate of symbolic mathematics that the perceived limitations of any two or more numbers can be transcended through interpretation.

We will work extensively with the marvelous tool of symbol interpretation throughout the remaining pages of this book. Our goal is to build a basic working concept of the interpretive process that can be indefinitely expanded as additional concepts and principles are learned. The first step of learning is to know the meanings of the numbers 0 through 9. The nature of the chart also needs to be thoroughly grasped. Finally, it is necessary to understand the meanings of any two or more numbers in combination. Analyzing a numerology chart will constitute the beginning of our study of the interpretation process. This, in turn, will enable each individual to learn mathematical symbolism by working with material with which he identifies very closely and about which he cares very deeply—his own chart. In this manner, the fundamentals of interpretation may be mastered at a basic level.

Many people are accustomed to think that if they have all the necessary information on a particular subject, and if they understand the information, that is all there is to the interpretation of that information. This is not so. Understanding information is a passive activity in which the views and concepts of another person are grasped. Interpretation, on the other hand, is only possible when the subject matter has been mastered. Prior to such proficiency, personal ideas on the matter are likely to show poor judgment or to be incorrect. Once mastery is attained, interpretation involves developing a personal concept of the material in question, plus the ability to take responsibility for the viewpoint. This type of interpretation is common in life, and is made routinely and continuously throughout adult life. The quality of our interpretations determines the quality of our lives. The study of a spiritual symbol system provides a means to learn to interpret more consciously and more deeply.

There is a more fundamental level of existence upon which "objective knowledge" is based. That level is *Meaning*. Numbers are archetypal Units of Meaning. The study of mathematical symbolism begins with learning and understanding the facts: the Force of each number and the types of experiences associated with that Force. Thus, while we use objective knowledge ("the facts") as a vehicle of learning, this is not our goal. What we seek instead is to live the experience of that Web of Significance upon which the objective has its basis.

Some people will think, upon reading the above, that Meaning must therefore be subjective, that is to say, strictly a matter of personal opinion and individual understanding. The subjective, however, is no more capable of explaining the world than the objective is. They are, in fact, two sides of the same coin; it takes both for either one to exist. The objective-subjective duality develops out of enigmatic Meaning, which is whole and undifferentiated. Both elements are necessary to the successful understanding of symbolic mathematics. Therefore, as the objective information about numbers is being learned, it also needs to be internalized as personal, subjective understanding. If one learns the objective facts but fails to find personal significance in them, those facts are empty and lifeless. Conversely, if the facts are learned only subjectively without the grounding effects of objectivity, that learning can be no more than vanity, tying the ". . . knot of egoity . . . ,"[4] as James Powell so aptly expresses it. Therefore, in the beginning stages of learning mathematical symbolism, one learns the facts—the nature of the number forces along with their characteristic effects, the definitions of the chart positions, and the standard results of two or more numbers in combination—and *at the same time* understands all this in personal terms.

At first thought, such total deep learning of a symbol system may seem too great a challenge. For one thing, there is so much to know. Also, there is no specific, measurable goal on which to set one's sights and toward which to strive. How do you know when you have arrived? With spiritual symbol systems, the goal is, by definition, at least vague if not entirely undefinable. That notwithstanding, all of us routinely fulfill this symbol-learning process many times over through the course of our lives. Ours is a world of symbols. We are so closely bonded with many symbols, our understanding of them is so comprehensive, our experience is so immediate, that their use is virtually instinctive and automatic. Such proficiency must be the goal when we seek to master a spiritual system.

Learning the interpretative process is in itself a search for Meaning. As one perseveres with its study, it becomes clear that the basic elements of Meaning—the numbers—have a definite, precise organization to them. The major part of interpretation is knowing the mathematics of number symbolism. Initially, the numbers and the mathematics seem highly abstract, with no direct or practical means to apply them to the physical world in which we live. The whole system looks complex (and it is), with meanings on many levels (and there are). There is no quick way to acquire understanding of mathematical symbolism. This only occurs over time as its essence is gradually absorbed and integrated. The knowledge is only assured validity if it is claimed in a deep, personal way. The numerical complexities must become second nature until at last they evolve into being our ABCs of thinking, our vocabulary of living.

To put all this into perspective, consider a symbol system that is universal in today's world: the English alphabet, which consists of twenty-six letter symbols. From this small group of elements, perhaps as many as 900,000 words have been derived in the English language[5] (not to mention the words of other languages that use the same alphabet), allowing for a truly vast use of the twenty-six letters of the alphabet. As adults, most of us have forgotten that learning to read and write is a very lengthy and complex achievement. It requires many years of childhood education to gain proficiency. Eventually, literate people come to possess a phenomenal facility with this symbol system.

As a result of that achievement, symbols and their significances are the same. Reading a written word and understanding it occur simultaneously! To see a written word is to experience its meaning at the same time, sometimes so strongly that it causes an emotional outburst, reveals an insight that takes our breath away, or provokes a deep laugh! When this is the case, the alphabet symbol system has been fully mastered indeed! Results from a spiritual symbol system can be expected when an equivalent degree of proficiency has been attained.

The numbers of a chart should be analyzed together as a group for their composite, gestalt significance. This is accomplished by going from one position number to the next, gradually building up a comprehensive picture of the whole. The interpretation of individual position numbers in isolation is essentially meaningless, unless and until their relation to the chart as a whole is established. Think of it this way: if the whole chart spells out the phrase "the nature of a person," then focusing on the significance of only one of the position numbers is like determining the meaning of "u" in "nature" without including any of the rest of the letters or words. On a similar basis, interpreting all the numbers of a chart, but without correlating their meanings into a coherent whole, is like interpreting all the letters of "the nature of a person" in no particular order, producing a random and confused result:

a p e e s t u h f n n e r t a o r o

A numerology reading should explore the full range of meanings, both positive and negative, even if it is painful to do so. An analysis that glosses over problems, difficulties, or shortcomings is incomplete, perhaps even misleading. Mathematical symbolism is a spiritual discipline and, therefore, should always aim to present the truth and to raise consciousness. Its purpose must be to clarify, to inform, to foster understanding, to build confidence, to generate hope, to heal, and in every way possible to aid in the development of spiritual life. All of this is accomplished by finding the purposeful connections of all the position numbers.

Interpretation is an art in addition to being a skill. Art is the organizing principle. It brings balance, harmony, proportion, and beauty to the process. It is through this kind of artistic activity that the diverse elements of the chart take cohesive form. It is artistic form that allows Meaning to emerge.

It is not possible for any two people to make identical interpretations of the same chart. Interpretations by experienced numerologists invariably differ in many ways. Disparities include not only the kinds of conclusions and the things that are emphasized, but even the types of basic approach. Some numerologists focus on making predictions of the future, others on past lives and karma. Still others determine lucky numbers or make psychological analyses. Finally, there is numerology as a philosophical system and spiritual discipline, the approach taken in this book. It is only natural for there to be such differences. Every person alive is unique. Different viewpoints are the way of things. Indeed, it would be strange if there were not such variations due to temperament, interests, education, career, life experience, age, sex, cultural identity, spiritual beliefs, and so on. These kinds of factors produce idiosyncrasy of understanding. Despite the inevitable range of interpretations, every numerologist believes strongly in the accuracy of his own interpretation, even though it sometimes hardly resembles the analysis of another. This is an apparent paradox: how can perceptions of different people vary tremendously, even conflict with each another, and yet all be true? In large part, the answer is that truth is a matter of perception.

To illustrate this point, consider how interpretation works in the case of a social stereotype we call a "bookworm." Our society has been developing a collective image of bookworm since the term entered the English language around 1600 C.E. It has become a very comprehensive concept with deep feelings. Within those wide parameters, however, it is possible to have an almost unlimited number of partial views that are true as far as they go, and that, due to their incompleteness, sometimes contradict each other. Who is to decide which partial view is the most correct? No one has a full grasp of the total bookworm concept. Limitation and incompleteness are the human condition.

In the passage below, physicist Stephen Hawking discusses the apparent conflict of partial viewpoints in terms of physics:

> The Weiberg-Salam theory exhibits a property known as spontaneous symmetry breaking. This means that what appears to be a number of completely different particles at low energies are in fact found to be all the same type of particle, only in different states. At high energy all these particles behave similarly. The effect is rather like the behavior of a roulette ball on a roulette wheel. At high energies (when the wheel is spun quickly) the ball behaves in essentially one way—it rolls round and round. But as the wheel slows, the energy of the ball decreases, and eventually the ball drops into one of the thirty-seven slots in the wheel. In other words, at low energies there are thirty-seven different states in which the ball can exist. If, for some reason, we could only observe the ball at low energies, we would then think that there were thirty-seven different types of ball! [6]

In this manner, there exist many versions of the truth, all of which are also correct. Incarnation into the ego state, which occurs at densest levels of gross matter, is definitely "low energy" existence. Spiritual consciousness, on the other hand, is traditionally associated with "high energy." That which is One in Spirit is broken apart into infinitely diversified forms on the earth plane, just as light is separated into different colors by a prism.

The interpretation process is essentially a storytelling method based on the use of two techniques: identification and comparison. The numbers of numerology are forces that tend to engender certain kinds of experiences. The chart position of a number limits the number's range of experience to a certain theme. The analysis begins with a discussion (an identification) of the number in the Participation position. This position is generally considered by numerologists to be the most important position in the chart, and, therefore, the one with which to begin. The interpretation of a chart tells the story of a person's life. As the Participation number is described, a concept begins to build up. In this first step of identification, the scope of the number is discussed in all its pros and cons, all its mental and emotional considerations. When the elements of the Participation number have been sufficiently discussed, the tale moves on to the second most important position number, the Character position. Once the nature of this element of the story / interpretation has been established, comparing their respective experiences links the two positions. This shows how these two dynamics function together. As the story moves from position to position, key themes begin to develop, along with many modifying factors. These imbue the analysis with a wealth of meaning, revealing the action-packed story of a person's inner psychological and spiritual life.

To illustrate the mechanics of the interpretation process, I will use the metaphor we discussed earlier: a bookworm; the one who is known for having her nose in a book twenty-four hours a day. For the purposes of our story, "Bookworm" is a woman (although Bookworm could just as well be a man). We begin our tale by "identifying" her:

> *We all know Bookworm. She is timid and withdrawn, preferring to spend much of her time alone. Her world consists of thinking, reading, and speculating. People overwhelm her, and she assiduously avoids close personal interaction. She is hiding from life, and especially contact with the opposite sex. She*

feels profoundly awkward and inadequate. She dresses to look plain and incon-
spicuous. She keeps conversations brief and superficial, rarely maintaining eye
contact. She is alone.

Yes, we all know Bookworm. Like many society-wide images, Bookworm is so appealing to the popular imagination that, upon mention of her, a rich scenario of thought and feeling swells in the mind. Concepts deep within our subconscious, absorbed over many years, are touched. Each of us, if pressed, could describe her at great length. We could go into considerable detail about her lifestyle, habits, attitudes, dress, appearance, favorite recreation, relationships, psychological make-up, and so much more. We could go on to cite examples of people in our lives who are bookworms; and we could easily tell how we would feel living that kind of life. This is because "bookworm" is a collective stereotype of society. The dictionary defines "bookworm" as: "a person devoted to reading or studying."[7] But there is certainly more to the overall meaning than this factual, rather dry statement. Part of what this dictionary definition does not include are all the unflattering feelings and connotations people have about bookworm types who are so absorbed in books and obscure areas of learning that they exclude everything and everyone else. All these kinds of ideas form the objective concept of bookworm because they derive from the general definition held by society at large. At the same time, bookworm is a subjective concept for everyone because each of us personalizes bookworm in our own terms. We have our own ideas on the matter, our own attitudes and examples, our own way of explaining it, each of which is a legitimate version of the "objective bookworm" concept. In this manner, something objective (from outside ourselves) is thoroughly blended with subjective understanding (from within ourselves), producing a concept that is both objective and subjective at the same time. It is not possible to be purely objective or purely subjective.

All those who have a concept of bookworm—and that is just about everybody who speaks English—give a "true account" of it. Each account begins with all that an individual person has heard, read, or experienced with regard to bookworm; it ends with the personal understanding that the individual has come to have of bookworm. As discussed earlier, my idea of this societal image is *Bookworm*. Now, each of us has our own reaction to the way other people envision a bookworm. We may feel one view is "right," another "wrong," and still another "distorted," "compelling," "lacking in insight," "universal in its implications," "innovative," "educated," "sincere," "beautifully told," or any of an infinity of other reactions. The point is, each viewpoint is the self's spontaneous take on the matter. We see what we see and that is our truth. It cannot be otherwise. Every single person alive on this planet shares this restriction of perception. This is humanity's Common Ground of Understanding Truth. It is always incomplete, always limited.

This is all modified when we interrelate with other people. Through the process of comparing ideas and disagreeing with others, gradually we learn and refine our own perception of truth. It causes us to examine our own thoughts. But there is a deeper significance to the opposition of ideas. The true meaning of conflict is not how the lower self sees it: as two opposites—sometimes interior, sometimes exterior—battling it out. Rather, the true meaning is how that conflict functions within the individual's system of ideas. Conflict is really a device of the self to bring about spiritual growth in order to attain higher consciousness. It causes us to reevaluate and reprocess our thoughts, feelings, and ideas. All interactions with others and the world, whether positive or negative, is experience that causes us to evolve.

Personal concepts are like numbers. When numbers are in stasis—not in relationship with other numbers—they are states of existence. They are neither right nor wrong, good nor bad. They simply are. When numbers are dynamically connected with each other by mathematical principles, change and growth are the result.

In our story, the concept of bookworm is handled in the same manner as the interpretation of a number. When I stated my ideas about Bookworm, I "identified" her, just as I suggest identifying numbers. This was a general characterization of her, applicable anywhere and anytime. Shortly, we will place Bookworm in a specific situation that limits and focuses her activities. Bookworm's upcoming situation is comparable to the function of a position in a numerology chart.

The reader will note that the character traits attributed to Bookworm correspond closely to those of the number 7. As we follow Bookworm's activities in our story, we will be metaphorically examining the number 7 and how it works. To continue our story, let us now identify a second common societal image, the playboy, a term that has been in the English language since about 1620.

> *Playboy is a dynamic and controversial type of man. He is good looking, a flirt, the veteran of many sexual encounters and short, superficial relationships.*

Clever with words, elegant of dress, he always seems to be reporting on a recent conquest or working on one. He is a hard one to catch in a committed relationship, or even in a moment of real intimacy. To some, he is a good time, an adventurer full of smiles, charm, and wit. To others, he is no more than a snake, a cheat, a conniver, a manipulator, and a breaker of hearts.

As we examine Playboy's behavior, observe that his nature correlates closely with that of the number 5. Furthermore, the interactions between Bookworm and Playboy will serve to illustrate what becomes of two numbers—the 5 and the 7—when they are in relation.

Societal images, like numbers, depend on each other—on the relationships they share—to bring out their qualities and characteristics. If Bookworm or Playboy were alone in a world of their own, they would possess no traits as such. With no other person around, Bookworm just *is*. She cannot be a recluse if there is no one from whom to hide. Likewise, she cannot be considered socially awkward if there is no other with whom to feel ill at ease. Playboy cannot be considered to have powers of charm without the presence of someone else whom he can entertain and delight. Characteristics are by definition comparisons. They are qualities that exist only because different natures contrast with each other.

It is the same with numbers. They are considered to be the basis of certain characteristic experiences *only* because of their connections with each other. This is a deep and abstract idea. A part of the difficulty in understanding this is that we are so accustomed to think that everything in life has qualities on its own. This is because everything in life exists in combination, a part of the whole. All ten single-digit numbers exist together simultaneously and perpetually define each other. Relationship, then, is crucial to understand, whether it is between social images or numbers.

Having identified Bookworm and Playboy, we come now to the question of their relationship.

Bookworm and Playboy: this is no easy association. What could they possibly see in each other? Bookworm knows she has no allure, no sexy self-assurance, no coy come-hither look to attract and intrigue him. She is a thinker, an intellectual, after all. Playboy is way out of her league. He scares and confuses her, completely upsetting her world. He is so raucous, uncouth, and exciting. From

*Playboy's perspective, Bookworm is dull. She lives in fear, and never does any-
thing of any interest. It would take a great deal of effort on his part to stir her
passions, if there even are any inside that plain, uninspiring exterior! And he
certainly wants to avoid work whenever possible. He finds her penchant for
reading, reflection, and alone time to be monotonous.*

Even before we begin the tale of Bookworm and Playboy together, we have established the main dramatic conflict of the plot: how can two people who are so different find common ground on which to share a relationship? This same dilemma is
also at work between 7 and 5 when those numbers are together.

The great challenge of interpretation is to know the meanings of two or more
numbers in combination. It is very educational to study and meditate on the combinations of 1 with 1, 1 with 2, 1 with 3, and so on, through 9 with 9. Such drills are
necessary to the craft, just as it is necessary for a musician to play the scales over and
over, or for a school child to practice the multiplication tables again and again.

To accomplish interpretation, more is required than mastering the factual information. Ultimately, the subject matter must be translated into a personal frame of
reference. Numbers are no more than acquired facts until we see *that* as part of ourselves and accept that we are *that*. Once numbers have become internalized to this
extent, they become part of our experience. Then, and only then, does it become
possible to know them intimately and insightfully, and to speak of them confidently
and with authority. Only then is it possible to make true interpretation.

In order for Bookworm and Playboy to be in relationship, they need to be in a situation of some kind in which they can function together. It will serve to define their
roles together. It will offer them a context within which they can relate, and give
them a reason for being together. Consider, for example, the manner in which they
would be thrust together if they went through a crisis in a foreign country, the language of which only Bookworm speaks, and how much that situation would dominate their thoughts, feelings, and actions. Consider how differently all the relationship dynamics would play out at a New Year's Eve party, around the dinner table
with Playboy's family, or sitting in a college classroom together. These and many
other situations in life consist of circumstances that determine to a great extent the
type and content of experiences people share. This is the role, also, played by the
positions of the numerology chart. Each position represents a different part of

human nature. The number in a given position is conditioned to express according to the character of that position. If the same number appears in five different positions of an individual's chart, that number is the same Force in all five positions. But each position has its own terms and conditions that cause the number to manifest in particular ways, just as circumstances in our lives necessitate particular types of thinking, decision-making, and behavior.

We are accustomed to believe that the circumstances in our daily lives are what motivate us, and sometimes force us, to keep striving to do or to be what is necessary. But the real "circumstances" with which we deal are the components of our inner nature, as represented by the positions of the chart. These are the inner, spiritual situations in which the soul lives and functions here on earth. The exterior, physical conditions reflect the inner, spiritual/psychological state of being. To continue our tale:

> *Let us now imagine Bookworm in the downtown library of a large city. She is quietly relishing an afternoon of reading and solitude in the rear area of the deserted fourth floor. Outside it is a warm and sunny spring day, the kind of Saturday afternoon everyone looks forward to enjoying. Playboy is intently prowling the busy downtown streets for possible conquests.*

The busy downtown is Playboy's "position," his prowling grounds. The library is Bookworm's "position," her intellectual sanctuary. The action in our story will take place mainly in the library, which thereby loosely corresponds to the Participation position of the numerology chart. This is because the library represents the conditions that determine how they "function in the world."

So now we have the characters, setting, and even plot of our story. Our purpose in telling the story is to explore the relationship between the two main characters in a meaningful way. We will want to gain a feeling for who they really are. If they have problems, conflicts, or limitations, we will want to see those deficiencies examined, then worked through, resolved, or transcended. As I tell this story, I will adhere faithfully to the societal stereotypes, as I understand them. At the same time, I have full freedom to direct the story line as I choose. I can use the full resources of my imagination in order to achieve results that are to my liking. In this way, Bookworm and Playboy can legitimately have experiences that would ordinarily be out of character. This is creative storytelling. In number symbolism, the same purposeful management of numbers is true interpretation. The efficacy of interpretation leaves a person with the odd feeling that no situation is unalterable reality. There is the nagging feeling that *any* circumstance, condition, or character trait represented in number symbolism can be transformed if sufficient ingenuity is brought to the interpretation of the numbers. This is a heady idea—that *everything* can be worked out, uplifted, prospered, *healed*. But how? This entire book is the attempt to answer that question.

For the time being, our immediate concern is to determine the goal in interpretation: what do we seek? If the goal is spiritual life, then we want to know the truth—who we really are and how best to live. We want to face Reality. We want to strip away fears and illusions, and all that would keep us from our highest potential. We want to replace ignorance with sure knowledge. We want to find and become that ineffable state of being called Spirit. This is our goal in interpretation. To bring this about, we are willing to aim high, to experiment, to take risks, and to develop new attitudes. We must be willing to own up to our fears and be honest about ourselves. We accept any idea, attitude, or philosophy, no matter how fervently we cherish it, if it becomes clear it is wrong or blocks our way to Highest Experience.

This, at any rate, is something of my goal in interpretation. What is yours? A person's Real Goal in interpretation—his Deep Purpose—has a profound generative effect in working with mathematical symbolism, and in living life. It mobilizes unknown causes and invisible forces. It is the seed of life, which is always and forever in the act of germinating. It is the tiniest nexus of vibrant potentiality that faithfully turns into life experience.

As I unfold the account of how Bookworm and Playboy meet and get on with each other, note how logical and natural it all is. It has an "of course!" feeling at each moment. Of course they act and behave as they do, for that is exactly *who they are*. This is so because there is an inner logic to these two, just as there is to numbers. Once the basic idea of each character (or number) is grasped, everything that follows is a logical consequence.

> *So Bookworm is spending the entire afternoon hidden away in the library—not that a day at the library is really her idea of a fabulous time. She never does anything that is too exciting or too fun. Instead, she is relatively content to read*

and think quietly and inconspicuously in a spot where she can remain unnoticed. Meanwhile, on the Avenue, Playboy is performing his Saturday ritual of Flirt-and-Conquer. He moves confidently from one familiar haunt to the next, when suddenly the gleam in his eye dims. He realizes that he has become bored! He feels unchallenged! Every female face is explored territory. Crestfallen, he concludes he needs a whole new arena to explore, some virgin territory. He is now willing to consider trolling places he has always shunned, simply on the off-chance he might find someone new and interesting.

In this moment of perplexity, he comes to a standstill. Across the street looms the hulking public library. Suddenly, as though seeing the library for the very first time, he envisions it as a place of opportunity to which he can go. He slowly intones the words "the public library" with a certain reverence and incredulity.

The library is the last place we would expect to find Playboy. Literature, research, and quiet are out of character for him. But this is no problem for our story. We needed only to find a reason *from his viewpoint* for him to choose to enter the library. From Playboy's frame of reference, he is totally bored. Consequently, he is willing to reconsider alternatives he had previously rejected. This is his kind of thinking. It is the same type of resourceful flexibility that allows us to create desired ends when working with numbers. It is simply (and it is not always simple or easy) a matter of finding the reason from within the context of the number.

*As Playboy enters the library he is astonished! How had he never known about this place before?! Immediately he is curious. "What is all this?" he whispers to himself excitedly. Of one thing he is sure: this is an **opportunity**. And so he proceeds to scour the library for someone or something that catches his eye. Everything is of interest; everything is novel. There is so much potential for . . . ? If only he could put his finger on it. Yet the answer somehow eludes him.*

At her table, all is quiet and undisturbed. Bookworm is engrossed in her book, Jane Eyre, *a romance novel. Her keen mind races, stimulated by the book's wealth of insight. The beauty of the writing uplifts her, while the characters engage her imagination. And her feelings! Nothing shows outwardly, but deep within she yearns for soul union with a man. Toward that tender aspira-*

tion her emotions lurch awkwardly. She so desires to piece together the neces-
sary psychological components within herself to make it all possible. She sighs
deeply, knowing love is not her lot in life, and gazes longingly into the book.

Playboy, leaving no stone unturned in the aisles and byways of the library,
finally spots Bookworm in a distant corner. She has none of the good looks that
usually lure him. But today he is after something different. He immediately
assesses everything about this lady: lonely, insecure, secretive, defensive, yet vul-
nerable, caring, and reachable through her intellectual interests and her emo-
tional naiveté. He makes a note of the book she is reading. Picking out a novel
in a related genre, he seats himself nearby. He reads just long enough to have a
grasp of the literary territory so he is able to initiate a conversation with her, a
seductive conversation. He is a quick study. He knows people and how to work
them. "Excuse me," he observes thoughtfully, " it looks like you're as fascinated
by nineteenth-century romantic literature as I am." He smiles vulnerably as he
moves a seat closer, fully confident of his charms, fully enjoying his conquest-in-
progress.

Her response is equally predictable. She squirms uncomfortably and turns
away, scared. Who is this guy? This man represents danger, disruption. His
casual grace and alluring charm seem cruelly threatening. More importantly, he
is obviously consumed by the sensual. How easily she could be won over by him.
But he is totally unattainable. She plunges into a vortex of confusion. Every
word of the conversation—the one with him and the one inside her throbbing
head—becomes the subject of intense speculation. Her feelings rage and soar.
Her vision blurs as she sits utterly immobilized.

So here is the basic rapport between Bookworm and Playboy. Their "relationship"
has all the earmarks of a psychological chasm that cannot be bridged. Normally, this
is as close (if you can call it that) as these two stereotypes ever get. Such will not be
the case here, however, because, contrary to his customary attitude, Playboy has
decided to connect with Bookworm. What can be the outcome of this liaison? A
union of any type between these two is so improbable, so unlikely, so fraught with
obvious conflict that it is very difficult to imagine them together. Yet, at the same
time, we know there will be *some* kind of relationship, because what Playboy wants
he usually gets. He is that good.

There is nothing new here in what is being said of Bookworm and Playboy. Their story is playing out strictly according to their stereotypic natures. It is the same with numbers. As their respective forces are discussed and compared in an interpretation, concepts and conclusions issue logically one from another, thus building up and establishing the interpretive concept and the lines of reasoning that support it.

> *Playboy is stimulated by Bookworm's diffidence. He is too quick, too resourceful, too hungry to chase an opportunity to become discouraged by a moment of aloofness. It is true that he is completely unfamiliar with* Jane Eyre, *the author, Emily Brontë, the literature of the period, or any literature at all, for that matter. But it is sufficient for him to read the dust jacket quickly to find out the gist of what he needs to know to start up a conversation. "I am amazed," he interjects after a few moments, "that a frail, inexperienced girl like Emily Brontë could have created such strong, savage characters as the Heathcliff family." He glances up at Bookworm to see if she realizes he is shamelessly reading from the flap of the dust jacket. "It is such a . . . how shall I say it? . . . such a passionate story, but so unsentimental, you know? What do you think?" Playboy certainly sounds like he knows what he is talking about. Bookworm cannot help but be intrigued by his thoughts, his sexy thoughts. Not many men could discuss Emily Brontë intelligently. He is a thinker, this one, and he has managed to engage her interest. Well, on that narrow basis she can see talking to this man—no harm there—just for a little bit. He, on the other hand, is doing no thinking at all save what his next tactical move will be. He deftly expands the range of their discussion until he, at last, is openly flirting and she, enjoying this rare moment of intellectual attention, hesitantly plunges her mental toe into the playful waters of conversation.*

The above developments between Bookworm and Playboy demonstrate how they enter into relationship. It is all plausible. This discussion is also a metaphor of the numbers 7 and 5, which parallels Bookworm and Playboy and their relationship. It is an extremely unlikely association due to their radically different natures. But relationship has been established nonetheless in a genuine way because the story line adheres strictly to the nature of each social stereotype, ensuring that the sequence of developments was real and not forced or contrived.

This story illustrates many of the considerations when numbers are interpreted. It is also the simplest interpretation to make in a numerology chart: two numbers in two positions. The interpretation process becomes much more involved and intricate when a third element is introduced. So much more needs to be taken into consideration. A rapport needs to be established between each of the three elements. To illustrate this, I will now add a third character to our story: Do Gooder. Previously, we needed to only be concerned with the interaction of two dynamics. Now we have three in operation, as illustrated in Figure 10.

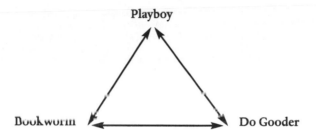

Figure 10. All three characters are in relationship with each other.

An additional complexity with three elements is this: when one element is being discussed in relation to another, the influence of the third must be taken into consideration also. Thus, if the rapport between Do Gooder and Bookworm is being analyzed, the simple presence of Playboy has an effect on each of them that must be taken into account at every moment. In other words, when Do Gooder is speaking to Bookworm, she cannot avoid being aware that Bookworm is with Playboy, and that definitely affects how she relates to Bookworm. At the same time, even though Playboy is not actively interacting with her, Do Gooder is fully conscious of him, and that mindfulness is itself a dynamic of how she acts and what she says. Consequently, although we are interested in knowing the relationship each shares with the other two, it is of greater interest to know the nature of the group as a whole. This is always the goal of interpretation: to determine the cumulative meaning of all the numbers together as one multifaceted whole (see Figure 11).

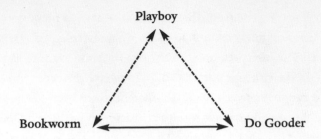

Figure 11. All elements of the story have an impact on each other, whether the elements are active or passive.

To continue our tale, I now identify Do Gooder. Although this societal image could equally be a man or a woman, in this narrative I have made her a mature woman.

> *Do Gooder is a selfless volunteer for humanity, forever joining worthy causes that have nothing in them for herself. Her devotion to good works is such that one wonders if she has a life of her own. She is there for the betterment of everyone, whether they want her efforts or not. She is often surprised at the indifference of people to the great spiritual causes, but this does not diminish her own devotion. Do Gooder is earnest, and everything she says has a moral tone and point. She functions with the appearance of humility and genuine cheerfulness even in the most distressing of circumstances. Her spirit is indomitable, strong but genteel; she is a helper to those "not as fortunate" as her, and treats everyone the same, whether young or old, good or bad, family or stranger, rich or poor, with courtesy and an air of charity.*

The qualities of Do Gooder are comparable to those of the number 9. In the story, Do Gooder's "position" is on the sidewalk outside the entrance to a large department store, where she solicits volunteers to work on behalf of abandoned children. There is a natural affinity between Bookworm and Do Gooder, just as there is between 7 and 9. Their strengths and characteristics tend to complement and reinforce each other, generally. They share a certain mutual sympathy. On the other hand, Do Gooder's characteristics (like those of Bookworm) generally contrast and conflict with those of Playboy. They operate strictly at cross-purposes.

After Playboy had worked his charms on Bookworm long enough to advance his flirtation to the next stage—having a romantic dinner together—they leave the library, still engrossed in matters of a literary nature. Bookworm is pleasantly elated to be in the company of a man with intellectual curiosity like her own. For his part, Playboy loves seeing his plan coming together. On the inside, Playboy is intently planning how to work on her at the restaurant in order to complete his sexual conquest. How he loves the challenge of strategy-making, and the warm day along with the sights and sounds of the city in the spring.

Just then, Playboy overhears Do Gooder up the block ask loudly if anyone will give freely of their time to help destitute children who are not able to help themselves. He cannot help remarking to Bookworm, "With all the fun things to do in the world, who wants to spend all their time nurse-maiding some unfortunate kids?" This startles Bookworm. Not only because it is such a callous and insensitive remark, but because, from a very young age, she had always felt abandoned. She can certainly identify with the plight of those helpless, little children. Intuitively, she feels their pain. She withdraws immediately from Playboy, plunging her hands deep into her pockets and gazing down at the sidewalk as they stroll along.

There is a silence between them now, a state all too familiar to Bookworm and a curious oddity to Playboy. She morosely ponders the dilemma of anyone who is abandoned and lost, and alone. Bookworm keeps her thoughts and feelings to herself. She knows Playboy is uninterested in what she might have to say. And she is not one, either, to confront him on his selfish attitude.

Do Gooder sees the couple coming. She always recognizes people that she can, well, talk into doing good. She thinks the woman is definitely one of those people who is easy to persuade, that's for sure; and as for the man with her, he just might be vulnerable because he has an interest in the woman. She embraces them with her mind. A look of piety veils her face as she lures them to her with a sweetened smile and a pose of modesty, hands clasped demurely in front.

Playboy is kicking himself for his frank (and unreflected) comment moments earlier. Now he is going to have to do a little fancy footwork to regain her confidence and her affection, which he lost through his one reckless statement. He is resourceful, though. He can use even the awkwardness between them to his advantage. He will show her his flexibility and demonstrate a willingness to be generous. He takes the initiative as he and Bookworm near Do Gooder. "What a wonderful thing you are doing to help children," he observes disarmingly, without so much as slowing his pace. Bookworm keeps on walking with Playboy, but she is confused.

This is Do Gooder's perfect moment to launch into a magnanimous sermon about dispossessed children. "There are so many, so very many," she moans piteously, just beginning to warm up to her topic. Bookworm is more than willing to listen to this, mostly out of curiosity and a desire to know. But Playboy has no intention of letting this go any farther. "I am sure you are doing all you can, thank you," he says as he pushes on by, pulling Bookworm along with him. He has won; Do Gooder has lost. Bookworm was receptive to Do Gooder's pleas, but not assertive enough to voice her position, allowing herself instead to be romanced by this clever, charming fellow. And so they continue walking up the sidewalk, holding hands, talking pleasantly about one thing and another. Do Gooder turns toward another passerby, the gleam in her eye undiminished.

And so our story draws to a close for now. The very charming and resourceful Playboy (number 5) dominated this trio. The potential rapport between Bookworm (number 7) and Do Gooder (number 9) was too weak to come about. The rift between Playboy and Do Gooder is complete. Bookworm and Playboy may have begun a relationship, but it is bound to be difficult for both of them to manage successfully.

It would be easy to go on spinning this yarn indefinitely. Playboy could drop Bookworm (the kind of thing he is famous for doing) in order to begin courting Do Gooder. Bookworm could decide to work for Do Gooder's cause, or even to become friends with her when Playboy is not around. Do Gooder could stray from her sober life, tempted by Playboy's pleasurable lifestyle. You get the idea. We stop here—for the time being—because certain principles of interpretation have been sufficiently explored and established.

It should now be clear how this group of three interacts, with one drawback. Being social clichés, they remain no more than impersonal stereotypes. So, while the story does demonstrate how to make an accurate interpretation through the dual technique of identify-and-compare, it is entirely lacking in personal meaning. The problem of going deeper with these three social stereotypes is the same as it is with numbers. In the beginning stages of learning interpretation, we master the common definitions void of personal relevance, except in a most general way. The study of numbers and their interpretation are initially stereotypical. At that level, analyzing combinations of numbers is purely mechanistic. Later, when intuition and creativity and other advance skills play a major role, the basic principles learned in the beginning continue to remain valid, just as addition and subtraction continue to be valid in physics.

It will perhaps help to learn the numbers and to develop interpretation skills by working with stereotypes applicable to each of the nine numbers. Bear in mind that none of the suggested images for each number in the chart fully encapsulate that number. Each image is very suggestive of certain aspects of the number Force with which it is associated. Analyzing any combination of these social clichés is a useful way to experiment with numbers.

Social Stereotypes Comparable to the Numbers

1 Egomaniac; Number One; Self-Starter; Leader of the Pack

2 Wall Flower; Help Mate; Nervous Nellie; Team Player

3 Layabout; Word Smith; Chatter Box; Song and Dance Man; The Good Life

4 Drudge; Honest Abe; Workaholic; Never Say Die

5 Life of the Party; Wheeler-Dealer; Glad Hander; City Slicker; Playboy; Roustabout

6 Homebody; Doormat; Florence Nightingale; Shrink; Family Man; Pillar of the Community

7 The Thinker; Egghead; Strong Silent Type; Bookworm; Hermit

8 King of the Hill; Top Dog; Social Climber; Mr./Mrs. Millionaire; Overachiever; Power Broker

9 Armchair Philosopher; Do Gooder; Sacrificial Lamb; Saint; Miracle Worker

Endnotes

1. Dion Fortune, *The Mystical Qabalah* (York Beach, Maine: Samuel Weiser, Inc., 1989), 43.

2. Ibid., 165.

3. Ibid., 168.

4. James N. Powell, *The Tao of Symbols* (New York: Quill, 1982), 55.

5. Edmund H. Harvey, Jr., Editor, *Reader's Digest Book of Facts* (Pleasantville, N.Y.: The Reader's Digest Association, 1987), 93.

6. Stephen Hawking, *A Brief History of Time* (New York: Bantam Books, 1988), 71–2.

7. *Webster's Encyclopedic Unabridged Dictionary of the English Language* (New York: Gramercy Books, 1994), 170.

chapter 7

A Numerological Interpretation

So, that's the way destiny is: simply the fulfillment of the potentialities of energies in your own system. The energies are committed in a certain way, and that commitment is out there coming toward you.

—Diane K. Osborn, Ed., *Reflections on the Art of Living*

The interpretation process consists of identifying each number and comparing back and forth, gradually building the concept until everything has been discussed. This is the heart of the matter. We have seen this function theoretically in chapter 6. To demonstrate how it works in reality, meet Wilma Dawn Thomas, a fictitious personality I invented for this purpose. The phrases in the margins follow the structure of the reading; they let you know which number is being identified, or which numbers are being compared.

```
    9    1   1          6   1      = 9 Heart's Desire
 W I L M A   D A W N   T H O M A S
 5   3 4   4   5 5 2 8   4     1    = 5 Personality
 5 9 3 4 1   4 1 5 5   2 8 6 4 1 1  = 5 Character
                    April 16, 1951  = 7 Participation
```

Wilma's Reading

Well, Wilma, before I begin your reading, I want to explain briefly my views about numerology. I believe that before we're born, and while we are still in the Spirit State, our soul plans out our life here on earth. It envisions the kind of person we will be, our special qualities, the challenges we will face, the learnings we will achieve, and so on. In a mysterious way, the details of that plan are encoded in the birth information: the birth name and the birth date. My job is to get a sense of what your plan is, to see how it is going at this time, and to suggest what you might do to improve your life. In view of this, I consider a numerology reading to be a spiritual report.

Needless to say, if the divine part of ourselves designed this life for us and determined the combination of numbers we would have, then it is perfect. That is to say, it is perfect for us and exactly what we need even though we might not understand why we need those particular numbers or why we have this or that challenge. This is why I say that your chart is all to the good, no matter what the difficulties and negativities are. It is all purposeful. My job is to *see* that good and that purpose, and to communicate it all to you.

Nothing in this reading is dogmatic. The interpretation I am about to give you is my understanding of who and what you are based on what I see in your chart, but it is *your* life. So, you decide for yourself what to accept and what is of value to you.

On your chart you will notice four little words: Participation, Character, Heart's Desire, and Personality. These are called *positions* on the chart. Each position represents a part of human nature. The number in each position shows what that part of you is like. What I will do as I begin your reading is to identify, or describe, the number you have in the Participation position. I will tell what it means for you to have that number in that position. As I go from one position to the next, I will compare the numbers back and forth to show how they all work together.

I begin with the Participation position because it is considered to be the most important position of the chart. This position represents how you function in the world. It is the role you play on the stage of life, so to speak. It shows how you handle relationships and how you take part in situations. The number in this position is the energy, or aspect of human experience, that you mainly work with, and experiment with, as you go through your life. Consequently, this is the indicator of a major lesson in your life. After all, it is like the big project your soul decided to work on during your time on earth. It makes sense that in the course of trying to accomplish the goal, you will have some big learning as a result of making that kind of effort.

In the Participation position you have the number 7. Each number in numerology is associated with certain kinds of experiences, characteristics, and attitudes. But more basic than that, each number is a Force, a deep, spiritual Force, operating within each of us. Everything associated with each number is a result of the primal Force that is its essential nature. The spiritual-psychological bottom line of the 7 is this: to discover and to live the truth of the self. As a 7 person, this makes you a seeker of truth. Now, the term "truth" covers a lot of territory. A lot of people have their own ideas about the meaning of truth. I don't have any single, specific form of truth that I am trying to sell you on. What I am saying is that, in your own terms, you look for the inner essence of things, situations, people, and yourself. You are one of the thinkers of the world, and much more mental than most people. It is your nature to think things through, to analyze everything, and to look for understanding. This makes you an intellectual kind of person who tends to develop skills more thoroughly and deeply than most people. This is because, as a 7 person, you spend most of your time on the inside, in the privacy of your own mind. Any skill area you are interested in receives a lot of attention. You mull over it, think about it, work with it, analyze it, and so on. You really master skill areas you like. For this reason, 7 is known as the professional number.

Seven is also known as the metaphysical number because its focus is inside of the self. Your attention is attuned to what is within you and, ultimately, to your true nature, your Higher Self. You are always partially in meditation, as it were. If you are interested in spirituality, you hear the still, small voice. This means that you have a strong intuition. What is intuition, after all, but listening to Spirit? And that is what 7 is all about at its heart.

So, as you function in the world, the search for truth and wisdom is a main preoccupation for you. The two most spiritual numbers of the nine numbers of numerology are 7 and 9. Seven is the inner search for the truth of the self, and 9 is the outer drive to become one with the world and with life. The big lesson I mentioned earlier concerning your 7 has to do with having the courage and the faith to stand by the truth you find, no matter how the world reacts to it. This can be difficult for the 7 for several reasons. One is that 7 is inward and private, and likes to have time alone to reflect and to think. You cannot have that kind of quietness if you are confronting the people you know over the validity of what you believe. Another reason for difficulty is that it is not the nature of the 7 to be sociable and to communicate, to share feelings, to commune with others, and so on. Seven goes within, and stays there. So, it takes courage and effort for you to come out of your 7 shell and to assert your feelings and ideas. This requires intense concentration on what is inside, and the courage to be honest about it. Superficialities will not do the trick.

Every number has both a positive and a negative potential. The negative characteristics are simply the other side of the coin of the positive ones. If you're feeling stressed, angry, antisocial, or insecure, that kind of attitude can turn the positive qualities into their negative counterparts. In this mode, you can be very difficult to know—aloof, distant, incommunicative, critical, and even emotionally disturbed. If you are in such a negative state, you can be very hard to get along with because you're mentally absent. You're not connecting with those around you, or even with yourself.

Due to your 7 Participation, you are your own person, an individualist with your own attitudes and ideas, your own thinking and perceptions, your own philosophy and understanding. You make up your own mind based on your personal concept of things, not based on what others say or think. All your individuality and inwardness make relationships challenging for you. It is not your nature, from the perspective of your 7, to exhibit the kinds of attitudes and behaviors that create and maintain relationships. The other three numbers in your chart will change this whole picture, based on what *their* natures are. We will be discussing them shortly. Considering the 7 alone, for the moment, activities like communicating, sharing, being involved in other peoples' lives, being there for other people and meeting their needs, and being accepting of the quirks and oddities of others simply are not you.

These kinds of "people" behaviors might collectively be called "relationship skills." For you, good relationship behaviors do not come naturally, because 7 has another agenda, a different purpose. This is why relationships tend to be difficult for you. Even if you know exactly what to do to keep your relationship healthy and fun, it is hard work and effort for you. Many people with a prominent 7 feel socially awkward and find it difficult, even fearful, to express thoughts and feelings. The good news is that creating and maintaining relationships is a skill like any other. It is a skill you can learn, if you really want to, because 7 masters skills of any type. Even if you become an expert in this area, it will always be a struggle for you because relationships simply do not come naturally to the 7. They will always take more perseverance for you than for most people who have other numbers in their charts, numbers that naturally facilitate relationships. All this doesn't mean that you can't have good relationships, such as with a husband or close friends. You can have fully satisfying relationships. What I am telling you are important considerations, not impossible blocks. These are things to think about and to be aware of as you work on developing your relationship skills.

Identification of the number 7

In terms of work, 7 is a strong number. It is considered the professional number. With the 7, you have excellent mental and intellectual abilities. You are able to develop deep understanding and insight into any subject area. This, of course, is an asset in any kind of work you do. I said "any kind of work," but I really meant mental work, work in which you think, reason, and use your education. You would do well to avoid purely physical work or manual labor. Some numbers, like 4, 5, and 8, have the need to be physical and hands-on. This is not the way of the 7.

I like to give an image for each of the numbers, otherwise all the qualities and characteristics I discuss during the reading risk blending together into an undifferentiated mass of abstractions. A strong, clear image, on the other hand, is easy to remember and helps you to focus on what the number is all about. You can think of the 7 as the research scientist. She[1] is very at home in the laboratory working alone with her experiments, and not very comfortable having other people intrude into her private world. She's an intellectual and a skilled specialist who works with ideas and concepts.

The Participation position, which we have been discussing, shows how you function in the world. The next position I will discuss is the Character position. It shows the basic type of person you are, your overall nature, and the kinds of abilities you have. It is who you are. If you think of the Participation position as being the role you play on the stage of life, the Character position represents the person playing that role.

Identification of the Character position

In the Character position, you have the number 5, making you a person of freedom and opportunity. If you don't have freedom in all aspects of your life, you feel frustrated and limited, and you cannot function fully as the 5 person you are. This is because the spiritual-psychological bottom line of the 5 is discovering and living one's individuality. That is the basic Force of the 5. It is the mission of every 5 to claim her full individuality, and to go forth into the world accordingly. You can't do that unless you are fully free to be who you are, to come and go as you please, doing what you feel is necessary to do. Five's prime directive is to be its own individual. And so the 5 woman tends to be a seeking and searching kind of person. She seeks out the ways and means to fulfill personal wants and needs. She experiments in life, trying new things and ideas, taking risks—calculated risks, because the 5 is clever, not foolhardy, and it definitely likes to succeed. Five is the wheeler-dealer and, consequently, the number of prospering in this life. Five loves the earth and dealing with the earth more than any of the other numbers in numerology. For 5, life is opportunity: the opportunity to exercise all its talents and abilities and to have fun doing it.

A good image to represent the 5 is the comedian who performs before a live audience. In my view, people are not predisposed to laugh at a comedian's jokes. In fact, they are usually sitting and waiting to see if she can provoke them to laughter. It may not be a fully hostile situation for a comedian, but it is at least testy. Think of the strength it requires to take that long walk through the group of strangers to the stage; think of the adventurousness, the willingness to risk, the boldness, and the sheer audacity it takes to step before the crowd and say, "A funny thing happened to me on the way over here . . . ," and then expect to hear laughter. *That* is the 5.

This is basically *your* nature: to be a speculator and a gambler in life. You are vibrant, energetic, even daring in your creativity, a life-of-the-party kind of person, definitely an extrovert. Five people are usually talented and resourceful, so in a crisis you are almost always able to figure out a way to do what needs to be done. You are the idea lady, and the one who gets what is needed in a situation in which there isn't enough money, resources, or supplies. You break out of that limitation. You handle it. You figure out what to do and how to flourish in that situation. No one is more of a quick thinker than the 5, making you a quick study, versatile, able to handle fast-changing conditions. You are good at dealing with people, not so much in the sense of diplomacy or human relations, but more in the sense of strategy and the ability to cope and maneuver in any situation.

These are the positive expressions of the 5. There is also the negative potential of the 5, as there is for all the numbers. I am not saying *you* are negative in this way, necessarily. Rather, as a 5 person, these are the potential attitudes and behaviors to watch for. The same ability you have to seize an opportunity and maximize it can, if you are in a negative frame of mind, make you opportunistic. This is because you are so alert to opportunities and how to make the most of them that you are always way ahead of everybody else. If you are feeling impatient or insecure, if you see a chance for a big financial windfall or a way to get on the good side of an important person, well, it is child's play for you to take advantage of other peoples' slow-paced thinking. In your mind, you have already taken the opportunity at hand while everyone else is just waking up to the possibilities. From there, all you have to do is deftly move in and take the prize. This is something to be careful to avoid. Nobody likes to be taken advantage of by an opportunist.

Another negative potential of the 5 is to be a rebel and a roustabout. This is because 5 has a deep need for the new and the different, something interesting happening all the time. The 5 needs to be entertained. In the negative mode, 5 is impatient and can't wait for things to change at their own pace. Instead, it forces the situation in order to create the new and the different by doing something unconventional, wild, or even immoral, in order to bring it about. Five has a potential for great frustration at the slow pace of life. In this regard, all people with a prominent 5 are restless. I don't make many absolute statements in my readings, but over time I have found that 5 people are invariably restless. During a positive period, that restlessness translates into constructive seeking and searching. You *discover* life! In a negative state, though, that same restlessness can result in the inability to stay with anything, a complete intolerance of everything that smacks of routine, responsibility, commitment, restraint of any kind, or even putting up with something unpleasant or frustrating. You probably often simply flee from such situations.

This is why the 5 is a challenging number when it comes to relationships. Healthy and happy relationships require attitudes like commitment, being there for the other person even when he is really slowing you down, putting your needs aside for the sake of the other person, agreeing to do what the other person wants, and the like. This is all opposite to the nature of the 5 and its strong need for freedom, its anytime-anywhere syndrome. When your relationship gets slow, routine, testy, or requires you to be home at regular times (so you satisfy the other person's agenda instead of your own), you are tempted to say something like: "This is all too much for me. I am out of here. I am taking to the open road. Have a nice life and maybe we'll meet again someday." In other words, you've got a low boredom-frustration threshold. As a 5, it is hard for you to stick with responsibility or anything that seems to slow you down or impose on your spontaneous lifestyle. Your instinctive response is to get away, to be free.

Does this mean you can't have a good relationship? No, of course not. These are simply thoughts to bear in mind when it comes to being in relationship. On the positive side of relating to people, 5 makes you a delightful and ever-interesting companion, an excellent conversationalist, clever, witty, and entertaining. With all these strong people qualities, you also would do well on stage or anywhere you can perform for people. Of course, you are always performing, whether you are on stage or not!

Another area of potential difficulty for you as a 5 person has to do with the sensual appetites: sex, drugs, food, alcohol, and so on. This is due to the 5s need to experience widely and to indulge in all the pleasures the earth has to offer. Think about it: if you are fleeing from the responsibility of living your life in a positive and constructive way, there is a good possibility that you'll be attracted to the sensual appetites that, in turn, can eat you alive. One thought that may help you to deal with these impulsive urges and temptations is to deliberately and consciously apply your need for seeking and searching to something positive. If, for example, you put all your seeking-and-searching energy into being responsible, that could turn out to be quite an interesting journey of inquiry and discovery. That would satisfy the seeking and searching need, and you would find that there's more that is interesting about being responsible than first meets the eye.

The point is that 5 explores and experiments: the individual chooses what to focus on.

Identification of the number 5

It is the nature of the 5 not only to cope well with change—that's clear from everything I've said—but even to need some change and some risk happening all the time. If things get too staid and settled for you, too organized and routine, then you're likely to have to tap your head with your hand and wonder, *Is Wilma alive in there? Is she awake?* Change, risk, uncertainty—these kinds of conditions are quite stimulating to you.

In terms of work and career, 5 is very strong and positive. This is the number of prosperity, opportunity, salesmanship, wheeling-and-dealing, strategy in negotiation, and taking the calculated risk, all of which can be a tremendous asset in work. Add to that creativity, inventiveness, resourcefulness, having fun all the while, and 5 is wonderful when it comes to work. Another good image for the 5, other than the comedian, is the salesperson who loves to travel about, loves to meet new people all the time, and loves the challenge of selling a product time after time.

Comparison of the 5 Character and the 7 Participation

Now, as I've been discussing the 5 person that you are, you may have noticed how different the 5 and 7 are in every way. They are opposite. The 7 is quiet, reserved, private, and intellectual, and its purpose is to go within to look for insight and understanding. Experiences in the world serve to stimulate 7s thinking process. Noise, commotion, conflict, and a fast pace are all disturbing to the 7 part of you, whereas the 5 part of you not only needs boisterous activity but also thrives on it. The difference between these two energies is tremendous.

This is your great inner conflict. The combination is also extremely dynamic and has great potential. On the one hand, with the 5 Character number, you are a vibrant, active, resourceful person who stirs everyone around you into activity. That is who you are *sometimes*, I should say. At other times, with your 7 Participation number, the role you play on the stage of life is opposite to the 5. It's quiet and reserved, intellectual, searching for knowledge and learning in a contemplative, undisturbed way. These two numbers are like oil and water. Imagine a teenage rebel who is trying to pull a fast one with his girlfriend's father by pretending he's a scholarly thinker whose area of expertise is Sumerian archaeology! This example gives you an idea of the contrast between your 5 and your 7. I am sure there have been many times in your life when these two parts of you have faced off against each other and you've been *miserable!* Sometimes, I would say, the extreme difference between the sedate, secretive 7 and the raucous, unconventional 5 has had a paralyzing effect on you. In this condition, tremendous inner turmoil causes each number to negate the other so that they cancel each other out. In this state, which I think occurs only infrequently, you find that you simply cannot act.

You may be wondering if you can *ever* come to terms with this. Of course you can, but it will take some serious work on your part. That work involves accepting, and being at peace with, the 5 person that you are, and doing the same with the 7, the way in which you function in the world. The next step in this process is to make friends between the 5 and 7. If, from the perspective of the 5, you can be happy with the private, inward 7, and vice versa—if, in other words, you feel affection between those two basic parts of yourself —in the moment that they become friends, they unite with each other and become one. Then, the differences you have always experienced between them—your intractable inner conflict—disappear. In place of the conflict, you find you have the strength and vitality of the two numbers functioning harmoniously in partnership.

As different as these two numbers are, it is no easy matter to resolve the differences. But it can be done. Both are numbers of seeking and searching: the 5 explores the world around us and the 7 explores the inner world of the self. So you are a true seeker. When these two kinds of seeker energy are unified so that they pursue the same goal, there is no more dynamic, inventive, electric combination because the combined energies of the two numbers are so very potent. It's similar to holding onto a bare electric wire with current coursing through it. If you can bear the high voltage of high creativity and daring and ingenious inventiveness, you can do remarkable things.

Both the 5 and 7 are challenging when it comes to relationships. On the one hand, with the 7, you have a hard time relating and "being in relationship." On the other hand, with the 5, your tendency is to want to flee at the appearance of frustrating difficulty or stagnant routine. About the *last* thing you are prepared to be is a homebody whose time is spent tending to someone else's wants and needs. Does this mean you cannot have successful relationships? No, of course it doesn't. But it does mean that you need to keep your wits about you all the time. You need to focus consciously on what you want in relationships. You will have to figure out for yourself what your priorities are. It won't do you any good at all to rely on society's conventional ideas. You will have to determine what works for you. It is also worthwhile mentioning that there are number combinations that are attracted to the 5/7 combination and that respond to it. So it seems to me that your challenge is to be aware of the type of nature you have, to decide what you want, and to know what your strengths and limitations are. Then, go for it.

Comparison of the 5 Character and the 7 Participation

In addition to the Character position we've been discussing, numerology identifies two other parts of your nature: the Heart's Desire and the Personality. We'll begin with the Personality position. It represents your style of presenting yourself to the world and the kind of person you appear to be. It is the surface you.

Identification of the Personality position

With 5 in the Personality position, you present yourself as a warm, lively, vivacious, life-of-the-party kind of person. You also come across as upbeat, resourceful, full of ideas, and the one who can be counted on for solutions. You are certainly a lively conversationalist or debater. The downside of your high-energy personality is the tendency to have a short attention span. It is not your personality to linger on slow-moving, in-depth discussions. After a few moments of leisurely pauses and belabored details, you are *so* ready to move on to another topic. Your personality is ideal for activities that involve quick thinking, flamboyant behavior, fast-paced and witty talk, or arguing the pros and cons of some hot topic. You have a personality that is effective for such occupations as salesperson, comedian, debater, negotiator, advertising executive, actor, explorer, lawyer, travel guide, fireman—anything that has risk and excitement. This also applies to your 5 Character.

Identification of the number 5

Now, the 5 in your Personality position and the 5 in your Character position are the same Force. Since the numbers are in different positions, we are looking at them from different perspectives, which causes different characteristics to be highlighted. This is because each position induces its number to manifest in certain ways. So, 5 expresses in particular ways in the Personality position, while in the Character position 5 expresses in other ways. Also,

Comparison of the 5 Personality and the 5 Character

whenever someone relates to you and you respond, the 5 energy of your Personality is activated. This, in turn, emphasizes by association your 5 Character. This makes 5 the strongest number in your chart. This is a strength because it means that your Personality is the perfect outlet for your 5 Character—the person that you are.

There are four positions in your chart: Participation, Character, Personality, and Heart's Desire. Two of the four positions have the number 5, making them the dominant force. So, between the 7 Participation, your two 5s, and the 9 Heart's Desire (which we'll be discussing shortly), you are first and foremost a 5 person. On the positive side of this, you are a real live wire. You bring energy, enthusiasm, ideas, and innovation to any enterprise you're involved in. You have an incredible ability when it comes to coping in fast-changing, risky, or adversarial conditions. These kinds of situations would be debates, arguments, high-stakes negotiations, legal battles, improvisational theater, political campaigns, or even war strategy. You are a very quick thinker and very resourceful. When circumstances become desperate, you can be counted on to come up with some kind of solution, recourse, or the required supplies. You thrive when you cope with risk, danger, or uncertainty. Precarious situations motivate you.

The liability of such strong 5 energy is that all your positive strengths have the potential for equally strong negative counterparts. You have an almost extreme need for freedom, regardless of the consequences. Even a hint of being penned in by routine or a schedule, someone else's expectations or needs, drives you crazy. I would say that you instinctively pull away from anything that constrains your ability to do what you want. You like to obey your whim, which is not always practical, or even possible, to do. For example, you can't act according to whim if you accept certain responsibilities in life. Every responsibility automatically limits personal freedom because you have to fulfill your obligations regardless of what you want to do at the time. So, with those two 5s, I would say that unless a responsibility is significant for you in personal terms, you could easily let that responsibility slide, or abandon it altogether.

Relationships, of course, are all about responsibility and commitment at their core. This would make the idea of being in a long-term, committed relationship a scary proposition. At the very mention of marriage, you are bound to be thinking to yourself something like, "Yes, but what if I want to take off by myself for a weekend to ski in Colorado, or to hike the Appalachian Trail? And what if I want to do it right now, no questions asked?" I think you view a marriage commitment as an almost cruel form of confinement. It's a very distressing prospect for you. Now, if you have a partner who is also a free spirit and who also experiences the need for spontaneous freedom, this is the kind of person with whom you could pull it off. You would certainly understand if your husband said to you with no advance warning, "I'm camping out this weekend with Bob and Joe and I'll see you afterward." You would be all right with that, wouldn't you? You would also be compatible with someone who is very deferring to you, who accepts your unconventional ways without upset or without demanding that you meet up to your responsibilities.

The challenge is mainly yours, Wilma, when it comes to maintaining a healthy relationship. Your success in this matter depends on making some decisions and setting priorities where relationships are concerned. Ask yourself, "What do I want in a relationship? What am I willing to do in order to have a special someone in my life?" These are the kinds of questions you need to answer. This will help you to formulate some guidelines for handling relationships.

Also, consider this: there is adventure to be found in relationships. If you learn to apply your strong need for seeking and searching to exploring the enigma of relationships, that will change everything. There is mystery in the nature of another person, and all that is necessary to negotiate the path the two of you tread together. It can take every bit of resourcefulness and ingenuity you have to make it work. It can take all the guts for risk-taking you have at your disposal. This is not the normal form of "worldly adventure" the 5 person generally seeks. But if, through a creative act of understanding, you envision relationships as an activity to which you can apply all your restless needs to explore and experiment, you will have made a giant leap in personal growth. It will give you a measure of peace of mind. Also, it will change everything in your dealings with others. To put yourself in this frame of mind, conceptualize relationships as a very risky adventure. See them

Comparison of the 5 Personality and the 5 Character

fraught with unforeseen traps and unexpected developments requiring frequent solutions and the constant need for bold, innovative initiatives. If you do this, you will find it much more rewarding and satisfying to deal with the events of your relationship experiences. Do I think such a major change in perspective will be easy? Not a bit. I simply propose to you a method for enhancing the quality of your relationships.

Now that we are talking about the effects of having *two* 5s, I reemphasize the need to guard against being an opportunist. Those are strong words, and painful, too. But a numerology reading that doesn't tell the truth—the negative and painful right along with the positive and uplifting—isn't going to be of any real value. I say this about being opportunistic because, in any situation involving a good opportunity, you are way ahead of the game. Few can compete with you. At the very outset, you have already seen the outcome and know instinctively how to bring it about before anyone else has even begun to examine the situation. It is understandably frustrating for you to sit by twiddling your thumbs while others plod through the process at a painfully slow pace. But no matter how slow others are, it is worth it for you to restrain yourself so you don't take advantage of them. Or, you can develop the opportunity for the good of all concerned.

Needless to say, nothing in life is simple and one dimensional. Here's another way to look at this: when the opportunistic ability is used in business, it is a different matter altogether. The ability to spot a prime opportunity and to zero in on it first is a great and usually well-paid talent.

Comparison of the 5 Personality, the 5 Character, and the 7 Participation

Now, the fact that you have the 5 Personality and the 5 Character, both of which must function through the 7 Participation, makes living something of a conundrum. That 7 is so unnatural to the 5. So confining! So disturbing! Here you are, such a vibrant and alive person, and your only recourse is to express all that raucous vitality through the staid, private, inward 7! That's tough. When I see this kind of inner difficulty, I always wonder, *What can be the purpose of it?* In other words, why would your soul set you up in this life with such a difficult dilemma?

In your case, I think it has to do with learning self-discipline. How does this work? Well, the only way for the 5 to survive in a 7 mode is for the 5 to conceive of its "bold adventure in life" in 7 terms. Those terms are the inner search for the truth of the self. When the inner search is pursued consistently and with dedication, it becomes the spiritual path. That is what the 7 is really all about. In contrast, the natural inclination of the 5 is to explore the external world far and wide. For the 5 to limit its energy and resources and to focus them consistently within the parameters of the 7 requires discipline, *great* self-discipline. When this has been accomplished, you will understand that the *real* adventure in life is the spiritual quest.

The spiritual search requires the maximum of courage, audacity, and adventurousness. It challenges a person to her core, to her innermost self-identity. Now, the most common way 5 energy is used is to explore the world and to express individuality "out there," regardless of the hindrances and obstacles. To anyone on the spiritual path, all that outer activity is understood to be illusion, which is no more than a reflection of our inner selves. There is no number in numerology more dedicated to the courageous search than 5. So, if a 5/7 person such as you can bring all that 5 energy to the 7 spiritual search for the truth, this results in the potential for phenomenal spiritual progress. This is supremely difficult for the 5. It requires great control to continue to apply the 5 energy toward the attainment of the 7 goal. So, the spiritual purpose of the 5/7 conundrum is, in my opinion, a kind of trial by fire. It is a purification rite the soul must pass through on its path to perfection and transcendence.

You will notice that the 5/7 combination doesn't leave much room for relationships. Almost none of the impressive strengths, abilities, and interests of 5/7 supplies what is needed to stay in a good relationship. I would say that for you to keep a relationship positive and constructive, you have to work at it very hard, constantly making conscious decisions that you know are necessary. Without that kind of effort, I think you will find that your relationships dissipate one after the other once the initial blush of interest has worn off. I don't see any reason why you can't have fully satisfying relationships despite what I've just said. It's simply a matter of doing what needs to be done. However, even after you've developed strong relationship skills and know them by heart, it will always take conscious effort to follow through. They will never just flow naturally for you like they do for other people who have what might be called "relationship numbers."

*Comparison of
the 5
Personality,
the 5
Character, and
the 7
Participation*

With your 5/5/7 combination of numbers, the type of work you would do best involves great mental and physical investigation, lots of mental problem solving and physical exploration. For an example, I am now thinking of that great investigative anthropologist Graham Hancock. While he was in the Near East some years ago doing research on his book, *The Sign and the Seal: The Quest for the Lost Ark of the Covenant,*[2] he went on an incredible hunt for archaeological and historical clues, a trip that was arduous both mentally and physically. He exercised incredible persistence and ingenuity in piecing together scanty bits of information in order to reach very insightful conclusions. That's the 7 part. He also went physically to many isolated and sometimes dangerous places at great personal risk, negotiating his way through many kinds of situations. That is the 5 part. This is admittedly an extreme, one-of-a-kind example. But it does give a good illustration of a work activity that combines strenuous physical and mental activity. Although this is only one example, I think all real 5/7 kinds of work have in common their uniqueness. These are not your run of the mill, commonplace, garden-variety kinds of enterprises. Each is unique and quite individual. One thing is for certain: the successful union of the two 5s and the 7 in your chart is a daunting task. Its achievement is a true accomplishment of significant personal and spiritual growth.

*Identification
of the
Heart's Desire
position*

Now we come to the fourth and final position in your chart, Wilma—the Heart's Desire. This position shows your motivation, your inner drive, the kind of person you admire, your hopes and aspirations, and things that make you happy.

*Identification
of the
number 9*

In the Heart's Desire position, you have the number 9. This shows that it is your desire to be a humanitarian, a universal kind of person. You are happy when you are giving unconditionally, whether its love, friendship, assistance, knowledge, or creative talents. You yearn to see the big picture in life and to relate to all aspects of it, with compassion and understanding. When this is combined with your deep intuitive understanding of life and a need for high ideals, it makes you a person who strives to be philosophical in the way you live your life.

It is very important to you to be idealistic in the work you do. The kind of vocation in which you are happy is one that serves a high ideal, spiritual principle, or aspiration. You want your occupation to be a calling whose purpose is to work for the benefit of all. Examples of this would be work that preserves and protects the environment, shelters abandoned children, or brings peace, healing, or better race relations to a segment of society—any endeavor that has a spiritual or idealistic purpose to it.

Identification of the number 9

With all that heartfelt need for pursuing idealism, you are not especially practical when it comes to business. Such practicality can be seen in the common ambitions people have for money, power, advancement, and prestige. Those interests are simply unrewarding and unsatisfying to you. This is in black-and-white contrast with other parts of your nature. With your 5 Character and your 5 Personality, you are definitely one to get ahead in this world, to make the deal, to promote yourself, to beat the competition, to outwit your adversary, to win at the game of life. The problem here is that those 5 kinds of personal ambition and personal gain simply don't mean very much to you in the area of happiness and satisfaction—your Heart's Desire. Very often, those kinds of personal desires work directly against the greater good of everyone. This is why the 9 does not make a practical, realistic, competitive kind of businessperson.

Comparison of the 9 Heart's Desire with the 5 Character and the 5 Personality

The 9 has a related difficulty when it comes to relationships. You tend to be a little impersonal. This is because the 9 part of you is focused primarily on the many: *their* good, *their* needs, *their* aspirations, leaving one-to-one intimacy out of the picture. If you are mainly interested in satisfying the wants and needs of those who are close to you, you're not going to have much left over for the mass of people. Think of Martin Luther King, whose life exemplified a 9 type of existence. He dedicated his life to the Civil Rights Movement. How do you think he would have reacted if his wife had come to him and said, "For heaven's sake, Martin, *every* Saturday for the past several months you're working on *this* speech or *that* speech! When is there ever going to be time for *me,* your wife? I have needs, too." I am sure Dr. King loved his wife very much. But I am also sure his response would have been to continue working on the speech. It's not that he didn't want his wife to be happy, but that he—like the 9—was dedicated to the larger purpose, first and foremost. Next to the needs of an entire people or a nation, the needs of just one person don't count that much for the 9.

Identification of the number 9

Of all the numbers in numerology, 1 through 9, 9 is the number with the greatest potential for spiritual growth. I say "potential" because you can always ignore it. That is your choice. The spiritual-psychological bottom line of this Force is "to be one with life and with the earth." All of the qualities and characteristics of 9 are extensions of its fundamental Force. Since 9 strives to be united with all it encounters, its great challenge is to transcend the ego of the lower self. The ego is preoccupied—consumed!—with fears and desires. It is the cause of feelings of separation from the rest of creation. To the extent that the personal ego is alive and well within your nature, the energy of the 9 is diminished and made impure to that same degree. To understand this idea, think of Martin Luther King again. His life exemplified nineness. He gave up almost everything of personal interest in order to succeed in his humanitarian goal of civil rights for blacks. Imagine the effect on his historic effort if, privately, he had been fantasizing about the pleasures of being wealthy or famous after the civil rights crusade had achieved its goals. Any type of egotistical motivation like that would surely have weakened or even disabled his drive to improve the lives of many other people. Similarly, any personal motivation you might have that creates a separation between you and those around you takes away directly from your happiness. So, it is of major importance to work on your ego in a spiritual way, to face your fears and to resolve your desires. I am emphasizing the need to work *spiritually* on your ego because that is the only approach equipped to do the job. Only the spiritual path has as its purpose and its goal the transcendence of ego. So, ultimately, your happiness-goal is to transcend the ego of the lower self—to put it behind you, so to speak. Believe me, in the long run you will be considerably happier.

Since 9 is determined to become one with all that is around it—physical, mental, emotional, and spiritual—you are happy when you give yourself over completely, 100 percent, to projects and activities, to work and relationships you commit yourself to. It is not your desire to hold back any part of yourself. You want to give everything you have to it. If you do this lovingly and selflessly, your presence is a blessing to those with whom you are involved. Your participation and contribution are gifts. But if your ego-interests are what really motivate you, the whole picture changes. The 9 is a bigger-than-life energy. It is flamboyant, dramatic, possessing great charisma. Consequently, 9 is a center that people gather around, listen to, and follow. Now if, privately, you are nurturing desires for personal gain, and if your personal ego-motivations determine what you do, then you risk becoming a fanatic. You exclude everyone's viewpoint but your own. So, instead of being a person who is uplifting, inspiring, and liberating to be around, you zealously promote *your* own agenda.

Identification of the number 9

Since the 9 keeps your ego-issues in the frying pan twenty-four hours a day, the 9 is a spiritual test and an indicator of spiritual growth. Like the 7, the 9 part of you is very intuitive. The reason for the strong intuition of the 9 is that, being connected with all of life, you are open to the signals that life sends you, including those that come from incorporeal life—from Spirit. Now, if you receive a clear, unmistakable intuition from Spirit, and you follow your guidance even though you really *do not want to do it,* that is spiritual growth. It means that you are being spiritual and that you are in harmony with Spirit, because you are putting Spirit first in your life. It is quite another matter if you beg off, so to speak, saying something like, "Oh, come on, Spirit, *please.* Be reasonable here. You know that I am with you 100 percent. But doggone it, I mean, what you are asking me to do right now means that I've got to drop everything that I've worked so hard for, and, anyway, I just don't have the money. Can't you see it in your heart for me to delay this just a couple of months until I get on my feet . . . ?" This is the ego getting in the picture and blocking the spiritual way, keeping you from *living* spiritually When this occurs, 9 is known as the number of pain and loss. After all, Spirit is going to have its way, one way or another.

So, taking into consideration now all four of your numbers, I would say relationships are very difficult for you to establish and maintain. Everything within you has needs and priorities other than relationships. By this, I mean attitudes having to do with commitment, dialogue, compromise, diplomacy, and intimacy. For you, maintaining successful relationships requires making good choices consciously and working hard to do what you know you have to do. You will have to learn—and to accept!—how to be in a healthy relationship, and then be disciplined enough to carry it through consistently.

Comparison of the 9 Heart's Desire, the 5 Personality, the 5 Character, and the 7 Participation

Comparison of the 9 Heart's Desire, the 5 Personality, the 5 Character, and the 7 Participation

In this reading, we've discussed a lot of things going on inside you—the things that make you tick. This should help you live better and more happily because, if you are unaware of those dynamics, they drive you. When those impulses and needs are subconscious, you have no ability to make conscious choices. When you become aware of what those inner dynamics are and how they work—as we have been discussing throughout your reading—they become conscious. Then you can decide what you want and choose how to act. So, I think it is a matter of deciding what your priorities are in terms of relationships. And it is a matter of accepting your limitations and being resolved to do what it takes to make your relationships work. Know this also: if two people love each other, the supposed limitations and incompatibilities of the numbers take a back seat. They are still there in latent form, but the love is stronger. It harmonizes and completes what otherwise might be wrong or conflictive. Love smoothes out the rough places, and that's all there is to it. So, of course you can have a wonderful, fully functioning, fully satisfying relationship, if that's what you want. The difficulties and challenges I have been discussing with you are not permanent and unalterable; they are things for you to think about; they are notes (or warnings) for you to keep in mind as you go about living your life. I say this because there are too many people who receive numerology readings and take the opinions of the numerologist as gospel. Numerology was never meant to lay down the law for someone else!

Comparison of the 9 Heart's Desire and the 7 Participation

Now, there is a strong compatibility between your 9 Heart's Desire and your 7 Participation. These are the two main spiritual numbers of numerology. Seven is the inner search for the truth of the self. Nine is the outer search to be one with all life. Earlier we discussed the spiritual purpose behind your 5/7 combination. Briefly, what I said was that the pain and frustration of that conflict could cause the wild 5 to discipline itself to carry out its seeking and searching in the 7 way. That is a very difficult transition to make, but then, what spiritual goal isn't highly challenging? Your Heart's Desire clinches the spiritual purpose I see in you. Nine is more than a number of being philosophical. Nine's nature is to live the spiritual understanding that 7 creates. So, your 9 yearns to have a spiritual kind of life and, with your 7 Participation backing that up, you are working on that spiritual philosophy all the time.

The key to bringing all this spirituality about are those two 5s. They are half of your basic nature. They are the strongest element in your chart because they are two out of the four numbers. You need their support, so to speak, in order to tread the spiritual path. The dilemma, of course, is that the 5 can be so nonspiritual and so totally focused on this world and all that it offers. If you can pull off a little numerological trick and cause the 5 part of you to join the spiritual program, then you will be on the path in the way your soul hoped and envisioned. Without this kind of spiritual effort, you are likely to be split right down the middle, with the 5/7 conflict and the 5/9 conflict hampering you at every turn.

I haven't yet mentioned the rapport you have between the 9 and the two 5s. Having heard all that I have said, you can appreciate the tremendous difference between your two 5s and that 9. Nine is self-sacrifice and selfless giving for the greater good. Five is personal freedom and worldly prosperity. There is no common ground between them.

I feel that despite the differences between your 5 Personality, 5 Character, and your 7 Participation, you will learn to make those three numbers function together one way or another. As a 5 person, you are too practical when it comes to living in this world to allow that 5/7 conflict to hogtie you indefinitely. The 5 intends to prosper, even if it has to go through the 7 to do it! But it is a different matter with the 9. Being in the Heart's Desire position, 9 doesn't carry as much weight in your chart as the 7, so there isn't the same degree of need to find a way to link the two 5s and the 9. It is left out in the cold. Living, thinking, and behaving exclusively in the 5 manner will never give you happiness. The 7 won't bring happiness either if you establish a working relationship between the two 5s and the 7. In this situation, in which your 5/5/7 manage to get along, I see your 9 Heart's Desire being odd woman out, so to speak. In other words, if you live a worldly life, your spiritual yearnings from the 9 perspective will have no support from the rest of you. The 9 won't be part of the 5/5/7 combination. It will be isolated. So, by leading a mundane, materialistic kind of life, you will never be very happy. If, on the other hand, you unite the four different parts of yourself by working spiritually, this will provide them the means to function together as one undivided unit. You will be united as a person. The various inner dynamics that

Comparison of the 9 Heart's Desire, the 5 Personality, the 5 Character, and the 7 Participation

Comparison of the 9 Heart's Desire, the 5 Personality, and the 5 Character

Comparison of the 9 Heart's Desire, the 5 Personality, the 5 Character, and the 7 Participation

make you who you are will exist together harmoniously because they will all be working toward a common purpose. Ergo, no debilitating inner conflicts, plus you live constructively. You will be happy and fulfilled.

That completes my interpretation of your numerology chart, Wilma. Remember: nothing I have said here is the dogmatic truth. I have told you what I think about your nature based on the numbers in your numerology chart. You are the one whose job it is to live your life, so it is up to you to decide what is valid for you. I hope my thoughts have been helpful, and that they have given you some guidance for living your life.

Endnotes

1. "She" is used here out of respect for the person getting the reading, who is female.

2. Graham Hancock, *The Sign and the Seal: The Quest for the Lost Ark of the Covenant* (New York: Touchstone, 1992).

chapter 8

Acts of Living

It was inherent in Pythagorean doctrine that arithmetical relationships were a manifestation of the divine . . .

—Kieren Barry, *The Greek Quabalah*

The goal of interpreting a numerology chart is to harmonize all the numbers in such a way that they are mutually purposeful. Those numbers are the givens of a person's life, the spiritual structure upon which his life is fulfilled. A truly spiritual life is achieved when all the diverse parts are made to function together, each supporting and cooperating with the others. The ramifications of this accomplishment are wide and deep.

Interpretation is an act of creative spiritual potency. Interpretation is much more than a clarification of the numbers and an explanation of their interrelationships. If a higher potential can be glimpsed, it enables the individual to understand in his own terms how to proceed in order to realize the desired goal. This is a path of learning, of evolution, and of what is sometimes called initiation. Ultimately, the object is to attain spiritual consciousness.

Thus far in our discussion of interpretation, we have explored the technique of comparing numbers. This is the exclusive method of interpretation used in Pythagorean numerology today. Some will say this is not so, that mathematical procedures are sometimes used in Pythagorean numerology, and more commonly in Kabalistic numerology. It is true to a limited extent that addition and subtraction are used in both numerologies, and certain additional procedures in Kabalistic numerology. Their use, however, is purely mechanical, and only for the purpose of producing symbolic numbers that are subject to interpretation.

The mathematical procedures themselves are not considered to have symbolic meaning.

Mastery of the technique of number comparison means having full conscious awareness in this life. This involves having in-depth understanding of all combinations of the numbers from 1 with 1, 1 with 2, 1 with 3, and so forth through 9 with 9; 81 combinations in all. This is a *passive* activity that enables one to discern the dynamic elements at work inside a person or in a situation. One is able to perceive the underlying matrix of forces of which a person or a thing is composed. The use of number comparison is observational, analytical, and capable of detailed scrutiny and wonderful acumen. Great insight and understanding of people, situations, and life itself are possible, but that discernment is idle and latent. It *observes;* it does *not participate.* Numbers alone have no power to be or to do; no ability to create, to initiate, to persevere, or to accomplish. They exist only.

With mathematical functions comes the ability to live. Those functions include all principles, formulas, and equations of all branches of mathematics. Each branch represents a different level, aptitude, or special aspect of living. Some are basic, some advanced, some specialized, some powerful, some magic, and some are transcendent. All have the potential for spiritual growth depending on the individual's intent. The use of a particular mathematical function performs a certain act of living. If a person's desire is to *reach* a certain goal, to *work* through a problem, to *master* a spiritual principle, or *do* anything, it is a matter of performing the proper calculation of the applicable branch of mathematics. When numbers are manipulated according to the proper mathematical principles, the elements of one of life's experiences are resolved to a proper conclusion.

In this book, we will be concerned mainly with the four arithmetic functions that represent the basic skills of living: addition, subtraction, multiplication, and division. We will also examine squaring numbers and finding square roots. With the enormous body of mathematics now available for symbolic use and interpretation, a discussion of only six principles may seem a drastic limitation. I agree. However, I have taken this approach for two reasons. The first reason for limiting discussion to six basic functions is that the task of interpreting the symbolism of mathematics has barely begun. Mathematical knowledge today is extensive, and it is the result of innumerable mathematicians working throughout many centuries. Analyzing the symbolic dynamics of mathematical principles is deep work, very slow and painstaking. It will require considerable time and effort on the part of many before the symbolic meaning of mathematics as a whole will be understood. Mathematical symbolism is at the beginning of its quest.

Second, although these six functions are rudimentary, it is with these aspects of living that the world is mainly preoccupied. For the most part, our daily lives consist of the ordinary and the mundane. We deal with family members, friends, and people in society. We cope with anger, stress, and personal problems. We struggle with how to get what we want, how to achieve our goals, how to succeed in work, how to prosper, how to maintain healthy relationships, how to have intimacy, how to make difficult communications, how to compromise when dealing with emotionally-charged issues, how to demand our rights or graciously defer to another, how to deal with social issues (poverty, prejudice, injustice, or war), and so on and so forth ad infinitum. These kinds of things largely fill our daily lives, stimulating our thoughts and charging our emotions. And, they are *all* activities of the four basic functions! It sounds simple to master symbolic addition, subtraction, multiplication, and division ("That's stuff you learn in *elementary* school!"), but it is, in fact, no easy matter. Its attainment is an accomplishment indeed! The process of learning these functions requires more than reading and understanding information. It involves creating basic techniques of living for oneself.

With that perspective in mind, we will now consider the symbolic meanings of the four basic functions.

Addition

The act of living: union

Type of act: passive

Types of decisions associated with this act: mutual attraction, involvement, bonding, love, integration, synthesis, courage, hope, positive attitude, respect, confidence, finding common ground, understanding, communication, harmony, grace, flow, cooperation, sharing, fulfillment, friendliness, relaxation, enjoyment, light heartedness, happiness

Subtraction

The act of living: separation

Type of act: passive

Types of decisions associated with this act: being fearful, scared, isolated, uninvolved, preoccupied, distant, withdrawn, secretive, having alone time, meditation, self-evaluation, feeling weak, empty, suspicious, defensive, irritable, being fault-finding, critical, disrespectful, conflictive, argumentative, trouble-making, sorrowful

Multiplication

The act of living: attainment

The type of act: active

Types of decisions associated with this act: having vision, purpose, determination, goal-orientation, self-control, self-discipline, being constructive, hardworking, competitive, responsible, problem solving, overcoming obstacles, handling adversity, dealing with reality, being powerful, steadfast, persevering, nurturing, bringing to fruition, experiencing growth, new beginning, birth, transmutation

Division

The act of living: destruction

The type of act: active

Types of decisions associated with this act: having self-doubt, fear, abandonment, rejection, despair, decline, inaction, hurting others, meanness, loss, pain, sorrow, cruelty, negativity, weakness, brutality, betrayal, immorality, evil, depravity, desolation, murder, death, elimination, fasting, sacrifice, getting rid of negative attitudes and habits, renewal

These, then, are the meanings of the four basic functions. Presently, we will examine their use in sample *mathematical sentences* called equations. First, we will need to know the meaning of the ubiquitous equal sign (=).

Equal Sign

The act of living: becoming

The type of act: active/passive

Types of processes associated with this act: having trust, having faith, being curious, willingness to adjust, to change, to grow, to embrace the new, to adapt, to be open to new possibilities, to evolve, to transform into, to transmute into

Addition and subtraction are characterized as *passive* acts. This is because they represent acts that occur according to mood or circumstance. They are acts performed without self-determination, goals, or enduring purpose. Addition and subtraction are opposite sides of the same coin. The one follows upon the other cyclically—sometimes quickly, sometimes slowly—according to the natural pace of events. Neither is permanent. What unites together today will separate again tomorrow, just as day turns to night, then back to day again. It is the way of things.

Instances of addition and subtraction are equations that we read as *mathematical sentences.*

Addition: The equation "$x + y = z$" reads: when "x" unites with "y," together they become "z."

Subtraction: The equation "$x - y = z$" reads: when "x" separates from "y," they become "z."

In contrast to addition and subtraction, the acts of multiplication and division both pursue attainment of a goal. They are considered *active* acts because underlying them is self-determination to achieve a goal until it is realized. The individual decides to persevere and overcome adversity until that goal has been attained. Like the first two mathematical functions we discussed, multiplication and division are cyclical, alternating between periods of building up and tearing down. There is a further link between these four functions. When the same addition is done again and again, it can develop into multiplication. This is because, over time, a repeated action becomes established as a determination, turning mood into decision. Similarly, repeated application of an act of subtraction may eventually solidify into division. The reverse process can happen also. If one fatigues from the sustained effort of multiplication, and thereby loses the motivation to do it, the commitment can weaken, effectively breaking down into addition. Likewise, when too much energy is expended in division, the determination to be negative may wane, assuming the less intense form of subtraction.

You may have noticed during Wilma's reading that I discussed many acts and decisions that go beyond simple number comparison. This is because it is a *natural human need* to form conclusions. Highly experienced numerologists may be able to make good assessments of particular combinations of numbers, but their judgments can never be complete. Their conclusions can only be speculative because, without use of the mathematical system on which to base thinking, there is no principle to guide us to accurate conclusions.

Some examples of my conclusions taken from Wilma's reading are listed below. Words that determine the mathematical function are italicized.

Addition

5 + x: "With 5 in the Personality position, you *present* yourself as a warm, lively, vivacious, 'life of the party' kind of person."

5 + x: "You *thrive* when you cope with risk, danger, or uncertainty."

7 + x: "She is *very at home* in the laboratory working alone . . ."

9 + x: ". . . you are *happy* when you give yourself over completely, 100 percent, to projects to which you commit yourself."

Subtraction

x − 5: "I would say you *instinctively pull away* from anything that works to constrain your ability to do what you want."

x − 5: ". . . your *tendency is to want* to flee at the appearance of frustrating difficulty."

x − 5: "The downside of your high energy personality is the *tendency to have* a short attention span."

x − 5: ". . . all people with a prominent 5 are (*feel*) restless."

Addition and Subtraction

5 + 5 + 7 − 9: "Nine, being in the Heart's Desire position, doesn't carry as much weight in your chart as the 7, so there isn't the same *inclination* to link the two 5s with the 9. It is *left out* in the cold."

Multiplication

7 x x: "So, it *takes courage and effort* for you to come out of your 7 shell . . ."

9 x x: "So the 9 *supports*—no, I would actually say it *yearns to have*—a spiritual kind of life."

5 x 5 x 7: "Somehow, I feel that despite the differences between your 5 Personality, your 5 Character, and your 7 Participation, *you will learn* to make those three numbers function together, *one way or another.*"

5 x 7: "I would say for you to keep a relationship positive and constructive, you have to *work very hard at it, constantly making conscious choices that you know are* necessary."

5 x 5 x 7 x 9: "If, on the other hand, you *unite* the four parts of yourself by *working spiritually*, this will provide the means to function together as one undivided unit."

Division

x ÷ 5: "In a negative state . . . restlessness can result in the *inability to stay* with anything . . ."

9 ÷ x: "To the extent the personal ego is alive and well within your nature, the energy of the 9 is *diminished* and *made impure.*"

9 ÷ x: "That type of *egotistical motivation* would surely have weakened or even *disabled his drive* to improve the lives of many people."

7 ÷ 5 & 9 ÷ 5: "Without this kind of *spiritual effort*, you are likely to be split right down the middle with the 5/7 conflict and the 5/9 conflict *hampering* you at every turn."

x ÷ 5: "Your *instinctive response* (to responsibility) is to get away, to be free."

All of the previous examples are conclusions that were reached regarding the inter-action of two or more numbers. Every number has certain characteristic energies. When any numbers x and y are together, it is our instinct to contemplate them, then to decide upon a meaning. It is a natural thing to do. At every moment of our lives we assess where we stand and what we're going to do about it. We have an in-built need to know what the consequences are. We have a particular attitude toward a given situation and customary ways of handling it. We do all this because to live, we must (and do) function. We must handle things. We must *act*. Whether we approach life confidently and effectively or passively and weakly is irrelevant at the philosophical level. Both positive and negative approaches are simply different styles of making decisions. They are different ways of coping with events. The decision to act is represented symbolically by *mathematical procedures*.

Previously, I stated that the mathematical system currently has no role in Pythagorean numerology, or any other branch of number symbolism, for that mat-ter. Interpretations like those cited previously are common in numerology, but they are routinely made by numerologists without regard to the mathematical principles on which they are based. The examples of addition, subtraction, multiplication, and division clearly demonstrate the need to handle symbolic numbers mathematically.

What is missing from current numerological understanding is the knowledge that (1) mathematical functions like addition, subtraction, and so on are symbolic dynamics in their own right, and (2) each function has a specific numeric result. The previous examples represent the activity of mathematical processes but not the out-comes. The example below shows the multiplication of 5 x 7:

> I would say that for you to keep a relationship positive and constructive, you have to work very hard at it, constantly making conscious choices that you know are necessary.

The meaning of this multiplication concerns Wilma's need to work hard at rela-tionships and to make the difficult, but necessary, choices to keep them happy and healthy. However, the *form* that success will take is not given in the quote because there is no way to know it without multiplying 5 times 7. The answer is, of course, 35, which reduces to 8. We are now able to understand Wilma's decision to change, *and its outcome,* in the following mathematical sentence:

5	x
When Wilma's individualistic nature	fully works through

7	=
her deeply private way of relating,	she becomes

35/8
a master of handling relationships.

In this scenario, the 5 and 7 cease to be independent from each other. As a result of working them together over time, Wilma learns how to be happy and successful in relationships, and those two numbers come to form an indissoluble partnership. They become the 8, in other words, which handles relationships very capably. Thus, the specific result of Wilma's efforts to be successful in relationships is the 8. When problems come up for Wilma, she resolves them with dispatch. She has earned the ability to do this by persisting through the difficult growth process described as 5 x 7. The result, 8, is the number of empowerment, taking charge, making the difficult decisions, and being tough and competitive. Thus, she has learned to face the issues and to deal squarely with the fear and pain that so often arise in relationships. She has developed the ability to be strong when she needs to be strong, to be firm when she needs to be firm, and to see issues clearly. She has perfected expert knowledge in the management of her relationships. She learned it through hard-won experience by persevering through the multiplication process. This taught her to stay in charge of that which needs tending.

You may wonder how it was determined that 5 and 7 were the numbers at issue in the statement quoted at the top of this page, and how it was decided they were being multiplied. Five and 7 are Wilma's two most fundamental numbers: her overall nature (5 Character) and the way she functions in life (7 Participation). These are the two key positions to consider when personal growth occurs. The growth process can only be multiplication. Wilma is working toward the achievement of a goal. So 5 x 7 is one solution to Wilma's relationship dilemma. A more inclusive and detailed resolution of her relationship challenge would be the multiplication of all four of Wilma's numbers: 5 x 7 x 5 x 9 = 1,575/18/9. This multiplication is much more involved and complex because so many more factors are part of it. Using the 5 and 7 alone, she becomes fully competent to handle relationships, but not necessarily happy (because her Heart's Desire was "not consulted"). The process involving four numbers takes much more work than is required by the multiplication of just two numbers. On the other hand, the outcome is far deeper and more rewarding. In the example of four numbers, Wilma not only manages relationships successfully, but she is also well adjusted, confident, and happy.

A striking realization that comes to mind when all four of her numbers are multiplied is that the outcome is 9. Since 9 is also the number of her Heart's Desire, she would be doubly happy functioning in relationships in a 9 manner. The 1,575/18/9 approach would bring a Big Heart to her relationships. She would be philosophical, very inclusive, full of understanding and compassion, and have deep awareness, intuition, drama, emotion, and insight. She would love deeply and learn profound lessons in the crucible of marriage and friendship. These would include not only personal relationships, but also anyone or any group in life with whom she associates, from people she encounters once to close friends, family, and even pets.

Having completed the multiplication process, the issues with which she struggled for so long and that caused her so much pain and fear have now been put to rest. Those earlier experiences have not been forgotten. Rather, everything she has been through in the past now forms a broad base of experience and understanding. She is at peace. When trouble arises in relationships, as will happen from time to time, she takes it all in stride. She has tremendous heart. She has become a lover of life.

It is near universal practice in number symbolism to use positive, whole numbers, as with the multiplication example of 5 x 7. At the same time, it needs to be recognized that this alone is simplistic. Most areas of life are an inseparable melange of positive and negative. Consequently, symbolic numbers representing the ordinary and mundane in life should symbolize both potentials. Thus, a more accurate way to write Wilma's multiplication is: ± 5 x $\pm 7 = \pm 35 / \pm 8$. In general practice, positive numbers, "x," are understood to represent both positive and negative. Most positive symbolic numbers, such as those in Wilma's chart and in Pythagorean numerology, are in actuality *generic representations* of $\pm$x. Therefore, unless there is a real need to be precise, positive whole numbers are understood to represent positive and negative.

In this book, it is necessary to be very exacting in differentiating these distinctions. It is worthwhile to examine the subtler aspects of mathematical processes for several reasons. One is that exclusive use of positive whole numbers is simply too general to be useful in in-depth symbol work. Another reason is that, since the mathematical system has been excluded from the discipline of number symbolism for over two thousand years, we need to gain the fullest understanding of what is possible in the use of any aspect of mathematics that comes under our scrutiny. Only in this way can we truly know what each function is capable of doing. Anything less would be superficial.

In addition to the multiplication of "generic" numbers we discussed, there are also multiplication situations in which the numbers are either positive or negative. Let us begin with a discussion of purely negative numbers. These are numbers that manifest the worst aspects of their Force. A truly devastating prospect for Wilma would be $-5 \times -7 = 35/8$. In this case, both -5 and -7 are at their most harmful. We can imagine how Wilma, during an especially trying period of her life, comes to feel terribly defeated with regard to relationships, particularly with men. Her 5 nature has become defiant and rebellious due to frustration. She is determined to stir up trouble. Being afraid, her 7 Participation mode is also withdrawn, antisocial, and deceitful. So she withdraws from social intercourse and she *stays* withdrawn.

It is a curious fact that when two such negative states are multiplied together, they produce a positive number! We know this is so because in mathematics when two negative numbers are multiplied, they produce a positive number. In some respects, this positive outcome is comparable to the generic number x (that is, $\pm x$). It can even appear to resemble the $+x$ that results from the multiplication of two positive numbers $(+x) \times (+y)$. The key to understanding the differences between all these similar outcomes lies in contrasting what was multiplied, for the multipliers determine the specific nature of the outcome. It is clear that there is something rotten about the outcome of multiplying two negative numbers, no matter how positive the result appears. It is a "positive" outcome because the negative elements have been absorbed into a number that has stabilized, albeit at a negative level. The negativity that is present is active, but only in the form of *limited expression*. This means that the number is not harmful to those around it, but the individual is confined to a narrow range of unrewarding experience.

In the example we are focusing on (–5 x –7 = 35/8), –5 x –7 is the same thing as 35/8. Proper interpretation of equations includes all pertinent elements. The commonality between these three 8 outcomes (±5 x ±7, –5 x –7, and +5 x +7) is the power, the commanding strength, and the determination of the 8. They all have it. As previously stated, the ±5 x ±7 is a mix of positive and negative, such as is found in everyday life. This 8 does its best to live each day with the all too familiar ups and downs, successes and failures. It handles them as best it can as circumstances arise. In contrast, the –5 x –7 results in an 8 that also is powerful, has commanding strength, and is determined. But here, it is focused negativity and limitation that drive 8s potency. The effect is to make a lifestyle out of coldness, isolation, and cruelty. This is more than being momentarily defensive and stand-offish. It is backed by the resolution that Wilma will spare no mental or emotional effort to keep herself from the companionship of others. She accomplishes this by dominating all those around her and by never allowing anyone through her impenetrable, impersonal facade.

Purely positive numbers, +z, in contrast with generically positive numbers, ±z (generally written z), is the result of adding two positive numbers, (+x) x (+y), and indicate a strong and disciplined aspiration to experience the higher levels of a number. So, +8 is the product of +5 x +7. Since both multiplicands are positive, it is evident that Wilma has struggled hard to learn the skill of relationships in the most healthy, constructive way. What is indicated here is that Wilma set a high goal for herself, and that she followed through with consistency and persistence. She knew what she wanted and she kept her sights on that ideal. When difficulties arose, or when she was nearly overcome by fear, pain, or some other form of compelling discouragement, she persevered until she learned how to create and sustain wonderful, satisfying relationships. This multiplication, +5 x +7, is a significant accomplishment in which inner negativities are worked through and eliminated so that they no longer occur. In the process, she gained substantial knowledge and the understanding of how to use it. This is empowering to Wilma because the benefit of all her work tangibly improves her quality of life. This is a +8 that has been purified and raised up. It holds on to what it loves with an open hand. The stresses and dilemmas of daily existence do not threaten it. It consists of the most commendable qualities, such as being appreciative, astute, candid, honest, gentle, strong at all times, fair, kind, even humble and gentle.[3] This is 8 at its best. It is truly empowered.

The final form a number can take as a result of multiplication is negative (–x). This occurs if one of the two numbers being multiplied is negative. The minus sign before a number indicates that it is in a failed or fallen state, defeated and hopeless. Thus, our continuing example could be either –5 x +7 or +5 x –7 equals –8. In this example, it matters a great deal which multiplier is negative, the 5 or the 7. Since 5 is the stronger, more dominant number in Wilma's chart, the likelihood is that 7 will be the negative number.

So, let us now consider the implications of 5 x –7. In this scenario, the resourceful and freedom-loving 5 functions in a positive, normal way. Instead of cooperating with 7 as equals, 5 takes over with or without 7s consent. Wilma is trying to sidestep the 7 part of her nature by focusing exclusively on the 5. Wilma would give anything to have a 5 Participation. As it is, the private and analytical 7 is ignored and shut out. Seven, of course, cannot "just go away" and will not be subverted. However, it does collapse into passivity and inactivity. It is critical and moody, sullen, incommunicative, and elitist. At times, it is even backward and incompetent, silly, naïve, and has no depth. So, while the 5 Character does its best to cope day by day and to manipulate 7 into being something it is not, the 7 Participation thwarts every single one of 5s innovative efforts to induce it to "live well and prosper," like a proper 5 should. Remember, Wilma's 7 Participation is the role she plays on the stage of life, and it is her 5 Character that plays that role. There is no way for Wilma to get around her 7. Her 5 lives, loves, and works within the context of that 7, which is a flat tire.

What is happening to Wilma is that she is at war with herself. She is making a good and legitimate effort with her 5 to live her life well, but she is using only one part of herself to do it; her 7 is in denial. The result is disastrous, a bit like adding wonderful, tasty ingredients to rotten, stinking food, then cooking it. Like the other three 8s, this –8 has the core qualities of power, commanding strength, and determination. The way it expresses them as a –8, however, is by being combative and intolerant, narrow-minded, ill-bred, disreputable, and vulgar. The –8 offends everyone, as only 8 power and authority can. In this mode, Wilma is extremely alienating, pushing everyone away in ways that are callous and crude.

Briefly summarized, the four types of multiplication are as follows:

±x x ±y = ±z: Unreflected maturation that has its good points and its bad points.

–x x –y = z: Negative growth that significantly diminishes an individual's ability to function.

+x x +y = z: Transcendent maturation that raises an individual's consciousness and quality of life.

–x x +y = –z: Destructive growth that causes an individual to be adversarial with those around him.

Division is a process of destruction, purification, or renewal. Like multiplication, most division occurs *generically*. That is to say, it takes place in the normal course of living and without a great deal of thought and reflection. It is usually a time of difficulty, frustration, and pain. Feelings of anger, failure, and impotence frequently accompany division until despair and ruin occur when the process reaches completion. If, however, division is deliberately carried out for spiritual reasons, it can bring renewal and release. Once again, *intent* is the key element.

Division often produces very long quotients. Some numbers divide evenly, or almost evenly, into each other. For example: $4 \div 2 = 2$, $6 \div 4 = 1.5$, and $5 \div 2 = 2.5$. Other numbers do not resolve as simply. Pi is the most famous example. Pi is the ratio of the circumference of a circle to the diameter, whose solution begins $3.1416 \ldots$, then continues indefinitely with no repeating numbers. Computers have carried out the calculations to billions of digits without any end in sight. When single-digit numbers are divided into each other, the answers sometimes involve endless repetitions of numbers. Examples are: $9 \div 6 = .666666666666 \ldots$ ad infinitum; $6 \div 7 = .857142857142 \ldots$ (in which 857142 endlessly repeats); $5 \div 6 = .83333333333 \ldots$ ad infinitum. These latter divisions, whose answers contain infinite numbers, have very subtle effects that go deep into our psyche. This is a great mystery because the full extent of the division is never complete, never fully resolved, and never definitive. Instead, these divisions keep dogging a person, penetrating deeper and deeper into his intimate self. In the case of division with an endless quotient, there appears to be no simple, straightforward method for reducing it to a single digit. For example, $4 \div 7 = 0.57142857142 \ldots$, and the sequence of numbers continues repeating endlessly. The first two digits reduce to 3: $5 + 7 = 3$; the first three reduce to 4: $5 + 7 + 1 = 4$; the first four digits reduce to 8. Subsequent reduced numbers are 1, followed by 9, then 5, then 3, then 4, then 8, then 1, and so on. The question is where to stop, or even whether to stop. For reasons that will be discussed in the last chapter, only the first nine digits (if there are that many) should be totaled, and then reduced to a single digit. The first nine numbers of $4 \div 7$ are: $5 + 7 + 1 + 4 + 2 + 8 + 5 + 7 + 1$, which total 40, then reduce to 4. If the tenth digit is 5 to 9, the ninth digit is rounded up to the next number. In the number 1.86775436873, the second 8 is the tenth number. Consequently, the 6 preceding it is rounded up to 7. Thus, the number to be reduced is: 1.86775437 = 48/12/3.

The reader may wonder how it is possible for a decimal fraction to reduce to a whole number. Further, how can it be that .5714, 5.714, 57.14, and so on through 5,714 all reduce to 8? The answer is that these same four digits are all added as whole, single-digit numbers, regardless of where the decimal point is. Consider 5,714. The "4" has a value of "4," but "1" really represents "10," "7" is actually "700," and "5" is "5,000." Each of these numbers represents a different power of 10. Seven hundred, for example, is 10^2, which equals 100, multiplied by 7. If 700 is then reduced, the result is 7: $7 + 0 + 0 = 7$. On this basis, 7 is always the number used for reduction purposes, whether it is 7,000, 700, 70, 7, .7, .07, or .00000007.

By using this method, the number 5,714 can be expressed in a longer form to show fully what I mean: $5 \times 10^3 + 7 \times 10^2 + 1 \times 10^1 + 4 \times 10^0$. At first glance (and maybe the second and even third glance), this may look like a very long and complicated bit of mathematical notation. Please bear with me through this illustration and it will prove to be worth the effort. Let's see how this "long and complicated bit" works. The first part—5×10^3—breaks down in the following way: $10^3 = 1,000$, and when that is multiplied by 5 the result is 5,000. The next multiplication (as we discussed above) is 7×10^2; $10^2 = 100$, and when that is multiplied by 7 the result is 700. In a similar manner, $10^1 = 10$. When 10 is multiplied by 1 the result is 10. The final bit of multiplication is 4×10^0. When 10 is raised to the 0 power it becomes 1, and so when 1 is multiplied by 4 the result is 4. So the very long (and possibly intimidating) form of writing 5,714—$5 \times 10^3 + 7 \times 10^2 + 1 \times 10^1 + 4 \times 10^0$—is a mathematical way of saying: $5,000 + 700 + 10 + 4$. When these numbers are added together, they total 5,714. When 5,714 is reduced, all of the above is ignored so that only the 5, 7, 1, and 4 are added.

The same number with a decimal point in front of it—.5714—can also be written out as above using *negative powers* of 10. The difference is that a negative power (Y^{-x}) produces tenths, hundredths, thousandths, and so on, instead of whole numbers.

The long way of writing .5714 is $5 \times 10^{-1} + 7 \times 10^{-2} + 1 \times 10^{-3} + 4 \times 10^{-4}$; $10^{-1} = .1$, then $5 \times .1 = .5$; $10^{-2} = .01$, and then $7 \times .01 = .07$; $10^{-3} = .001$, and $1 \times .001 = .001$; Finally, $10^{-4} = .0001$, and $4 \times .0001 = .0004$. When these four separate results—.5, .07, .001, .0004—are combined together, the result is .5714. The *only* difference between 5,714 and .5714 is *different powers of 10*.

It does not matter where the decimal point is. All of the numbers are *whole numbers* multiplied by different powers of 10. This is why 5,714 and 0.5714 both total 17, which then reduces to 8.

It has already been established that most multiplications involve ± numbers, the "normal, average condition" of everyday life. The same applies to division. Division involving ± numbers gives expression to most of everyday living, which contains its ups and its downs, its good times and its bad times, its positive people and its negative people, and so on. It results in either a renewal of spirit or in abject ruination, depending on the individual's intent. The quote below demonstrates the 5 acting against both the 7 and the 9 in Wilma's chart:

> *Without this kind of spiritual effort, you are likely to be split down the middle,*
> *with the 5/7 conflict and the 5/9 conflict hampering you at every turn.*

These two divisions are as follows: $7 \div 5 = 1.4/5$, and $9 \div 5 = 1.8/9$. In the interest of keeping the present discussion to a reasonable length, I will limit my analysis to $9 \div 5$.

With her 9 Heart's Desire, Wilma yearns for a philosophical life of service to others, unconditional love, and selfless giving. This is the basis of her happiness and satisfaction. She desires to live a spiritual life, or at least an idealistic one, without having to be too concerned with the practical side of living. Unfortunately, her 5 nature is much stronger than her 9 aspirations. After all, the 5 is who she is, how she lives, and what she does. By contrast, the 9 is "merely" hopes and yearnings. The purposes of the 9 and 5 are very different, and they frequently work against each other. The 5 couldn't care less about the 9's need to live a spiritual life. To the 5, this is a nonstarter. The 9's dreamy philosophy is not going to bring in money, put food on the table, open up titillating opportunities, or even be any fun. So the 5 turns a blind eye to the 9 and all it stands for. In this way, the 5 is free to pursue a worldly life of pleasure and taking advantage of every opportunity it finds to prosper. In its zeal to get ahead, 5 places a high value on doing what it wants while ridding itself of any high-minded ideals that stand in the way. Every time one of 9's idealistic urges comes to mind, the 5 kicks it out and goes after what *it* wants with renewed vigor. Thus, the 5 strives to kill off everything that even suggests higher purpose, impersonal love, idealism, broadmindedness, self-sacrifice, and the like, and instead devotes itself to matters of adventure and personal satisfaction.

The result of Wilma's inner battle is $\pm 9 \div \pm 5 = \pm 9$, a morbid outcome. This change in Wilma's life through division is quite destructive. Both the 9 Heart's Desire and the 5 Character are losers here. This is a morose result because, with her 9 Heart's Desire, Wilma takes masochistic pleasure in the ± 9. This is a 9 that has been gutted of its Big Heart. Consequently, after the division process is complete, Wilma is callous and disloyal, listless and tactless, petty and self-centered, superficial and foolish.

Division of the very same numbers could result in a renewal of Wilma's spirit if she approached the issues differently. If over the course of her life, for example, Wilma had always followed the urgings of her 9 Heart's Desire for a spiritual life to such an extent that her devotion to good works had suffocated her personal life (just like Do Gooder), the 5's rebellion would be a productive event. It would bring her back to reality, freeing her from an unreasonable and confining attitude. The reckless, raucous 5 is no respecter of the sanctimonious and highfalutin 9. It would run roughshod over the arbitrary standards and phony niceties of the out-of-control 9 by confronting them, breaking them down, mocking them, forcing them to own up to what they really are, and making them be honest. The ± 9 that results from $\pm 9 \div \pm 5$ has come to its senses. It has its head on straight.

Whether $\pm 9 \div \pm 5$ results in destruction or renewal for Wilma, both alternatives are based on $\pm 1.8 / \pm 9$. If the intent of 5 is to defeat 9, the benevolent intentions of the 9 are beaten down, causing the 9 to give up and be apathetic, indifferent, and callous. It becomes detached and intolerant. Its high aspirations are ruined, disillusioned. If the intent of 5 is to free 9, the result is a resurrection of that energy. Wilma finds herself feeling normal and happy "for the first time in *years*" because she is not on "another one of those crusades" that everyone she met rejected and scorned. What a relief!

It is an interesting twist that Wilma's ± 9 quotient is the same number as her Heart's Desire. This means that the ± 9 quotient is not only very familiar to Wilma, it is also satisfying. From time to stressful time throughout her life, she is bound to have felt that way briefly and temporarily. Consequently, the change to the ±9 quotient probably feels like nothing more than a shift of emphasis. Although the ±9 quotient has its drawbacks, it is something she can live with. Sooner or later, she probably will want to have a healthy, fully functioning, balanced 9 again. For the time being, however, the ±9 quotient is an accommodation she has reached between a 9 that is weak in her chart and a 5 that dominates it. Perhaps at this stage of Wilma's life she needs to focus on her 5 Character to the exclusion of her 9 Heart's Desire. At a later stage, she can reverse the process and restore the ±9 quotient to its original 9 status by multiplying it by 5.

The outcome of division (or any mathematical process) and the form it takes (relationships, work, creative expression, problems, goals, and so on) is entirely the result of the issue and one's intent. The division process is painful, and even devastating, for it forcibly kills off a way of life. When the outcome is negative, it impairs or paralyzes the person's life. If the process is essentially positive, it is revitalizing and it frees him to live his life more fully.

Division involving two negative numbers, $-x \div -y = z$, occurs when a person is in real trouble. Minus numbers manifest weak, negative, or debased motivations. This type of division results in a catastrophic collapse of those two energies. When Wilma's Character is −5, she is agitated and heedless, erratic and thrill-seeking; −5 has lost it; it is debauched, bizarre, and dissatisfied. When her Heart's Desire is −9, she feels like being grasping and overemotional, capricious and bigoted. She is isolated from life and filled with inhospitality, stubbornness, and dogmatism. When the energies of the −5 set out to undermine the −9 at any cost, the resultant 9 quotient is perverse. A state of profound weakness and hurt is reached, like a tiny figure riding the crest of a tidal wave without purpose or control. This is a state of depravity, despair, and total loss. It is perhaps akin to self-murder, in which the lowest common denominator of human behavior is reached. It is a destruction process in which fear and loathing, pain and despair create and sustain the experience.

Two points bear mentioning. First, every numerical situation may be remedied through the mathematical manipulation of numbers. Wilma can restore her $-5 \div -9 = 1.8/9$ by "putting Heart" back into it. Her Heart is 9. It should come naturally to Wilma to bring herself back up from the lowest of low points because she loves the very solution she needs in this case. In other words, if she applies the transcendent energy of her 9 Heart to the failed 9 quotient, it can be reawakened to its serendipitous potential: 9 x 9 = 81/9. Second, what division is really about is flushing out fear and desire in order to transcend the personal ego. Division involving two negative numbers is a sickness of the soul, a spiritual cancer that must be expunged. If Wilma were to ruin her life in this way, she would either bring herself out of it eventually or it would be her demise. In the short term, this division is devastating. In the long term, this is probably the first phase of a growth process that will ultimately result in a renewal of her being.

Another destructive form of the division process occurs when just one of the numbers is negative. The result is a negative quotient, causing the individual to subvert and undermine the people around him. In the case of our ongoing example, either number could be negative: –9 ÷ 5 or 9 ÷ –5. Since 5 is the stronger number in Wilma's chart, it is more likely that 9 will be negative. Thus, when the adventurous, risk-taking 5 takes on the –9, its drive is to free itself from the –9's stubbornness, dogmatism, and sullen detachment. Five would dearly love to rid itself of this monkey on its back. It cannot, of course, because this is a case of the self fighting itself. It is a desperate inner conflict with serious repercussions. The 5 is over its head trying to free the listless, half-hearted –9 from its misery and dissatisfaction. The egocentric 9 sours them both, and that produces the –9 quotient. In the company of others, Wilma is in their face. She uses the power and charisma of her –9 to force her bigotry and dogmatism on them. One moment she is petty and demanding, the next she is unsympathetic, forbidding, and uninvolved. She causes hurt and disruption wherever she goes. This is a formidable dilemma for Wilma. The –9 quotient is the same as the –9 of her Heart's Desire before division. The difference is that the –9 quotient is much more deeply troubled and agitated than the –9 prior to division. Oddly, she likes the –9 quotient even though it is so ruinous for her life. This makes things excruciatingly difficult—it's a kind of death wish.

When the quotient is "±," it mainly affects the individual on the inside. The back and forth interaction of the ± number keeps the individual self-preoccupied with its activities. On the other hand, a quotient that is purely negative or purely positive tends to affect those around it. So, Wilma's –9 quotient exerts a constant negative influence on those around her. She "subtracts from" or "divides into" them. A profound hopelessness engulfs Wilma. She is embittered about life. Her moods run riot. She uses her considerable 9 charisma and persuasiveness to preach the virtues of material well-being and prosperity, but she has no real involvement with other people. They find her opinionated, outspoken, and selfish. She makes philosophical and spiritual principles out of her arbitrary personal opinions, and she pushes her prejudices on everyone. She is fundamentally compromised. Her spirit is broken.

Division involving two positive numbers—$+x \div +y$—cuts away all but the truth. It is based on a sustained discipline to live at the highest levels of each number's range of experience in extremely limiting or devastating circumstances. The payoff for this worthy effort is an abiding self-confidence and self-love. In her everyday life, Wilma lives her 9 Heart's Desire at an average level. It is generally healthy, but cluttered with the usual assortment of self-doubts and fears, emotional dramas, conflicts between being a universal woman and being egotistical, between her faults and not living up to her ideals. She has no special awareness of her spiritual potential, no particular understanding of her deep need to love unconditionally, no special urge to give herself over to grand and worthy causes. The exquisite potential of Wilma's 9 has yet to see its fulfillment.

Fortunately for Wilma, this is not the end of the story. Due to her 5 Character, true seeking and searching is her nature. This includes investigating the mysteries of her inner self. The ingenious and resourceful 5 has the ability to discover what the potential of the 9 is at its best. The 9 may not like the ride during which the 5 takes the 9 apart only to put it back together again, centered and self-aware. The end result is a clearing out of any fuzzy thinking, impracticality, egotism, or extremes of idealism. Five will force the philosophical, good-hearted 9 to apply its ideals in a realistic, down-to-earth manner. In this "school of hard knocks" approach, the 9 and the 5 become good partners. They do not become an inseparable pair. These two numbers simply do not share a natural affinity with each other. Nevertheless, after the successful division of $+9 \div +5 = +1.8/+9$, they both function together very harmoniously and very productively on the level of practical living. Five has learned a lot as well by dealing with a number quite different from itself.

In the above discussions of multiplication and division, Wilma made remarkable and sometimes ruinous changes in her life. In each case, a single number replaced the two that were multiplied or divided. The difficulties, stresses, conflicts, weaknesses, and dysfunctions she experienced through the interaction of two numbers were permanently dealt with and resolved, for better or worse. It is not fully accurate to say "permanently," because, although a lot of effort went into every procedure, each one could be reversed at a later time. What was multiplied with such strength and perseverance could be divided back to its original state, and vice versa. It is reassuring to know that a difficulty between numbers may not only be resolved through the application of mathematical functions, but also that the nature of the outcome may be known in advance as well.

Briefly summarized, the four forms of division are as follows:

$\pm x \div \pm y = \pm z$: Self-destruction or self-renewal.

$-x \div -y = z$: Abject ruination and total loss.

$-x \div +y = -z$: The bona fide attempt to resolve a flaw or illusion fails, causing disruptive thoughts and behaviors.

$+x \div -y = -z$: A destructive part of the self causes a general degeneration of thoughts and feelings.

$+x \div +y = +z$: Ignorance and falsity are eliminated from an individual's nature, resulting in a higher quality of living.

Let us now turn our attention to the two *passive* mathematical functions with which we are concerned in this book: addition and subtraction. As previously explained, they are considered passive because through them the self bases its decisions and actions on mood, circumstance, fear, desire, and other changing or cyclic influences. In contrast, multiplication and division are *active,* because in them the individual sets for himself a certain course of action and does not allow changing conditions—whether they are inner or outer conditions—to deter him from his goal.

Many numerologists think addition is already in use in Pythagorean numerology for developing numbers to be interpreted. And so it is. However, its use is no more than a mechanical technique to produce numbers. The *symbolic meaning* of uniting numbers through addition is not given any importance. Thus far in my explanation of multiplication and division, I have only used numbers from Wilma Dawn Thomas' chart to illustrate methods of interpretation. For our examination of addition and subtraction, I will introduce the remaining single-digit numbers—0, 1 2, 3, 4, and 6—which have not as yet been made part of our interpretation discussion. By the end of this chapter, the reader will have some acquaintance with all ten single-digit numbers.

An example of addition taken from Wilma's reading is: "You thrive when you cope with risk, danger, or uncertainty." As I mentioned earlier, this attitude is typical of 5 energy. I further categorized this statement as addition, $5 + x$, because it is a reaction to circumstances, rather than a resolution to achieve a goal. The "x" is there because no experience other than 5 is involved. Wilma's ±5 Character is generally positive. She is usually sociable, outgoing, upbeat, fun-loving, witty, and constantly looking for something new and different to catch her eye, something a little risky. She yearns to break her routine, even if there isn't one. Being in this frame of mind, how will she fare with her coworker Amy as they spend the day together working on a project? Amy has a 6 Character and is in the same positive frame of mind today as Wilma. She generally feels quite sociable and is interested in everybody else's business. She is always on top of what is going on with the office staff. The company is like a big family to Amy, with herself as the mother in charge. Nobody in the office is as responsible as she is. Employees go to Amy with their problems. She is the best listener, and always finds reassuring words for those who confide in her. She is forever meeting everyone else's needs and wants—always giving, no questions asked—to the point that it hurts. Then she has to manipulate her friends to get those needs filled. Such is the 6 nature.

Ordinarily, a 5/6 combination is a testy one, with serious differences at every turn. But today, with both women in a pleasant and cooperative mood, they are in the addition mode. It is their attitude of *mutual affection* that is the dynamic of addition of the ±5 and the ±6. So, despite differing characteristics that could easily cause hurt and conflict, their two natures join happily together. In this scenario, we not only know the nature of their relationship, but also the outcome of this "union for a day": $±5 + ±6 = ±11/±2$. In this temporary partnership, Wilma is lively and unconventional, dramatic and resourceful, full of clever ideas and witticisms. For her, the relatively staid and conventional Amy is an opportunity to shine. In contrast to careful and conservative Amy, Wilma stands out as wild and free. This makes Wilma feel good. She can be exactly who she spontaneously is with Amy without any competition.

Amy is the solid anchor in this relationship. She is the responsible, caring one. With Wilma, Amy's experience is rich and varied. She has so much opportunity to listen and empathize, and to meet Wilma's fast-paced and ever-changing needs. Further, she enjoys the fact that Wilma challenges her standards and ideas, and questions her convictions about community and friendships. This is interesting to Amy. But oh, how she admires Wilma's ability to be a free agent in life! Amy never allows herself to be so loose and unrestrained. With Wilma she can experience it vicariously. Wilma makes Amy learn and grow. Amy is also able to help Wilma by showing her how to balance her raucous, rebellious 5 energy so that her life can run more smoothly.

The nature of the friendliness that they share together as a result of uniting ±5 and ±6 is not random or arbitrary: it is ±11/±2. Two is all about relationships. The 2 is a constant surprise for Wilma, and a welcome complement to Amy's concept of what life ought to be like. This number is open and receptive, and only really functions well when it is in partnership with someone else. It is gentle, helpful, considerate, and cooperative, so *very* cooperative. Two's hallmark is its sensitivity. This number has a strong empathy for, and a high awareness of, other peoples' feeling states. It is so emotional! Two feels in its gut what others want and need as well as what they expect of it. Because the 2's focus is so wholly on others, it is exceedingly vulnerable to their opinions, expectations, and negativities. Two is subordinate by nature, and it can easily slip into a subservient role. Then it is weak and dependent, relying on the other for everything. Until 2 learns who it is, it is very easily hurt by harsh anger, criticism, hostility, hatred, insults, even indifference or aloofness. Two needs to be needed. In a positive mode, 2's strength is its ability to bond with others. It is caring and supportive, loving, quiet, and intimate. It loves to communicate and share back and forth, and treasures simply being with a special person. It is the relationship engine. In a negative mode, 2 can cling for dear life to another person. The negative 2 has a large capacity to be passive and put all the responsibility on another to make its decisions. It can express itself as weak, indecisive, and vacillating with no sense of itself. Here, the 2 tends to be picky and obsessed with inconsequential details. It complains a lot and bemoans its fate, which it considers to be the fault of the others. But, apart from its petty, petulant moods, 2 is the best of partners.

This, then, is the character of ±2. We will now try to understand how this ±2 links Wilma's ±5 and Amy's ±6. First of all, note how greatly the 5 contrasts with the 2. Five is bold, adventurous, freedom-loving, and opportunity-maximizing, while 2 functions best helping and deferring to another person—it is passive and unassertive when faced with opportunity or the need for initiative. The 2's emphasis on relationship is unfamiliar territory for the 5. Five energy is simply too frenetic, too novelty-seeking, too focused on freedom, too disinterested in quiet times and moments of intimacy to ever experience the mundane benefits of close relationship. This is why Wilma is continually and pleasantly surprised by the intimate rapport she finds in her association with Amy. She never expected *that!* Five is always on the move, with never a moment for rest. Yet with Amy, Wilma experiences quietness. This contented peacefulness eludes Wilma's understanding. It is outside all her frames of reference, and yet she finds it curiously soothing. Since 2 is one of the *relationship numbers,* Wilma finds a different kind of freedom with Amy: the freedom to open up to someone else and to be genuine. They really talk to each other. They share their innermost concerns. They cooperate with each other with sensitivity and unhurried interest.

It is all a first for Wilma; but for Amy it is normal and natural, except that she *never* expected to get along with Wilma of all people! Six is the other main relationship number. It is the nature of 6 to care for others and to be involved in their lives. Consequently, 6 and 2 thrive together. They complement and add to each other's qualities. So Amy takes comfortably to this relationship with Wilma.

The addition of two positive integers—$(+x) + (+y)$—occurs when, in addition to mutual affection, there is a focused determination to be positive and upbeat. Here, the assorted negativities that normally hamper every number are consciously set aside. The individual *chooses* to be positive. He sets his sights on the higher functions of the number Force. In this manner, he remains open and receptive to that which comes his way. He passes no judgments on what occurs. He has no expectations and sets no limitations on what may happen.

This requires continuous conscious attention to everything thought, felt, and experienced. Common weaknesses and negativities of the 5 include becoming easily bored, needing to be entertained all the time, overdoing sensual pleasures, taking advantage of others, being irresponsible, and being too restless to sit still for a moment. In a +5 mode, when any of those faults come up, Wilma deals with them. She finds the positive, constructive impulse that is at the root of the negative urge. Instead of becoming bored, for example, she finds something of interest in what she is doing. With regard to needing to be entertained, she takes responsibility for her needs and chooses to be intrigued by what is happening at the moment. Again, if she is tempted to be an opportunist and take advantage of the situation at hand, she chooses to share the benefits of the opportunity with all who are involved.

At first, each negativity appears to be immutable. At a deeper level, the surface negativity can be discerned as a choice between positive and negative. The negative choice, born of fear or desire, is often viewed as powerful and extremely tempting. The positive (and much less titillating) choice is for well-being, harmony, and balance. It lacks any aggressive lure; it simply pleases.

On the negative side of 6 are such attitudes as controlling and manipulating others, being a doormat for others and their needs, being a gossip, and interfering in others' lives. If Amy looks beneath the surface, she will see that the need to control and manipulate others originates from the fear of not being loved and of being left out. If she faces this fear, she can choose the positive of this dynamic: to allow others to love her on their own terms. If Amy discerns why she allows herself to be a doormat for other people and their needs, she will realize that her excessive desire to help others is really a mask covering her own low self-esteem. She places a much higher value on what others want than on what she herself needs— I am serving you *all the time,* so please love me, love me, love me!" If she looks beneath the surface of her need to gossip and interfere in other peoples' lives, she will see it is due to the fear of being unlovable or abandoned. She forces herself on other people in order to avoid being excluded and alone. If she acknowledges this fear and chooses to view herself as belonging, she will relax and participate in others' lives without intruding.

None of these kinds of personal issues is easy to handle. Each has a considerable emotional and mental investment built into it. Yet, if Amy has sufficient focus and determination to choose the positive alternatives consistently, she will remain open and happy. She will be honest with herself and take responsibility for who she is. She will function congruently in the continuous give-and-take of life, welcoming all that life brings her and giving of herself each day.

The +2 that Wilma and Amy share in their temporary relationship is an excellent basis for an enduring friendship. They are able to trust each other. Both are mature people who understand deeply. They experience warmth and affection together, a gentle acceptance of each other, marvelous communication, and attentiveness to each other's needs and expectations.

The two forms of addition may thus be summarized as follows:

$\pm\text{x} + \pm\text{y} = \pm\text{z}$: A generally pleasant temporary bonding with no commitment to hold it together when the mood passes.

$(+\text{x}) + (+\text{y}) = +\text{z}$: An impermanent union of two numbers based on disciplined openness and receptivity.

Subtraction is a temporary breakdown of, or separation from, a relationship. It can be due to a negative mood or feeling, disapproval, an attitude of superiority, hurt, distrust, dislike, disagreement, or conflict. It can also occur if there is a need to be alone or to withdraw for the time being from a situation or the company of others. Like addition, subtraction is a passive function because its basis is one's dislikes and reactions to circumstances. Whereas addition represents a state of openness and receptivity, subtraction indicates being closed off and preoccupied with oneself.

Our first example of subtraction involves Amy's 3 Heart's Desire and the 4 Heart's Desire of her husband, Bill. Amy and Bill have very different motivations. With Amy's 3, she is happy when she is free to relax and enjoy herself, to express herself, to be creative, and to socialize. She could do that all day long! Pressure, obligation, work, and responsibility she does not want. What she does want is to be unburdened, light-hearted, positive, and to play—to pursue her hobbies or wile away the hours somehow in fantasy. She seeks out activities that are fun or personally meaningful. It is nearly beyond her ability to stick with duties, responsibilities, and unremitting toil to which she cannot relate. That kind of thing makes her feel dismal. What also affects her 3 adversely is lack of appreciation, or worse, sharp anger or criticism, especially when she thinks it is undeserved. Just thanking her or telling her she did very well uplifts her spirits and gives her the strength to carry on for a long time. With negative feedback, the hurt is fearsome and she shuts down. When this occurs, Amy is experiencing a –3 with Bill.

Bill's 4 Heart's Desire generally runs counter to Amy's 3. His motivation is to be serious, purposeful, hard working, and to fulfill his duty. He is the soul of stability. Bill's inner drive is to be steadfast, persevering, strong, disciplined, and organized, so he has little tolerance for messing around, for wasting time in frivolous pursuits or senseless kidding around. Relaxing and having fun can actually be irritating for him, particularly if there is something else that needs to be done, and this is the big rub with Amy. To him, she never seems to want to do anything but chatter away about silly, unimportant things. He is further irritated by the fact that at the slightest hint of work or even constructive activity, she drops everything to make another cup of coffee, work on a crossword puzzle, or watch a romantic movie. She is so impractical. She can't stick to anything. If something is a matter of responsibility, she makes light of it and turns to something else that she finds pleasant. In this frame of mind, Bill is experiencing a –4 with Amy.

Here we have a $-4 -3 = -7$ situation. These two people are antagonistic toward each other, hostile, isolated, and alone. Both Bill and Amy feel ill will toward each other. Both refuse to accept the other's point of view, and the result of their dysfunction is –7. Seven is always an inward, reflective, thinking, and analyzing number. It is the inner seeker for truth and quiet; it is unassuming and private. Together, Bill and Amy have a –7 as their shared experience. The result is that they are withdrawn from each other and into their own worlds. They are critical and mistrustful. Emotions boil within them both, but they communicate nothing. Outwardly, they are aloof and moody.

Two negative numbers do not automatically mean the experience is disadvantageous. There is also a "positive aspect" to subtraction. This is the case when separation is due to an excess in a relationship. Such an imbalance might involve too much intensity, be too scary, require too much effort, be too demanding, or be too suffocating. Under these circumstances, it is natural and beneficial to separate after a while, whether briefly or for a long time, in order to restore the relationship. This could be the case with Bill and Amy if, for instance, they were together day and night until they got on each other's nerves. One way this might happen is if they were snowed-in in their vacation cabin and were unable to leave or see anyone else for weeks. At some point, they would crave being alone. It is normal! They would yearn for personal space and time to nurture themselves as is only possible when they are on their own. In such confinement, these normal needs for privacy would give Bill and Amy a very understandable –4, –3 situation. The –7 result would be an ideal time for individualism, self-reflection, and privacy—a timely vacation from the demands of "each other."

The opposite situation—$+4 +3 = +7$—can also have undesirable side effects and can thereby prove to be of a negative benefit. If, in maintaining a positive discipline, the effort if too earnest, too humorless, too dogmatic, too inflexible, too exclusive, or too stubborn, then it is obsessive. There is no longer any normal response to each other, and it is therefore no longer authentic, except as an attitude of ego. Such attitudes represent an unhealthy imbalance. Thus, what was initially a praiseworthy effort becomes very destructive.

Imagine that Bill and Amy agreed to work through all their difficulties and differences with each other, and to be fully open and receptive with each other all the time. This has all the qualities of a +3 +4 = +7 situation. Imagine further that they are always polite and courteous to each other, there is never a cross word exchanged, and they are never in disagreement. Superficially, they appear to share uninterrupted harmony. Their gleaming, positive glow gives the impression that they have achieved a perfect partnership. But this is an illusion and they know it. They are performing an exterior discipline but not an interior one. Instead of dealing personally with their negative thoughts and feelings, they deny and repress them. Their victory of +7 is hollow and impersonal, a facade with nothing but anger and resentment boiling inside. What appears to be a highly positive effort turns out to be painful and infuriating.

Quite a different situation emerges when one of these people is essentially positive while the other is negative. Let us say that for some time Bill has been down on Amy, consistently rejecting all her efforts to brighten his day and to love him. He allows nothing to bring him out of it, and he is boorish, dogmatic, stuffy, and insensitive. Bill is sticking stubbornly to being –4. Amy, on the other hand, decided long ago to rise above the frustrations, limitations, hurts, and criticisms of daily living and to be genuinely positive, cheerful, friendly, and charming, sometimes in very creative ways. What gives Amy the strength to go on this way day after day, month after month, is her deep love for Bill. Their love is personally meaningful to her. She remembers how strong and forthright, caring and supportive he was before they laid him off at the company where he had worked for his entire adult life. He has been down on himself and depressed ever since. At times, Amy succeeds in being an inspiration to Bill, but mostly he chooses to stay in his negative rut.

In this situation, the quality of their relationship together is +3 –4 = –1. One is the number of the self, belief in the self, independence, self-assertion, taking the lead in a situation (both with others and within oneself), initiating new ideas, and going one's own way without allowing peoples' ideas or feelings to influence him. In the negative, 1 has a strong and unrelenting ego. Everything revolves around self. Selfishness and self-absorption permeate the air. This energy can cause one to be bossy (or even a bully), opinionated, unwilling to cooperate or compromise, and to act alone or strictly on one's own terms without regard for the interests or needs of others.

It is in this atmosphere of –1 that Bill and Amy now face each other. Amy has a dire challenge to stay positive. Bill's unwavering negativity and ill will devastate her +3 nature. It is the ultimate lack of appreciation from him. Negativity usually causes the 3 to be self-absorbed. The –1 simply blocks Amy from any open sharing with Bill. Three is, after all, the number Force of developing a concept of the "I." It is very important to the 3 that those around it affirm its actions. If the 3's "I" concept is not accepted, it has to go back to square one, as it were, to rethink the whole thing. So Amy's perseverance in the face of Bill's broken spirit shows amazing strength and demonstrates the deep meaning her relationship with Bill has for her. It is that great personal meaning that gives her the strength to persevere in the face of odds that appear hopeless.

Bill shares the same –1 with Amy, but his experience with it is dark and unrelenting. His –4 is heavy and deeply depressed. When that 4 faces the hardened ego and self-absorption of the –1, the combination is a sobering nightmare with no exit anywhere in sight. He casts an unhappy pall over everything that Amy offers in her attempt to be loving. He hurts deeply but refuses every effort to bring him solace. Amy cannot help him. He cannot help himself.

What could possibly bring Bill out of his desperate misery? Many mathematical manipulations could be applied here to bring about a variety of results. We will content ourselves here with considering one such manipulation: the addition of Wilma's ebullient 5. Although Wilma does not bring a 5 Heart's Desire to Bill and Amy (it is her 5 Personality), a strong injection of +5 or ±5 energy of any type would make a strong impact. So let's say that the day Wilma goes to visit them, Bill and Amy are home on a typically contentious Saturday morning. Amy is making a magnificent effort to be positive and cheerful, while Bill is an angry and hurt brick wall. This is very thick and murky emotional soup. Then Wilma arrives. She is in a happy mood that just won't quit. Her +5 presence changes everything: +3 –4 +5 = +4. Wilma alters the "chemistry" of Bill and Amy. Bill, who is wallowing in a state of –4, now finds himself experiencing +4 and begins relating in that manner. This is magical for him. How did it *happen?* It is all mathematical. In a +4 environment, his mood switches dramatically. You can't be crying if you're laughing.

If Bill's and Amy's situation were reversed—+4 for Bill and –3 for Amy—an entirely different outcome would be the result: +4 –3 = +1. In this instance, it is Bill who is determined to remain positive in the face of Amy's negativity. Now it is he who is the steady rock of their relationship, very purposeful, and he works hard in every moment to ensure their relationship stays on solid ground and is constructive and productive. He works to lay the groundwork for the future they want together. Toward this end, he is disciplined and organized, refusing to allow Amy's selfishness and her complaining to take him off center. He is focused. He has great patience and tremendous strength to persevere and endure. Nothing can shake his single-minded resolve. He works at this with a mechanical efficiency and detachment. He impassively avoids any reaction at all to her negative behavior. He does not build negative behavior into the structure of their relationship. He is very businesslike, persevering, and hard driving. That is the support he provides Amy. But it is a dry, emotionless kind of support.

Amy, with her –3, is entirely self-absorbed. She is moody, critical, taking Bill's "unemotional ways" as a sign of his lack of appreciation. She tortures herself, thinking, "He doesn't really love me." She mopes around the house, dejected and defeatist, unable to contribute anything helpful. She is remarkably bored, bored, bored! No attempt to comfort her touches her melancholy state. When she isn't complaining, she won't say a word. In her moments of silence, Bill can see she's touchy, but also curiously unfeeling. Bill is resigned to the fact that, despite the most loving of his efforts, there is nothing he can do to reach her. Still, he trudges on like a real trooper. For Amy's part, she has lost her way in the relationship. In this situation, Amy and Bill's relationship functions as a +1. One is the number that focuses on the self and believes in the self. It has the courage of its convictions. It creatively envisions a new potential or beginning, then initiates making it real. This is the number of taking the lead, including the lead of one's own self. So, when the 1 has a goal in mind, it takes the lead in its own life and takes the first step toward the new beginning.

This +1 is compelling and assertive energy—very forward looking. It stirs Bill up and motivates him. Despite Amy's downcast negativity, he finds the more petulantly she acts, the more he comes up with ideas and constructive solutions, resourceful efforts and creative attempts. Amy finds Bill's many "niceties" reassuring. They make a difference and help her to get by. Three is an intellectual number, cultivated and aesthetic. Even in its negative mode of expression, 3 has the potential to be inspired to imagine, to take an idea and to fantasize about it. From this perspective, +1 can eventuate in lifting Amy out of her –3 rut, and sooner or later lead her to express herself as ±3, or maybe even as +3.

The only drawback is that 1 is not a "relationship" number. This is because 1 is all about independence and going one's own way with others following its lead. While many relationships do seem to function in this way, a more fundamental basis for healthy relationships relies on qualities like mutual cooperation, helpfulness, and being adaptable, which are qualities of the 2. So, while the +1 relationship shared by Bill and Amy doesn't serve to nurture them to warmth and closeness, it does help to heal Amy of her negativity and to believe in herself so that she can contribute positively to their relationship.

As we saw earlier, Wilma's +5 presence was extremely healing for Bill's crippling –4. What effect would she have on the reverse dynamic, in which Bill has a +4 and Amy a –3? Well, +4 –3 +5 = +6. This is tremendously beneficial for Amy because 3 and 5 go together very naturally, just as 3 and 6 do. But it is frustrating for Bill because his steady groundedness, his unwavering and unoriginal perseverance (his 4 qualities) tend to differ dramatically from Wilma's flexibility and élan (her 5 qualities). On the other hand, he recognizes that when Wilma is around, it seems to do Amy a lot of good. The benefit for Amy is immediate and substantial. Amy enjoys Wilma. Three and 5 are fun-loving together. Five is also a natural complement to the +1 shared by Amy and Bill. One has to do with independence and taking the initiative, and 5 is all about freedom, resourcefulness, and taking advantage of what the moment offers—they go together very compatibly. The real benefit of Wilma's presence is the +6 of the three of them together. Six is the number of nurturing, being involved in other peoples' lives, meeting peoples' needs, healing and balancing problems. The +6 indicates a shared experience that is warm, loving, caring, attentive, and that works to calm Amy's out-of-balance feelings. This is an ideal ambiance for uplifting Amy's downcast mood.

Stated briefly, the two forms of subtraction are as follows:

–x –y = –z: Complete separation due to such attitudes as isolation, alienation, hurt, anxiety, or fear.

x – y = z: Painful conflict that causes separation.

We now turn our attention to 0, which is something of a special case in mathematical symbolism. Due to the late arrival of this number in mathematics, it is not part of virtually any system of number symbolism. The only exceptions to this of which I am aware are the 0 card of the Tarot (The Fool) and one position in Pythagorean numerology (the Challenges). As a consequence, there is no tradition for the interpretation of it, and its use is subject to a high level of confusion and misuse. Before beginning the discussion of 0 as it is used in mathematical symbolism, it is worth our while to see how it is used in Pythagorean numerology to understand where the error lies.

To figure the four Challenge numbers, the numbers of the month, day, and year of birth are alternately subtracted from each other. Almost all numerologists use the reduced numbers for these subtractions. This can produce 0, when 9 is almost invariably the correct answer. For example, the numbers of the date April 29, 1973 reduce to 2, 2, and 2. The first subtraction involves the month and day, the second subtraction uses the day and year, while the third involves the results of the first two subtractions. Lastly, the fourth subtraction is based on the month and year. Using reduced numbers, all four answers are 0 (see Figure 12). However, the mathematically correct answer in all four instances is 9 (see Figure 13). The error lies in the fact that the three birth date numbers are subtracted as though 29, 2, and 1973 have the same value. They do not. Consequently, none of the four 0s is a true and accurate result. All four Challenges should actually be 9, based on subtracting unreduced

---

Subtraction Using Unreduced Numbers

The unreduced numbers of
April 2, 1973 are: **29, 2, 1973**

Challenges
#1 Month – Day: $29 - 2 = 27/9$
#2 Year – Day: $1973 - 2 = 1971/18/9$
#3 #2 – #1: $1971 - 27 = 1944/18/9$
#4 Year – Month: $1973 - 29 = 1944/18/9$

Figure 12. Subtraction using unreduced numbers correctly produces 9 and seldom 0.

Subtraction Using Reduced Numbers

April 2, 1973 reduces to: **2, 2, 2**

Challenges
#1 Month – Day: 2 – 2 = **0**
#2 Year – Day: 2 – 2 = **0**
#3 #1 – #2: 0 – 0 = **0**
#4 Year – Month: 2 – 2 = **0**

Figure 13. Subtraction using reduced numbers often wrongly results in 0, although 9 is nearly always correct.

numbers. Once subtraction has been completed, the numbers are then reduced to 9. Zero can only legitimately occur in the first Challenge, and only if the number of the day of birth and the number of the month are the same. For someone born on April 29, the first Challenge would be 0: 29 – 29 = 0. The other challenges can never be 0 because the unreduced number of the year is always greater than that of the month or day. This is why 0 is almost never correct in Pythagorean numerology. It occurs more frequently in mathematical symbolism.

You will recall that 0 is *nothing*. Zero is not of this world. It is *metaphysical*—beyond the planes of form. It can be exceedingly elusive to everyday consciousness. As long as we are caught up in sensual experience—experience related to the senses—we are in a state other than 0. Often when people think they are experiencing 0, in actuality they are *viewing* the 0 from the perspective of another number, where they are really focused. Even much of what passes for 0 in deep meditation does not involve 0. A high degree of focus and spiritual training is needed in order to clear away all thought and to be consciously open to *nothingness*. It is a number of pure bliss and manifestation of destiny. This is the spiritual experience of 0.

The experience of 0 at mundane levels is like being lost at sea, being without boundaries or definition. None of the usual approaches to living works. It is disorienting and unnerving. One flounders uncontrollably. The disarray is due to holding on to personal ego. Every element of ego has numeric value, and exists only in the manifested numbers. If one focuses on 0 from an ego perspective, a numeric value is thereby added to 0, and *that number* is the result; 0 is no longer present. If one approaches the 0 state of being as "an egoic vessel waiting to be filled," in effect one is a vacuum and brings a negative number, and that number is the result; 0 is not present. If the ego element is strong and determined to "multiply or divide the 0 into submission," 0 is indeed the result. But the tradeoff is that, in the course of the process, the highly esteemed ego element dissolves away into the nothingness. The individual is indeed in 0, but without the egoic foundation on which he had so relied. He now finds himself lost in the "great void," a place of great terror if the motivation is not pure; the 0 is not home to him.

Zero is a most curious number. The nature of its operation is a profound mystery. The ironic paradox is that any *something* that is brought by mental focus into that creative matrix is exactly replicated. And if that *something* is motivated by a sincere yearning or dreaded anxiety, the *something* will be perfectly duplicated *with the yearning or anxiety* now included as an integral part of it. The results of that recreation change nothing. This is because the problem itself, *and the attendant thoughts, feelings, and reactions,* are what the 0 faithfully recreates. When ego is present, 0 is merely a feedback loop, which calls to mind Dante's weary refrain: "All hope abandon, ye who enter here."[4] This is why 0 is useless if it is not approached in a proper and spiritual way. It merely serves to perpetrate what already exists.

The potential of 0 is to enable us to create any experience according to our wish. This ability is so far removed from what we are accustomed to how we think of daily life that it can be difficult to believe or even imagine we possess such power. Life doesn't often seem to offer us the chance to do something *exactly* the way we want it to be. Yet, this is precisely what 0 represents.

To illustrate this process, imagine a theater troupe improvising a difficult scene from a play it will perform later. As the actors go through the paces of the drama, they realize they are off the mark. At the same time, they also are committed to play it through to the end. And so they do. This is not unlike experiences in life. How often do we find ourselves feeling trapped in a situation going wrong, but haven't the least idea how to make it right? We do the best we can, calling on all the resources at our disposal. And yet, as though following some kind of predestined fate from which we have no appeal, such experiences can appear unavoidable, inescapable, and inevitable.

The theater troupe created its dramatic moments using essentially the same process. As the actors began the improvisation, each made certain decisions about the role he was about to play in the upcoming scene, and he committed to those decisions. As the scene progressed, each actor identified with his role, and the scene as a whole became personal. At some point in its evolution, the scene took on a life of its own. The actors found there was an inherent logic to the sequence of events and there was nothing they could do differently—just like in real life.

When the "wrong improvisation" came to an end, an objective reality had been created. The actors knew individually and as a group that they had fulfilled the scene in the only way possible, given the initial decisions everyone had made. When the dramatic experience was over and the actors were no longer in character, the director stepped forward to give them objective feedback on what had just happened. He explained, without judgment, what did and didn't work. He then asked the actors to reconceive the entire scene completely based on a more informed approach. The actors, being trained professionals, did not react personally to what the director said because their desire was to do the scene "right." They had the self-confidence and the self-discipline to let go of the "wrong" approach. When they began anew, they possessed the "enlightened approach" suggested by the director, and they invested themselves wholly in the new way. No one secretly held onto the old approach. The result was that the very same scene was repeated, but on an entirely different basis that produced an entirely different experience. The actors' ability to detach from the "wrong" improvisation and then to reenact it differently is 0 energy, as best as it can be expressed in metaphor. The "corrected" improvisation is a fresh and new experience, not a sequel to the "wrong" improvisation. As the scene is brought to life, it unfolds according to mathematical principles. The play is conceived in 0, but the role of 0 ends once action begins.

In life, the director's expert feedback is comparable to the wisdom we can use to guide ourselves through the days of our lives. If we approach what we do in life with "spiritual expertise," we can detach from our own ignorant, erroneous, and limiting ways. These ways are, in the main, deeply unconscious attitudes, beliefs, and habits. If asked, quite often we would identify with the flaw and believe that this is *who we are,* and believe firmly that nothing can be done to change it.

Such imperfections are the reality of the lower self, or personal ego. These are attachments of the lower self, and they are many and varied, and often subtle.

They are the product of "our world." They consist of our attitudes, beliefs, habits, abilities, talents, likes and dislikes, wants and needs, sex, age, health, successes and failures, moral sense, and many other things that make us "who we are." These characteristic self-concepts and all other ways in which we base our identity are representations of the numbers 1 through 9. They all originate in 0. They all can be modified, replaced, or eliminated in 0.

In life, each of us is highly challenged to do what was required of the actors in their improvisation: impersonal detachment. It is frightening to the ego, which reasons, "If I let go of all *that*, why, there will be nothing left of me!" The "director" in our lives is Spirit, whose voice is our Higher Self. If over time we develop wisdom and understanding, the voice is articulate. If wisdom and understanding are as yet unformed within our being, the voice is inaudible. As the Bible says: "Wisdom is the principal thing; therefore get wisdom; and with all thy getting get understanding."[5]

Consequently, unless there is spiritual ability to enter the void without the static noise of ego, the 0 answers no prayers, nor does it bring any discernable benefits; it is a waste of time and effort. This is a principle reason why many people are discouraged with spiritual life.

Let us now examine 0 as it applies to the other three mathematical functions: addition, multiplication, and division. When 0 is used in addition, at first glance there appears to be no change. "Nothing" happens. After all, x + 0 = x. But whereas subtraction produces the *opportunity* to create an experience, addition brings a *spirit of newness* to a given number. That number is seen afresh, as though for the first time. Most of us are locked into being who we are, as it were. We are accustomed to handle our lives in certain set ways. Even if our numbers accentuate freedom or independence, we are not even close to being free from, or independent from, our customary selves. We tend to customize our numbers according to the make-up of our nature. Wilma's basic nature, represented by 5, has certain enduring and unchanging characteristics. She *expresses* those 5 characteristics in consistent ways. The fact that 5 *is* the number of freedom and change does not mean that her nature is free to change from what it *is*. In a fundamental way, Wilma is in a rut with her 5 energy! Her fluctuating nature lives and breathes predictably. It is habitual with her. She is comfortable with certain aspects of the 5. She is not looking for a "bigger, better" version of 5 (and there certainly is one!) nor does she want to transcend 5 altogether.

It is possible for any of us to be lifted out of our numerical rut. Any extraordinary event can have that effect temporarily. It could happen to Wilma if something extraordinary happened in her life, like a fabulous love affair. That would certainly lift her out of her daily 5 routine. She would be inspired to look again at that 5 on an expanded level—new ideas, new approaches to handling life's situations, a willingness to take new kinds of risks (like intimacy with another person), and so on. Such an influx of new *vision* comes with the addition of 0. Even though for Wilma 5 + 0 looks as though it equals the same old 5 as before the 0, this is not the case. This new 5 has been reinvented, enlivened, stimulated, lifted up, and rejuvenated. At the same time, this is the same 5—"nothing" was added to it. It is simply in a higher, more expansive frame of mind, or, to be more precise, a more conscious state of being. The 5 Force is unchanged because addition doesn't "change" or "evolve" it. Addition *harmonizes* numbers so they coexist in a warm and affectionate partnership, the effect of which—apart from 0—is another number.

When numbers are multiplied, the numbers themselves do not evolve into other numbers. Number forces are constant; they are *spiritual elements* of life. Rather, the result of multiplication derives from the *interaction* of the numbers being multiplied, the effect of which is another number. The change takes place *within* the person who

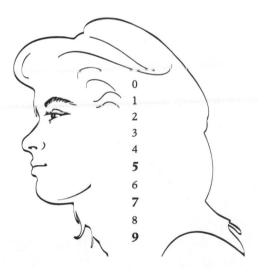

Figure 14. Wilma consciously experiences the numbers of which she is actively aware.

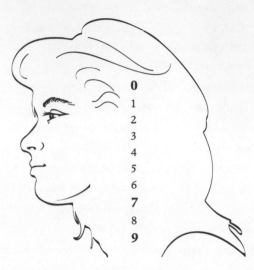

Figure 15. After multiplication of 0 x 5, Wilma's 5 becomes inactive and subconscious, and the 0 experience opens up for her.

multiplies, and, by extension, in the exterior world. Prior to multiplication, his being functions within the context of certain numbers. After multiplication, his consciousness experiences a different numerical reality. This is possible because all numbers are present in human consciousness, whether active or latent. Within the subtle structure of our natures, certain numbers are conscious and active while others lay fallow in unconsciousness. For Wilma, her conscious numbers are 5, 7, and 9. The other numbers are not accessible to her conscious awareness (see Figure 14).

It is possible to activate consciousness of a particular number and, conversely, to withdraw consciousness from a number. So, if Wilma uses 0 in multiplication, she makes a conscious decision to maintain a steady focus on the 0 and thereby to activate it. If over time she applies 0 consistently and persistently to the 5 until multiplication has occurred, the result is 0. The 5 is then quashed. This is only possible if she has an extremely thorough grasp of the 0 energy. She must have "owned" that number Force. She must understand it and have the ability to enter the 0 experience at will, to accomplish multiplication with the 0 humble and free of ego, and to apply it steadfastly. Gradually, the experiences and characteristics that result from the

Force of the number 5 dissipate, melt away, and disappear. The process involves ignoring all activity of the 5 Force (no easy task!) until it is lovingly erased out of her being. Wilma is then freed from the routine and limitations of 5, and she is able to use the 0 to create her life as she wishes. Such an expansion of Wilma's ability to live according to her true inner nature is not unlike an initiation.

Dividing 0 into 5 also results in 0, just like multiplication, but the process and the results are quite different. Instead of *lovingly expanding the potential of the self,* as in multiplication, division by 0 *surgically removes all traces of a number from the self,* creating an empty and hollow void. In $5 \div 0$, the experiences once generated by Wilma's 5 are cut away, leaving Wilma less than she was. The characteristics she once had—her vivacity and energy, her resourcefulness, adventurousness, curiosity, even her eternal restlessness—are now gone, and she is left with a vacant stare in her eyes and no mental or emotional capacity capable of stimulation. This is a troubling and devastating loss. Thus, division by 0 has the potential to produce mental illness, the loss of certain functional abilities, amnesia, or mental retardation.

In summary, the four functions when 0 is involved are as follows:

$x + 0 = x$: Temporary renewal of this number.

$x - x = 0$: Temporary release from ego into a pure spiritual state, *or* loss of self-awareness.

$x \times 0 = 0$: Achievement of ability to manifest one's life, *or* disorientation due to loss of egoic foundation.

$x \div 0 = 0$: Profound renewal of one's being or total destruction of one's life.

We now turn to examine two basic mathematical functions and their purposes: squaring numbers and finding square roots. These two functions represent highly potent *acts of being,* which, if used for spiritual purposes, can yield very high, even exalted, results.

When a number is squared, it is multiplied times itself: x^2. Squaring is a form of multiplication, but a specialized one. The goal of multiplying a number by itself—$y \times y$—indicates a *general effort* to evolve the two numbers toward their combined potential. It is a "general" effort because, apart from the individual's intent, there is no definite goal in mind. The subtle difference between the two processes is that squaring perfects the potential of a number. It is work on the inner self and it is very intense. It faces *all* the issues of a number—every aspect, behavior, characteristic, emotion, habit, attitude, and way of thinking of this number is examined and purified according to a very pure standard. Unyielding dedication and purpose are required in order to sustain the individual through the entire process. This makes squaring a number a spiritual act of being because it attains a high aspiration or metaphysical goal.

Consider the profound benefits for Wilma if she squares her 5: 5^2. Let's say for this illustration that Wilma is in great turmoil. She cannot figure out how to harmonize her 5 Character and her 7 Participation. Let us further say that the difficulty is mainly with the 5. All she has ever wanted is to be *free* to live and explore life. But this happiness and success has been relentlessly blocked by her need to find truth and to understand every darn thing (the 7). Recently, Wilma has been feeling especially limited by the introspection and intellectual nature of the 7. She is tremendously agitated and finds herself rebelling against anything quiet and thoughtful, and she seeks out whatever will thrill or entertain her. She says that nothing in the reading so far has helped to motivate her 5 nature to cooperate with the 7 part of her nature. She is split down the middle.

Her solution is $5^2 = 25/7$. The 5^2 paradoxically functions as 7, exactly what she needs in order to cope with her 7 Participation. This is a serious, spiritual workout, and very hard work. It requires clear vision and true courage. Every time her 5 acts negatively, she must instead choose the *Ideal of 5*. She must let go of her old attitudes, her deeply entrenched habits, all her long-term fears, and all other lower aspects of the 5. Her every decision and action in each moment must be based on rigorous discipline. She cannot lapse into temptation or what is comfortable, familiar, or pleasing. Any of that immediately negates the squaring process.

An example of the negative behavior of the 5 Force is opportunism. At its root is greed, resulting from either materialistic desire or fear of not having enough. In a 5^2 initiative, the question is, *How would 5 optimally resolve the quality of greed into a positive attitude?* The key issue is intent: what is 5 after? Grabbing opportunity is a passion for 5. It yearns to prosper in life. If 5 is negative, though, its needs can degenerate into wanting to take all it can get. In 5^2, the intent is to perfect itself. This requires a Way of Wisdom with which to develop opportunities. This, in turn, necessarily entails an inner search to discover and resolve impure motivations, fears, questionable attitudes, and so on. Note how 5 reflects on its own inner make-up as the method by which to envision higher consciousness. In this manner, the "unself-reflective" 5 develops an introspective quality as 5^2 evolves into $25/7$. As the arduous effort is made to square 5, each and every issue must be checked out according to wisdom, and higher choices must be set in place. Like the 7, 5^2 thinks deeply, analyzes, and seeks wisdom and understanding rigorously. This requires indomitable courage, determination, and hard work. For 5, however, truth and understanding are not the ultimate goal. Five's passion is innovative action and prosperity. Still, the 5 that has been squared makes a terrific working partner with 7.

The final mathematical function we will cover in this chapter is finding the square root of a number. This is similar to division. The difference is that division is a *general process of either renewal or destruction* in which a number is stripped down to its bare-boned essence. In the square root act of being, the quintessence of a number is extracted through a severe process, based on either a profound spiritual commitment or the direst of circumstances in life. If this is accomplished by ascetic means, which involve high purpose, unwavering discipline, and sacrifice, finding the square root is a deep purification. Only the true root, or seed, of the number remains, while the ramifications are burned away. The ascetic, during an intense period of fasting, meditation, and prayer, eliminates all illusionary thought and feeling until only archetypal truth remains. An individual then achieves an extremely penetrating and focused level of concentration, into which no distractions intrude. On the other hand, when a high and dedicated spiritual purpose is not the underlying motivation, the result of a square root procedure is likely to be devastation. This is the mundane square root experience. Here, a poisonous thought, issue, concept, or situation dominates everything in one's life. The result is that of overwhelming deprivation, loss, and extinction.

Earlier, we saw the result of squaring 5. Now, let's examine the opposite process by finding the square root of 5: $\sqrt{5} = 2.2360679775$. For reasons explained earlier, we will reduce only the first nine numbers: $2.23606798 = 43/7$. It is interesting that both procedures—squaring and square root—result in 7!

To understand square roots as a spiritual process, think again about Wilma. Imagine that several years from now she reaches a spiritual crossroads in her life. She finds that she can no longer continue to devastate herself with her $5/7$ conflict. She has become paralyzed in living, unable to function in most situations except those that are crucial to staying alive. Often, she finds herself spending the entire day in bed, unwilling to open the door to anyone. As this conflict reaches the boiling point, and Wilma is desperately looking for a solution of some sort, she realizes that she has developed strong spiritual beliefs. One day, to her great surprise, a stilling calmness comes over her as she recites a favorite prayer, "All is in divine order in my life." It suddenly occurs to her that fasting for several weeks in addition to three or four hours of meditation each day would help her to regain peace in her life. Although she had never thought of such a spiritual retreat before, she now finds the prospect enormously appealing. So she decides to do it, but the challenge lies in finding the time. For many years, her schedule has been frenetic. She has been on the go at work and busy in the evenings with socializing, attending meetings, hosting dinners, and throwing parties, not to mention babysitting her sister's kids every other Saturday. Further, she has developed a sideline business wheeling and dealing baseball cards, and many weekends she spends hours buying and selling cards at fairs and with friends. The hectic pace is finally getting to her. She feels profoundly exhausted and weary of nonstop activity. Finally, she makes a firm, conscious decision to find the calm eye-of-the-storm in her life. First, she makes the practical decision to slow down. But how? Her dramatic solution is to stop all activity—everything—for a period of time. She arranges to take a two-week vacation from work. She will be a hermit, leaving the house or answering the phone only when it is absolutely necessary to do so.

This is how it comes to pass on a Saturday in October that Wilma Dawn Thomas withdraws from the outside world and initiates the square root process. She enters an intense period of reflection, analysis, and spiritual discipline in an effort to understand her 5 nature at deepest levels. She fully accepts all that she must do and what she must give up in order to accomplish this goal. Since 7 is the reduced number of the square root of 5, this period of intense 7 activity is bound to be wonderfully productive for deep insight. After all, 7 is the number of seeking truth and developing understanding, and, synchronistically, it cannot help but resolve differences with her 7 Participation.

The previous scenario shows the positive benefits of the square root function when it is carried out as a spiritual discipline. Next, we will consider the very same circumstances to show the pain and heartbreak of a square root procedure in which egotistical motivations prevail. Imagine again that Wilma is leading the same frantic lifestyle as described previously. She gives herself over to every restless temptation and shiny opportunity that comes her way. Time just flies by because she herself is flying through life. Then one day she passes out at work. When she revives she is groggy and disoriented, and has trouble walking. Hours later, she seems well enough to go home, although she is still shaky and having difficulty coping. So, the company decides to have one of the clerks drive her home. When Wilma goes to her doctor, he tells Wilma that she is profoundly exhausted and stressed, and is at immediate risk of suffering a heart attack unless she stops all of her activities *right now*. He insists she spend two weeks in bed, and that she avoid all stimulation, including phone, TV, radio, newspaper, card games, reading, even visits from other people. She is instructed to draw the shades to dim the room. Meals will be catered and served on a tray placed outside her bedroom door. She is not to leave the bedroom except to go to the bathroom, and is only to leave the house in the event of a dire emergency!

This period of quiet and rest is not what Wilma wants; it is what she has been avoiding all these years. She is accustomed to accommodating her restlessness by filling her days and nights with people and amusements from the time she gets up to the time she turns out the lights at night. She has always loathed times when "nothing is happening," even if it is only for a few minutes. So, when the doctor tells her to spend two weeks without activity of any kind, or die, she panics. She cannot imagine even an hour with nothing to keep her busy and entertained. But *two weeks?!* She must do it, of course, to save her life, but she immediately sinks into a deep depression as the first few quiet moments begin.

Due to Wilma's attitude toward the austere two-week period, she experiences the square root process as deprivation and despair. She has lost everything on which she had always depended to keep herself sane. When she stops the diversions, she has to face all her fears that lurk so close to the surface. She has worked and played hard all her life to sidestep those deep-seated issues. Now, for "two eternal weeks," there is nothing else for her. The square root of 5 reduces to 7, of course, and 7 is the inward number whose Force seeks the truth of the self. If Wilma makes the decision to learn the truth about herself, she will then be working on the square root energy constructively and spiritually. The pain and fear will gradually subside. If that is her intent, she will be likely to reach a deep understanding about who she is and be able to make necessary changes in her life. But if she resists doing what is necessary and instead faces nothing, she may experience such emotional trauma and mental anguish that she needs to be under psychiatric care, commits suicide, or takes some other drastic step. After all, following the two weeks of rest, she can never again return to her fast-paced life without grave risk to her health.

In this chapter, we have closely examined six basic mathematical procedures. You, the reader, may initially have felt disappointed to learn that only the most basic of mathematical functions would be discussed. It should now be clear that even arithmetic is highly challenging to master on the symbolic level. Despite the "glamour and prestige" of higher mathematics like calculus, non-Euclidean geometry, and physics, most of us would be caught utterly unprepared to live at that extraordinary level, if given the opportunity. At the same time, it should be noted that human imagination has conceived a great deal in higher mathematics. At some point in the future, human beings will evolve the capability of living according to those higher mathematical functions.

A final word about this chapter. The goal in knowing numbers, their relationships, and mathematical principles goes beyond learning all the definitions and characteristics by heart. Full attainment of this skill means having the ability to live by mathematical symbolism with *instinctive knowing*. When one recognizes the numbers present in any situation, when one knows which mathematical functions will bring about desired results, and when one willingly endures the course of wise action, then one can be considered to be a *spiritual mathematician*.

Endnotes

1. It should be kept in mind that the full scope of the 8 is much broader than what is being discussed here. This discussion only concerns the characteristics of 8 that have a bearing on Wilma's relationship issues, because that is the theme, or purpose, of multiplying the several forms of 5 and 7. It is strictly Wilma's *intent* that determines the nature of the outcome.

2. Dante Alighieri, *Divine Comedy Inferno,* as cited in the *New Penguin Dictionary of Quotations,* by John Michael Cohen (New York: Viking, 1992), 131.

3. C. I. Scofield, *Scofield Reference Bible* (New York: Oxford University Press, 1945), 674.

chapter 9

The Mathematics of Becoming

But the universe begins a new cycle whenever we are ready.

—Marianne Williamson, *Illuminata*

Numbers alone are states of being—inert. Mathematics sets them in motion. It is difficult to discuss numbers without introducing a little addition or subtraction, as we did in the first part of Wilma's reading. But this does not begin to touch the issue of becoming. Here, in part two of Wilma's reading, we see how she can make the transition from Point A to Point B in her effort to evolve.

9	1	1		6	1	= 9 Heart's Desire
W I L M A	D A W N	T H O M A S				
5 3 4	4	5 5 2 8	4	1		= 5 Personality
5 9 3 4 1	4 1 5 5	2 8 6	4 1 1			= 5 Character
			April 16, 1951			= 7 Participation

Wilma's Reading: Part Two

Wilma, in the earlier part of your reading, we covered a lot of territory. We talked about your basic nature, how you function in the world, how you present yourself to others, and what makes you happy. We talked about how your numbers, or basic elements of your nature, work together. We were then able to discuss the strengths and weaknesses you possess, your inner conflicts, the types of abilities and limitations you have, your approach to relationships, and how you handle

*Review of
earlier
portion of
Wilma's
reading*

work. We discussed the role of spirituality in your life and, within that context, how your everyday challenges are actually spiritual challenges and what their purposes are. This was all accomplished through the interpretation technique of identifying each number and then comparing the numbers back and forth to see how they all work together. In this way, we discussed thoroughly who you are and what makes you tick.

*Identification
of
mathematical
functions*

What wasn't thoroughly talked about was what to do about your difficulties and challenges, and how to resolve them permanently. We didn't deal with these problems before because, in mathematical symbolism, it is the functions like addition, subtraction, multiplication, division, and so forth that represent how we live, the choices and decisions we make, the goals we pursue, the challenges we face, and so on. Numbers by themselves do not do this. They just *are*. So, when it comes to solving problems, one of those mathematical functions will need to be used.

What I do in a reading is choose two or three of the most important problems a person has in his life. For you, three main issues come to mind. The first one concerns your difficulty being happy and satisfied in life, and that, of course, is due to your weak 9 Heart's Desire. The second big issue deals with the challenges you face when it comes to relationships, and that has to do with the particular combination of numbers you have. Finally, the third issue concerns your major inner conflict, which, on a bad day, causes you to rebel and act out or withdraw and be aloof. And that, of course, is the difficulty you have reconciling your 5 Character and your 7 Participation.

You may be wondering why we are discussing only three problems when there are so many more that need attending to. Believe me, after we have discussed what it will take to resolve the three dilemmas I mentioned, you might decide that just *one* is too much to handle! Even though addition, subtraction, and so forth are the simplest of mathematical functions, it is still a serious proposition to apply any one of them to your life. If you do it right, each mathematical function is a full-time job. We are talking here about making basic, fundamental changes in your life. It isn't quick or easy. It may well take you years to do it. So, singling out three areas to work on is a lot to do. You definitely have your work cut out for you!

Let's talk first about how you can be happy and satisfied. As you will recall, it is your 9 Heart's Desire that determines whether you feel pleased with yourself and contented with how you're doing day-in and day-out. With your 9, you feel good if you are generous, express unconditional love, are nonjudgmental about people even though you disagree strongly, and if you are 100 percent involved in the relationships and activities of your life. Whatever you do, you like to give of yourself unreservedly. You also like to be a visionary and a philosopher, to use wisdom in your decisions and activities, and to work for idealistic causes that benefit humanity.

Unfortunately, this doesn't happen very often. The strongest part of you—your 5 Character supported by your 5 Personality—is opposite to 9 in every respect. You are the adventurer who intends to live well. You seize opportunities so that you can prosper. You place personal freedom above almost everything else. You definitely like to do what you want whenever you want to do it. You are first and foremost an individual, and you spare no effort to inject your unique self into every situation. And, if your freedom is blocked, that doesn't stop you or even slow you down. This is who you are. It is far stronger than your Heart's Desire, and it is going to win out over the 9 every time. When, for example, you have a strong desire to be generous and compassionate, then you—which is to say your 5 nature—won't stand for it. One thing is for sure: that 9 urge is *not* going to lock you into some idealistic or philosophical lifestyle, or "give everything away" cage that puts your personal or financial freedom on the back burner . . . no siree! You rebel. You mess it up. You make sure you don't waste any time on that! In this face-off, the 9 part of you wants to be a saint and the 5 part of you responds as the sinner. Since 5 is not only the number of the person you are but also of your personality, 5 dominates every other number in your chart, and your 9 motivational drive loses out every time.

Your other main number, 7, is in your Participation position. Ordinarily 7 is an ally of the 9. These are the two main spiritual numbers in numerology. Both are intuitive, philosophical, and truth oriented. Seven seeks its truth within, while 9 pursues its spirituality out in the world where it strives to become one with all that it encounters. But in your case, I think you made a practical decision very early in life to use the 7 for 5's purposes. You decided

Summary of weak 9 Heart's Desire in relation to strong 5 Character, 5 Personality, and 7 Participation

Summary of
weak 9
Heart's
Desire in
relation to
strong 5
Character, 5
Personality,
and 7
Participation

to use your mental abilities for material advantage rather than for noble work. This is strictly an arrangement of convenience. Left to its own devices, the 7 part of you would choose 9 for a partner, not 5. Seven is the thinker and the intellectual in a never-ending quest to understand what it decides to study. This part of you is quiet, introspective, private, and reserved. Most important of all, 7 is a studious, scholarly energy that is not very physical, adventurous, or outgoing. It wants nothing of 5's risks and hair-raising escapades, or all the intense wheeling and dealing and hard negotiating on which 5 thrives.

This is why 7 and 5 are not natural buddies. But I think your 5 decided long ago to make 7 work for it. You became, as it were, a thinking risk-taker. This is a dynamite combination. It has enabled you to develop great skill and insight in maximizing opportunity. You have great expertise and you are clever. You know how to survive both physically and intellectually. But when everything is said and done at the end of a day, I would say there is little left of 7 to work with 9. Once again, 9 is left out in the cold. You cannot be happy the way you are living.

Identification
of addition

Your best approach to become a satisfied, fulfilled person is to add all four numbers. During our discussion, remember one thing: this is a permanent solution. Basically, addition is loving yourself. You begin by accepting each number and being at peace with it. Then each number needs to be open, friendly, and receptive to each of the other numbers. In this way, you harmonize all four parts of yourself so they all get along famously. It is then that they are added together. When you add, you not only have to know how to complete the process, you also must know the outcome to expect! Five plus 5 plus 7 plus 9 equals 26, and that reduces to 8. So, if you successfully add those four numbers instead of having those four individual energies jostling and competing within you for attention, you will have just the one number with which to deal, the 8. Inner conflicts are gone, literally! You will find that your basic attitude in every situation is that of being open and receptive to whatever life brings you. It loosens you up and frees you so that you live in a much more loving, stress-free manner. This brings tremendous personal growth and marvelous benefits to the quality of your life, and that includes happiness and satisfaction in abundance. The price for all this is a lot of work on your inner self, on how you handle your life, on the attitudes and habits you have, and on all that you expect in a relationship. Everything depends on what you decide you *want*. I suggest that you study the nature of relationships so you know exactly what you are looking for. You might write out a statement of intent, then rewrite it as many times as necessary until you know precisely what you are trying to achieve. I guarantee you, the stronger and more definite your purpose is, the better the outcome will be. You are making such deep changes in your life, and this will take considerable doing on your part. In effect, you are retraining yourself to function in life on a completely new basis. It is definitely a process of discovery and reinvention, sometimes marvelous and inspiring, sometimes terrifying and astoundingly painful. The good news is that you are not doing all this struggling and relearning in the dark. You have your numbers to work with. You have the process of addition that we are discussing, and you know in advance what the outcome of all your hard work will be.

Identification of addition

It is a lot to do. Is this something you really want to take on? You're nodding. I thought you would, because this is an opportunity for you to prosper much better in life, and your 5, having recognized it, is anxious to step forward and accept the challenge. Good for you!

Now I need to illustrate the addition process with one of my stories to help you make the transition from wonderful theory to practical application. Otherwise, you're going to be wondering, *How exactly do I do this?* To start, I'd like for you to think of the number 5 as the Playgirl. Their qualities and characteristics are almost exactly the same. Playgirl is always on the prowl for adventure, a new experience every ten minutes, escapades, and relationships that titillate her, especially with men. She has wanderlust. She is definitely fun to be around, and always charming and engaging—just like you with your strong 5 nature. Playgirl also gets easily bored. She is so restless, she can hardly sit still for anything unless it is exciting or novel for her. She avoids situations that force her to be organized, accept responsibility, or to be in a rut day after day. This is why Playgirl sometimes flees for her life from staid conditions or rebels aggressively against them. Playgirl wants freedom, freedom, freedom . . . and if she can't have that, she will accept freedom as an alternative. Get the picture? Playgirl wants to live life to the fullest and

Addition of 9 Heart's Desire, 5 Character, 5 Personality, and 7 Participation

*Addition of 9
Heart's
Desire, 5
Character, 5
Personality,
and 7
Participation*

have fun, not be stuck in some dull routine all the time! Can you relate to that? I thought so. Playgirl is *you*, or at least a big part of you.

The first step in addition is to accept and to be at peace with this part of you, both the extraordinary talents and qualities along with all the flaws, weaknesses, and negative character traits that go with it. To do this, you need to avoid passing judgment on yourself. Love yourself unconditionally, whether you think you're doing something right or not. It sounds natural and easy to love yourself, but many times it will truly challenge you to do this. It will take clear purpose, strength, courage, and discipline. This is what you will need when you find that you are criticizing yourself, belittling or demeaning yourself, faulting yourself, rejecting yourself, putting yourself down, or in any way denying the wonderful spiritual being that you are. I do not mean that you should overlook or ignore any faults that you have. To be human is to have faults, and you need to continue growing as a person. But the key to this first step of addition is accepting yourself *as is*. Say to yourself, *This is who I am, and I am so glad!*

Once you get started on the addition process, you will begin to like it right away. Unconditional love is what your 9 Heart's Desire delights in. The more you get involved with addition, the more you will feel fulfilled and rewarded.

Then you need to apply the same attitude of loving self-acceptance to your personality. As you may recall, your Personality number shows the way you are comfortable presenting yourself to others. Since your Personality number is 5, the image of Playgirl also applies to your personality. So, what your Playgirl personality appears to be is "the life of the party." She is fun, outgoing, vivacious, charming, and a good talker. She always seems to have lots of ideas and is very resourceful. On the negative side, she has to be constantly entertained. The moment she loses interest, you've lost her, even if matters of importance are at stake.

This is the kind of person you seem to be, Wilma. Once again, the challenge is to accept your 5 Personality and to be at peace with it. If you have flaws there, it is important to recognize them. But you will never reach a state of perfection, so the healthy way to treat yourself is to be nonjudgmental.

Another part of yourself to love unconditionally is your 7 Participation—the way you function in the world. A good image for 7 is the Bookworm,

*Addition of 9
Heart's
Desire, 5
Character, 5
Personality,
and 7
Participation*

another type of person everyone is familiar with—we all know her. And she is just like the number 7: quiet, reserved, timid, and totally preoccupied with her world of books and intellectual matters. She is a thinker who has great academic and intellectual drive. She is hooked on pondering and analyzing the whys and wherefores of things. She is driven to find out what lies beneath the surface. But although Bookworm has professional expertise and success in her field, she rarely socializes. She feels awkward with other people. This sometimes makes her appear to be cold, aloof, even critical and demeaning.

All of this is also you, Wilma. You need to acknowledge fully that this is who you are. What you need to do is love yourself and honor yourself. Find as many ways as you can to be happy about the way you are.

Finally, we come to your 9 Heart's Desire, the "neglected you." For an image of this number, think of Do Gooder, the person who is obsessively on a mission for humankind. She is oblivious to all things merely human. Do Gooder has tremendous charisma. She relates to people of all walks of life, and they find they can relate to her. She likes to give and give, without ever asking for anything back except for loyalty and support for her cause. She is devoted, caring, and wholly involved in idealistic endeavors. Behind her views is a spiritual conviction about how she wants the world to be. As good as Do Gooder is, she can also be very dogmatic; then she listens to no one else. She doesn't talk to others—she preaches. You could say that she is at times an egotistical fanatic who relentlessly forces her views on everyone around her. Yet, when she isn't so self-preoccupied, she is one of the few people who is willing to devote herself to service to humanity. She asks nothing for herself. She listens to the still small voice that is always communicating to her and guiding her every activity. She yearns to be a philosophical individual. Everything she does, thinks, or feels is based on heartfelt thoughts about the nature of life and the role she has to serve on behalf of others. She is driven to lead a metaphysical existence full of meaning and purpose. At times, she is utterly selfless without an arrogant bone in her body. In this enlightened state, she understands her existence. She negotiates the eddies and currents of the waters of daily living like a champion swimmer who knows that she and the ocean of life are one and the same. Once again, you

*Addition of 9
Heart's
Desire, 5
Character, 5
Personality,
and 7
Participation*

are just like Do Gooder, or at least you would like to be. To add 9 to the other numbers, you need to begin by accepting the full scope of what you want, your inner drive, and to love that part of yourself without reserve. Since unconditional love is also a need of your Heart's Desire, I would say you will take to this requirement naturally and easily.

The second step of the addition process is for all four parts of yourself to become fast friends. This is mutual affection, and it depends on each number enthusiastically embracing the other three as bosom buddies—inseparable pals. Once they do this, addition has been completed. This means that your 5s and 7 need to develop a fond rapport. The way your life is right now, they already share a good working relationship, but it is all business and no affection or warmth. Your rowdy, wild, roustabout, restless 5s have to learn to love, value, and appreciate your reclusive, analytical, academic, judicious 7, and vice versa. In its heart, each number must champion the other, be pleased with it just the way it is, and rejoice in the opportunity each day to spend time together, relying on the others for qualities and abilities that it alone does not have.

The problem lies with the major differences between them. The thing is, what I have described to you is an active 9. But in your life, 9 is excluded from the company of others. The two 5 parts of you, both Playgirl, are too busy partying and having a good time to pay any attention to the 9 part, Do Gooder, which never gets a word in edgewise. Playgirl dominates every conversation with topics that are of no interest to Do Gooder. Meanwhile, Bookworm—7—would like to spend time with Do Gooder, but cannot. Playgirl always ties up all of Bookworm's time with projects and activities. So, Do Gooder sits idly by, hour after hour, year after year, twiddling her thumbs while Playgirl schemes and makes deals with the able assistance of Bookworm. We will deal with 9's isolation shortly.

Now, let's talk about how to add your 5 and 7. The challenge is the same as Playgirl and Bookworm trying to find common ground for friendship. *What* common ground? Yet, if each looks beyond the confines of her usual attitudes and expectations, and if they both have the willingness to accept the other without the customary judgments and criticisms; if, in other words, each opens up to whatever the other has to offer, they can do it! It does take two to tango, but here both numbers share the same goal and have the same purpose. *That* is their common ground. The differences between people or numbers are *perceived* differences that take on a whole new light when there is friendship. In the same vein, people or numbers can share every imaginable compatibility and yet be inveterate enemies. Friendship exists when there is a mutual desire to be friends. It is all in what you want.

It might help you a lot in this effort to think long and hard about what friendship is, even though I am sure you already have some pretty solid ideas on the subject right now. Look up the definition in a good dictionary. Read what psychology books have to say about friendship. Read a couple of novels about people who were lifelong friends, and reflect on how they became friends, how they endured all the slings and arrows of outrageous fortune, and yet never lost sight of their deep, loving, committed bond with each other. Study friendship. Meditate on it. Try to glean new insight into the process and the attitudes that it takes to be friends. Come up with your own definition and write it down. Recite it throughout each day like a mantra. Practice being friendly and affectionate with the people around you, even people you don't like. It is all the same process.

Another exercise that will help you to add your numbers is to write a story about how Playgirl, Bookworm, and Do Gooder become best friends. Explain exactly what each one is like. Fill your story with specific details about where they live, what they do for work, their likes and dislikes, their hobbies, their attitudes about politics and religion, and so on. Put all three characters in a situation that favors the development of a solid relationship between them. Then take them tiny step by tiny step through the process by which they come to love each other. Make sure every part of the story rings true. Tell how they survive a horrendous test of their closeness. Show how their relationships are strained to the very limits and how they get through it. The ending of your tale could take place years later, when they reminisce about what their lifelong friendship has meant to them. Once you've completed the story, it's important to realize that this is *you,* and those three people and their relationships exist within you. When you have figured out in writing how *they* can be happy and successful together, you will know

Addition of 9 Heart's Desire, 5 Character, 5 Personality, and 7 Participation

Addition of 9
Heart's
Desire, 5
Character, 5
Personality,
and 7
Participation

how *you* can be happy and successful. Your solutions for their most difficult trials are solutions that will work for you in your life.

You may be wondering why you need to create a bond between your two 5s and your 7 in order for your 9 to be happy. The reason is that *that* is your big inner conflict. You are not going to be happy if the two most important parts of yourself are locked in a feud. Plus, the process of addition is all about learning to be open and receptive. You won't achieve the goal unless you learn it comprehensively within yourself.

At the same time that you are adding 5 and 7, you also need to be adding 5 and 9. Five is just as different from 9 as it is from 7. Nine is more of a problem for you, though, because your Heart's Desire is so much weaker than your Participation position. It is easy for you to ignore your 9, but the price of that is your happiness. Your challenge is to figure out what Playgirl, your 5, needs and admires in Do Gooder, your 9. It may be that Playgirl is never able to figure out Do Gooder, and concludes that all she can do is accept Do Gooder as she is. Perhaps Playgirl broadens her perspective and sees a value in Do Gooder. Or, it could be that Playgirl unexpectedly sees practical worth in Do Gooder's humanistic philosophy, generosity, and selfless service. There are no easy answers. Each person who takes on the challenge of adding her numbers has to find her own way. I can only make suggestions based on what has worked for me. You, on the other hand, must chisel away at the granite of your nature until at last you sculpt your life experience in your own terms, according to your vision and your understanding.

To complete the second step of addition, you need to add your 9 Heart's Desire and your 7 Participation. This is not as difficult as the other additions, because 9 and 7 have a basic natural rapport. Both are inclined to be philosophical and to seek the truth. Both are on a spiritual quest. Bookworm's search is inward, and Do Gooder's is with all of life. Bookworm is a thinker amassing knowledge, while Do Gooder is a spiritual worker. There is a lot of compatibility between these two. The main challenge is for them to become aware of each other. Your 9 Heart's Desire has been asleep for a long time, and unaware because it hasn't been a functioning part of your being. You are not used to valuing what you want. You just live your life. Your 7 Participation is also unaware of your 9 Heart because you are so accustomed to putting all your intellectual and analytical abilities to work for your 5 nature. All your thinking goes toward making a living and surviving. You never use your thinking to find ways to save the world.

Some people wonder how to know when the addition process has been successfully completed. You know, that's all. Suddenly it happens. You see that a transformation has occurred. A feeling of peace courses through you. You are the same person as always, and yet you're not. You've grown. You've achieved a deeper knowing of who you are. You love yourself more and better.

So, there you have it. That's what it takes to add all four of your numbers. It is also important to realize that there will be times when you find yourself subtracting instead of adding. It is inevitable. Adding and subtracting go together. They alternate in cycles, just as periods of weakness follow upon periods of strength. It's natural. We humans think that when we decide to take on a discipline, we have to be perfect in our efforts. But this is not the way of things. A growth process always has some setbacks and failures. Subtraction is opposite from addition. It means withdrawing or separating from others, or even taking a breather from the work of adding. My point is that you need to make both addition and subtraction part of the overall addition process.

Addition is union and subtraction is separation. As I said, it occurs if a person needs to be alone, if she is angry or upset with someone else, if she needs time off, if she disagrees and goes her own way, or if she's fed up with being strong and disciplined all the time. These kinds of feelings are normal. To try to root them out and be rid of them is unhealthy. It is easy to imagine how this might happen to Playgirl and Bookworm. Playgirl, who is all about being playful, outgoing, and fun-loving, sooner or later is going to need some time away from Bookworm, who is serious, pensive, and analytical. Similarly, Playgirl, who is individualistic, rebellious, and interested in personal prosperity, will definitely need occasional breaks from Do Gooder, who is philosophical, selfless, and devoted to giving service to others. Such moments of subtraction are not only natural, they are healing. Don't let them throw you.

By now, Wilma, I think you understand how to add your numbers and what it will take to do it. The question now is, *What will the result be of unifying*

Addition of 9 Heart's Desire, 5 Character, 5 Personality, and 7 Participation

Identification of subtraction

*Identification
of the sum
of addition*

these four numbers? Well, as I said earlier, 9 plus 5 plus 5 plus 7 equals 26, and that reduces to 8. But what does 8 mean for you? It tells how you live after the addition is complete. Since your purpose in adding is to learn to be happy, you will experience happiness by living in the 8 way. For you, 8 will be synonymous with happiness. This is because day in and day out you work hard to achieve this goal, and it is all in terms of happiness. Every time you face a difficulty, every time you are successful in staying open and receptive, it is all about your happiness goal. In other words, that is your frame of reference for the number 8. Happily, your 8 sum isn't restricted to fulfilling your Heart's Desire. Your payoff is much more than that. You will have devoted considerable time and energy to training yourself to be open and receptive. But you will be able to apply that knowledge to *anything* almost effortlessly. You will have grown tremendously. You will have become an *expert* in "open-and-receptive." It is now just a matter of using your hard-earned awareness in other areas of your life.

*Identification
of the
number 8*

So, having added your numbers, you are open, receptive, and happy, and you live in the 8 way. Eight has to do with being empowered. It is strong, ambitious, determined, competitive, and realistic, and devotes itself to the achievement of goals. People with a strong 8 accomplish what they set out to do. For an image of this number, you can think of the boss who takes charge of her business, manages it, and who is commanding, authoritative, decisive, productive, efficient, and very, very serious. Eight handles what needs to be done. This is why is it known as the number of karma. When a karmic situation comes into a person's life, she takes care of it. As you can tell, 8 is mainly known as a number of work, power, and achievement. It is also generally considered to be a challenging number when it comes to relationships and to being open and receptive. I still think 8 is marvelous for you to have as the total of your four numbers. This is because you will have spent a great deal of time shaping 8 according to your needs, making you a *master* of openness and receptivity. So, once you are successful in handling your life in an 8 manner, you will be extremely strong and capable at the skill of being open and receptive. Nothing will have the power to throw you off track.

Eight is also a number your 5, 7, and 9 get along with well. In other words, it is a natural transition for you to go from each of these numbers to 8. Five and 8 make powerful partners. Five is freedom and 8 is the executive. An executive who is free to do what she needs to do is stronger for it. Seven and 8 is another good combination. Seven is knowledge and 8 is power, and that is an unbeatable combination for the achievement-oriented 8. Nine and 8 also go together well. Eight is the powerful executive and 9 is the humanitarian. An executive who puts all her ability to achieve for the good of all is a successful human being indeed! This is why I say that your 5, 7, and 9 will all take naturally to the 8 outcome.

Comparison of 8 with 5, 7, and 9

So, you will be happy with your 8 total, probably for the first time in your life. You will find that you are much more confident, much stronger, and much more capable. Having put all that work and effort into your own personal growth, you will awaken to the realization that you can accomplish anything you set your mind to. And as time goes by, your 8 will become a habit and a normal part of your life. When you have the occasional relapse. I think you will be strong in taking charge of the momentary mood and managing it. No problem. As you live your life in this capable manner, as you do what you have to do, as you accomplish your goals and meet your challenges day by day, you will find that you are pleased with the way your life is going. You will feel happy.

Identification of the 8 sum

As you can see, Wilma, this addition process is a full-time job that could keep you busy for quite a while, maybe even years. Now, I'd like to discuss your two other big challenges: relationships and your conflict between 5 and 7. When I first suggested upgrading your relationship skills, I thought that would require a separate mathematical procedure. I see now that if you add your four numbers as we discussed, it will also change everything concerning relationships. What it all amounts to is this: the addition of your numbers means the establishment of friendly relations between the different parts of yourself. The same thing will automatically be happening with the people around you. This one act of addition will transform your life in many, many ways. You are accustomed to being alone in the world without much support from others, without companionship or close friendships. But now, I think you will find people opening up to you, seeking out your company, and wanting to get to know you. I think your new popularity will catch you by surprise. You will be wondering, *Why is Joe or Mary coming on to me like this?*

Summary of (1) relationship challenge, and (2) conflict between 5 and 7

At first, receiving all this attention from others will take some getting used to. Pretty soon, I think you will begin to enjoy it.

Comparison of addition and multiplication

The last point I have to make in your reading is about that 5/7 conflict. During our discussion of addition, I did talk about adding 5 and 7. That will help, but it won't be enough to solve the problem. You will need to multiply these numbers to get satisfactory results. Don't get me wrong—addition is wonderful and will bring astonishing benefits to your life, but this conflict is, I think, very deep, and addition is not the right approach to resolve it. Addition has no driving goal. It isn't striving for anything. It isn't prepared to overcome any obstacles or to struggle and endure for the attainment of a highly-valued purpose. Addition wants to be friendly and get along, or it bows out with a good, solid subtraction! And even though you will make tremendous strides toward resolving your 5/7 conflict with addition, that is not an adequate solution. The goal of it is simply to be open and receptive to whatever comes your way. You go with the flow. And if something unacceptable comes along that you can't be open and receptive to, then you just subtract your way out of it. You withdraw. You close yourself off. You remove yourself, end involvement, and then you work as hard as you can all the while to stay positive in your thinking. That's why addition is termed "passive." You are basically interrelating with circumstances in praiseworthy ways, but not being proactive, as they say.

Identification of multiplication

You need the purpose and determination of multiplication to solve the 5/7 dilemma. The difference between addition and multiplication is that addition is a passive process and multiplication is active. With multiplication, you set a firm goal and you persevere until you reach that goal. You do not let any feelings, thoughts, or disruptions stand in your way. You endure until you tame the adversity. You stay the course of multiplication until you can function at that higher level in any situation. This is why multiplication and its opposite, division, are considered active processes.

Multiplication of 5 Character and 7 Participation

The key to multiplication, like all the mathematical procedures, is intent. You need to be clear on what you are trying to accomplish with multiplication. So, what is your purpose? That is what you must decide. Well, we were talking about that before the reading. You said you would be happy if you could figure out how to function smoothly in a job without rebelling against the boss and all his rules one minute and then withdrawing into your own little world the next. That is your 5/7 conflict in a nutshell. It is a very diffi-cult cycle to go through. I think you do it not only on the job, but also in many kinds of situations and relationships, particularly when you feel trapped or frustrated.

When we discussed addition, I said its purpose is to learn to stay open and receptive in a warm and friendly way. I further said that if you succeeded, happiness would be the result for you. The purpose of this multiplication is more specific: to cause the raucous, prospering adventurer part of you and the intellectual, analytical expert part of you to join forces in good times and in bad while you work. Those parts are, of course, your 5 Character and your 7 Participation. Like addition, in multiplication both parts must accept and befriend each other. But in multiplication, this bond goes deeper. It is proven trust, for it has passed every test, overcome every challenge, limita-tion, frustration, and argument, and has survived a veritable trial by fire. This achievement has its basis on unwavering commitment. A goal was set and it was attained. In other words, through the desire and the determination to change, you learn a different way of living. You train yourself to think and feel in a new way. You become a different person. And you do it all according to the sure guidance provided by mathematical symbolism.

To accomplish multiplication, you need to accept and be at peace with the 5 person that you are and the 7 way you function in the world. Each number needs to work with the other in the spirit of friendly acceptance. Then the real work begins. Each number takes on the other as its teacher. Now, since the goal of this multiplication is effectiveness at work, that is what you must keep in mind at all times, even when you're not on the job, because what you are changing is years upon years of old habits, your whole attitude, and your basic approach to work. This is a big job. It means uprooting familiar feelings. It means reconsidering what you think are nor-mal reactions and reasonable conclusions. You'll catch yourself a thousand times doing things and thinking thoughts that had always been second nature before. Now you are learning a new way. So it's very important to have a clear understanding of what you're doing and what your goal is, oth-erwise you won't have the capability to distinguish between what is produc-tive and what is harmful to your effort.

Let's talk about what to expect from 5 and 7 on the job. Five is an excellent number for work because of its resourcefulness, its vitality, its selling and bartering skills, and its ability to profit from opportunity. Seven is also excellent at work. It contributes analysis, in-depth understanding, and mastery of skills. It is the thinker, and will work over a problem and study it until 7 grasps the key principles. Your difficulty with these two numbers is their different styles and approaches. Always keep your goal in mind: effectiveness in work. Any time you are at work, keep your mental and emotional eye on your goal to be sure your 5 is supporting your 7, and vice versa, and that the numbers do not get in each other's way. And that's all there is to it.

Let's take a look at how all this works in a specific situation. Remember, I make up the examples I use in your reading from what I know about your life so I can communicate all this to you most effectively. Let's say that you are going to be out for a day selling your company's product to a man who loves river rafting. And so, on the day of the sale, you find yourself standing on the chilly bank of a fast-moving river about half an hour before dawn. Your client is having tremendous fun. You can tell by all the laughter you hear in the blanketing darkness. You realize that in just a few minutes you'll be hurtling down the rapids with nothing between you and the swirling waters but the earnest hope that you don't tip the boat over and drown. All throughout that exciting day, you have the prospect of lots of physical exertion and excitement, and the occasional moment to mention the product. This day is so perfect for your 5 nature. The wild outdoors, the thrilling adventure, the test of your physical strength, and the novel circumstances in which to attempt to sell the product. This is all tailor-made for the 5. Who could ask for anything more than to do *this* for eight hours a day?

Meanwhile, the 7 part of you hates everything about this day. It is in full retreat. It's all so messy and happening so fast. There's no time to think, and anyway, how can you have a decent conversation while you're spending all your time and energy using that damn oar? A person could get hurt. Besides, once you've seen one hard crashing wave, you've seen them all. This sale would be so much easier in a lab where there would be a decent chance to make a scientific study of wave motion in relation to floating objects. It would be far more interesting to know the dynamics of water at this rate of flow there than *be in it!* No chance here to engage the thinking of this other person. He won't be able to hear a thing. He'll be spending all his time rowing the boat! How can you develop a clear line of thinking when the boat is jostling back and forth a thousand times a minute? You can't. So the 7 part of you says, "I am getting out of here. While that 5 is being reckless and irresponsible, I have a good opportunity to try to figure out the Wiggins principle[1] as it applies to plastics heated to very high temperatures. Let's see now . . ."

Here, your 5 and 7 have gone their separate ways, and you wind up divided against yourself. Only half of you is on the job in the boat. River-rafting is not an activity the 7 takes to very easily or cheerfully. The question is, *How can 7 partnership with 5 constructively in this endeavor?* It's easy to see Playgirl having fun river-rafting, but not Bookworm. How can we imagine Bookworm putting her heart and soul into a day like this on the river? Here is what you need to do to succeed in this: you have to understand 7 as a partner of 5. So now, I want you to take a mental and emotional step back in your mind and see if you can imagine 7 from a completely different angle. What if it had always enjoyed stories of adventures in the wild, especially on the water? What if it also had a serious interest in the wildlife of this region and would welcome the opportunity to see it firsthand? See what I am doing? I am finding ways to link 7 with a situation that, at first, seemed exclusively for 5. Suddenly, we start to visualize 7 having a motivation to participate in the situation. Of course, the basic reason for this trip in the first place is to make a sale. Your boss sent you because of your intelligence, your insight, and your expertise, all 7 qualities. Anybody can spend hours river-rafting down the rapids and laughing with the customer. But how many can do that *and* engage the thinking of the customer at the same time? That takes both 5 and 7. Let's now say that a hobby of yours—that is to say the 7 part of you—is psychology and understanding people. You enjoy that. And let's further say that you find yourself relishing the mental challenge of figuring this guy out. *What makes him tick,* you wonder? *He is a serious and sober CEO of a large accounting firm through the week and an adventurous thrill-seeker over the weekend. What's that all about?* So now the 7 is not only enjoying the trip, but also the traveling companion. Seven is surprised to discover that this man has intellectual curiosity, and, in addition to talking about the product, he enjoys classical music, certain art films, and a good philosophical debate. For a change of pace in the conversation, 7 uses the stream as a metaphor of spirit. By now the customer is quite intrigued with you. You have impressed him. You are a thinking sportswoman! He likes that. Seven and 5 are successful partners in this endeavor in ways that seemed out of the question only moments ago.

Now, even in this happening situation, it will likely happen that 7 gets tired of all the hubbub, commotion, and physical exertion and says to itself, "Okay, so when do I get to have *some alone time?*" All the fun and frivolity have proven to be too much, and 7 just wants some quiet time in which it can reflect and do some serious thinking. When serious problems come up in multiplication, it is of crucial importance to figure out how the number can get satisfaction in the situation. So, the question now is, *How can we make 7 function positively in this moment of crisis?* Well, let us say that you and the customer have been intensely discussing river-rafting *and* your product nonstop for twenty-five minutes. The conversation has been good, very creative, interesting, and productive. The customer has already tentatively agreed to purchase a sizeable order. Now 7 has had it. It desperately wants to withdraw into its own thoughts. But this may work out nonetheless. Even though the conversation is peaking, it is important to honor the needs of 7, too. After all, it has contributed greatly to the success of this outing thus far. It would not be productive or fair to force 7 to be a team player all the time. But what kind of quiet and reflection could the 7 find here? Well, 7 enjoys contemplating nature, and so, as a compromise, 7 could call a short break in the intense sales conversation by calling attention to an unusual bird of the region, then use the opportunity to gaze off for a time into the woods and at rock formations along the water's edge. Your customer, who by now likes and respects you quite well, takes the cue. A period of silent thought follows. As it turns out, the two of you spend the next thirty minutes taking it all in, each in the privacy of your own thoughts. And 7 is satisfied. It bent a little and it found everything was okay. Will wonders never cease?

It is of special importance to find practical techniques by which 5 and 7 are able to function well together. Every time there is a flare-up between them, the real multiplication process takes place, and the most progress is made. I created the ways in which 7 decided to participate in the day on the river. It is up to you to find your own solutions to the situations that arise in your life. Those are really the only ones that will work for you.

In the opposite work situation, 7 is called on to perform in its area of expertise and 5 is left out. Let's say a group of well-known scientists (and you are among them) convenes to develop fresh solutions for the Wiggins principle. This is a group of very erudite, educated, intellectually curious people whose ability to scrutinize detail is renowned. And this is just what they need to do for this project. They must analyze the research already completed and try to determine if there is some subtle flaw in the assumptions or reasoning on which current understanding is based. In order to be most effective, the group has sequestered itself for several months in a local hotel, where they have rented the entire floor.

This is an event tailor-made for 7. There is nothing it relishes more than a good intellectual mystery. Seven cannot wait to begin the serious deep thinking and pour over reams of fascinating data, tirelessly assessing and reassessing the facts in order to find the clue in the haystack. There is nothing like the joy of teaming up with like-minded coworkers on a project like this one. No interruptions, no superficial chitchat, nothing to interfere with the process of searching for the answer. Everyone involved has developed expert knowledge and perfected skills. They have all earned the right to be here, and 7 respects that. This is an exciting adventure, with all the drama and suspense a person could hope for. Meanwhile, for 5, the very thought of spending day after day with nerds regurgitating reams of boring figures is more than it can take. In its desperation, 5 concocts a thousand schemes for escape, some quite creative. In one, it dreams of hiring a helicopter to rescue it from the roof of the hotel at 3 A.M. while everyone else is asleep. But 5 knows these 7 types. There is every possibility they will be up all night while on their quest. Five will need a reason to go to the roof. It will not be sufficient to claim an all-consuming yearning for fresh air in the crisp breeze atop the building. What if one of 5's friends phoned anonymously to warn that there is concealed electronic surveillance equipment, and only 5 has the knowledge and the courage to find and dismantle it. Well, by this point, 5 has long since abandoned 7 and the entire group of dedicated scientists. The breakdown of 5 and 7 is complete.

Yet, if your multiplication process is to be successful, Wilma, you must find ways for 5 not only to fit in, but to join in and make a constructive contribution. How can 5 relate to this scientific work that seems to be so far removed from its nature? Once again, we must find a way for 5 energy to participate cooperatively on its own terms. One thing we know about 5 is that it loves a good adventure. Is there any aspect of this work project that 5 could view as an adventure? Well, I've already explained that the scientists are on an "intellectual" adventure. Would that satisfy 5? Not as such. Nonetheless, 5 is quite inventive, and I am sure it could figure out a way to join 7's intellectual adventure, if it made up its mind to do so. After all, this is the adventure of a lifetime for 7. So, 5 might reason to itself, *Look at how slowly, methodically, and dully these people are plodding along toward the answer they seek. I am known for my quick wit and resourceful thinking. It just might be fun to stir things up with a few in-your-face ideas that would keep these stick-in-the-muds stirred up for a week.* And so, 5 is off and running. It will play the devil's advocate of unconventional thinking. It will be funny. It will use its uncanny creativity to offer fresh perspectives and metaphors drawn from fields not ordinarily associated with science. Suddenly, 5 is no longer idle and bored. It has figured out a role to play here. It finds this stuffy group oddly fascinating *and* it is now the center of attention. No one else in this black-and-white group stands out in technicolor.

For a while 5 has fun, the time of its life. It is the star attraction, the showperson, laughing and strutting, and provoking them all to think in ways they would ordinarily never have considered. Five specializes in unusual insights and the innovative approaches. It sees lots of progress being made. The group is pumping. As wonderful as all this is, though, it is not 5's element. Sooner or later, it is inevitable that 5 will suddenly back off like a cat who realizes growling canines have it trapped, and springs away. Five wants out of there badly— out of the stuffiness, out of the incessant mind chatter, out of the dullness. Five screams like bloody murder, "For God's sake, *let's do something!*" and knows deep in its soul it cannot stand being with these people *one more second.*

Once again, you, Wilma, must make a choice here. If your multiplication is to proceed, you must decide how 5 will rejoin working with this group. It again boils down to this: what do you want? If you want the multiplication, which I think you do, then the 5 part of you must choose to go with the program. Rebellion, stirring up antagonisms, or fleeing the scene is destructive and self-defeating. In fact, what you have here is division. The negativity is tearing apart your 5 and 7, and reestablishes their conflict all over again. Here, division is destruction. It clearly delineates the differences between the two numbers and sets one against the other in a range war to the death. Short of suicide, neither 5 nor 7 will perish from existence, and so it is a true battle of attrition. Both numbers lose. That is a worst-case scenario in which you give up completely on multiplication and, in your despair, lose all hope. You abandon any attempt to better yourself.

Still, it must be said that in multiplication, division has its place. It can remove a block when no amount of positive thinking does the trick. Let's say, for example, that you are doing the best you can to multiply, but you are dismally stuck in a rut. Every time you start being successful, your 5 rebels and wants to break out of the multiplication, no matter what the cost. It doesn't care. Let's also say that the reason behind that is immaturity and willfulness. Try as you might, you are unable to break the cycle. In this situation, division is occurring, and it will destroy the cycle of obstinacy. If you are resolute in your determination to complete the multiplication, the division will work positively in your favor. It will likely be very painful and cause you to think intensely about this issue. For an illustration, let's say that in the midst of a satisfying moment of rebellion, your boss, whose respect means a great deal to you, comes up and says, "I'm so sick of your adolescent moods I could scream. You are off this project until you straighten up your act. Until then, you'll work with Charlotte on the Harper account. I know you don't like Charlotte and you hate account work, but that's all I've got for you right now." After such a turn of events, you are faced with a clear choice. What do you want? If you want to succeed in multiplication, this interlude of division will be brief and will help you make very rapid progress toward a decision. Demotion from your position causes immediate pain, despair, humiliation, and lots of self-doubt. It floods your brain with questions about your real motivations. You feel intense pressure not only to figure out why you rebel, but, more importantly, to change your ways. In this way, division can be an essential part of

*Division of
5 Character
by 7
Participation*

the multiplication process. It can break down a block quickly that otherwise would stall the multiplication indefinitely.

Therefore, once again, 5 takes a mighty deep breath and reassesses how it might contribute to this 7 endeavor. Five is clever and insightful into human nature. Looking around the assembled group, it realizes in an instant that everyone is feeling bogged down. How bizarre! Five recognizes that it isn't the only one! Suddenly 5 has purpose once again. It sees a role for itself that it likes. These people are suffocating in their own stuffiness. In a moment of inspiration, 5 cracks a silly, irrelevant joke that is just what everyone needs, and the group is energized once again. And so is 5.

*Identification
of
multiplication*

Multiplication is hard. It will take everything you've got. It will require time to accomplish because you are doing two difficult tasks. You are breaking life-long habits that are deeply ingrained in your nature. You are also developing a whole new way of working. I might add that once you attain this goal at work, the same learning can be applied to any area of your life, like relation-ships, for example. After all, work involves relationships with other people, too. Success in this will give you confidence and insight. It is simply a matter of refocusing and applying your knowledge in a different way.

*Identification
of the 8
result of
multiplication*

So, what exactly have you accomplished when you multiply 5 times 7? What you have gained is 35, which reduces to 8. This is a very nice result! Both 5 and 7 are compatible with 8. Five thrives in an 8 environment, pro-ducing a combination of high energy and productivity. Seven also prospers with 8, and the combination creates the power that comes from applied knowledge. So, both parts of you will prosper in the 8 result. Eight is the number of empowerment, and one of the two numbers that have to do mainly with work. A common metaphor of the 8 is the executive. She is tough, competitive, ambitious, decisive, determined to achieve goals, and highly productive. Eight accomplishes. Eight does what needs to be done. It is practical, grounded, realistic, and has excellent judgment. It is authoritative and commanding. Your 5 and 7 will like being winners under the steward-ship of 8. So, not only will you remove your debilitating 5/7 inner conflict, you will be considerably more capable on the work scene than you have ever been before. You will manage your business life and your career with strength and knowing. I feel confident you will advance in your company very rapidly. What's more, successful multiplication of 5 and 7 has singular qualities. Both are numbers of seeking and searching—5 on the outside in the world and 7 in the world of the inner self. When you make them work together, you have it all—all the seeking and searching there is. This is extremely dynamic. It produces a level of astonishing insight and ingenious creativity. You are a master of discovery and invention. It may take you years to accomplish your multiplication, but in the end you will be amazed at what you are able to do. You will discover capabilities you never knew you had. You will unlock a very high level of job performance. You have a lot to look forward to.

Identification of the 8 result of multiplication

Well, Wilma, that completes your numerology reading. You are a complex, capable, and lovable person with many wonderful qualities, plus your share of challenges, of course. I hope this reading has given you a lot of understanding and insight into who you are and why. I have suggested two mathematical techniques for improving your life, or, as we say in metaphysical circles, raising your consciousness. You have your work cut out for you on that score. I believe you will accomplish these two goals because you are motivated and determined to succeed. Good luck!

End of numerology reading

Endnote

1. This is not a real scientific principle. I created the name to illustrate my example.

chapter 10

The Meaning of Time

. . . Einstein's theory leads us to regard (time) as an aspect of the relationship between the universe and the observer.

—G. J. Whitrow, *The Nature of Time*

We live in an era when science has fundamentally changed our basic concept of time. With the advent of Einstein's theory of relativity, we now know that time passes at different rates of speed, depending on an object's velocity. At the speed of light, time slows to a standstill. It is now believed that before the Big Bang created the universe some fourteen billion years ago, there was no such thing as time. Neither it, nor matter, nor any of the laws of physics existed in that primordial soup. Space (that is, matter) and time are now thought to be two components of the same thing, termed "space-time." This means that if space is altered, time is altered as well. At the subatomic level, particles operate outside the "laws" of time. In physics, the *arrow of time* expresses the idea that time moves in one direction, from past to future. According to current theory, it is possible to reverse time to a limited degree, and, consequently, to travel into the past. Yet, for all the new scientific ideas about the nature of time, there is still no understanding of what it is.

Whatever its true nature, our present concept of time has been made possible largely due to our ability to keep track of time accurately. Early precursors to modern timekeeping methods include the sundial, in common use up to the fourteenth century and useful only during daylight hours. There were also water clocks, some of which were extremely complex but not terribly accurate. Their principle limitation was that, because water freezes in cold weather, they were useless in winter, and so sand clocks were invented for year-round capability. The earliest mechanical clocks were invented in Europe in the thirteenth century, initially for the purpose of ringing cathedral bells on a schedule. The idea of dividing an hour into sixty minutes and a minute into sixty seconds was first used around 1345 for the purpose of timing a lunar eclipse. At that time, clock faces were only divided into quarter hours and featured just the hour hand, until the seventeenth century. Modern, accurate timekeeping first became possible with Galileo's invention of the pendulum around 1650. Today, our ability to keep time accurately has been astoundingly enhanced by using certain reliable rhythms in nature, such as electromagnetic waves and the radio frequencies of particular atoms. Caesium clocks have an accuracy rate of two parts in ten million million, far more precise than the daily rotation of the earth!

All these developments have led to the present concept of time as being linear. This is the idea that time is an irreversible, mechanical progression toward the future. The relentless and rational march of time with which we are all familiar, where minutes and hours reliably turn into days, weeks, and years, then entire lifetimes, centuries, and millennia, is viewed as part of reality. The basic assumption on which linear time is based is the belief that certain events occur only one time; in particular, the life of Jesus.

> The influence of Christianity on our modern concept of time is not restricted to calendrical details. It was far more fundamental than that. Its central doctrine of the Crucifixion was regarded as unique in time, not subject to repetition, and so implied that time must be linear and not cyclic.[1]

The advent of the Man from Nazareth was definitely a distinctive event in history, but not singular. We will examine the validity of this belief shortly.

As universal as this concept of time is now, it has only become entrenched in our consciousness within the past three hundred years. Prior to the present era, the dominant view was that time consists of cycles that endlessly repeat. In the ancient world, only Hebrews and Zoroastrian Iranians thought that history progressed. The vast majority of past peoples and civilizations understood time as a kind of meaningful experience that evolved through repeating cycles. Certainly this was the case with the Mayans, for example, whose calendar consisted of various time periods— *Kin* (one day), *Vinal* (20 days), *Tun* (about one year), and so on. Each period of time was governed by a god, which imbued it with a certain character. The particular combination of gods present at any given time was interpreted for meaning, similar to major events (the trend of the stock market, an uprising, having a major test, beginning or ending a job, extreme weather, a marriage, and so on) that provide a compelling context within which we change and grow. However, for the Mayans and many other peoples, the sequence of combinations provided meaningful understanding that connected moment to moment, day to day, and year to year, giving each person a sense of continuity throughout his life. Time had *experiential meaning,* which extended beyond the simple passage of time. The difference for us today is that we do not see the events of our lives and the world as a function of time.

Throughout recorded history, mathematical symbolism and astrology have been other methods of reckoning the meaning of time's passing. In these and many other ways, past societies interpreted their days to have an evolving significance. Implicit in those approaches was the idea of *repeated experience.* Individuals found themselves retreading the paces of earlier experiences again and again as they progressed through their lives. They did not repeat situations detail for detail, but rather *types* of situations, whether relationship- or work-related, disease, danger, difficulty, fear, deprivation, and so forth. They knew the same kinds of circumstances would arise again and again. Each time an event was faced it was from a slightly different perspective. They brought all their learning, experience, and wisdom from previous situations to each challenge. They learned something new about themselves and how to handle that type of situation better. As cycle succeeded cycle, the situations were gradually handled more proficiently.

It is a true skill and art to know the meaning of cycles and how to apply that knowledge. At any moment of time, there are cycles upon cycles within cycles going on in our lives. They contain both the problems to be faced and the solutions to them as well. As we move through them, we must take action. In mathematical symbolism, such action takes the form of mathematical functions—addition, subtraction, and so on. Cycles are *mathematical events.* We will return to this point in chapter 11.

A cycle can be of any length of time during which an event or process occurs. In science there are cycles that occur in thousandths or millionths of a second, and others that span billions of years. Although these and many other cycles of extreme lengths of time are valid, they are not useful for the purposes of this book, whose primary focus is the span of human life, approximately one hundred years. Pythagorean numerology interprets days and months, but its most common cycle is the year. In mathematical symbolism, the full complement of cycles includes all the normal divisions of time that we use in our daily lives. This begins with the second, then the minute, then the hour, and so on up to the century and the millennium. Each one of these standard cycles is deeply imbued with meaning that determines to a great extent the characteristic nature of that cycle.

Before proceeding further with the discussion of cycles, let us examine the assumptions underlying linear time in order to determine, if possible, its validity. As previously stated, the outstanding argument for linear time is the notion that certain events happen only one time. Therefore, it is reasoned that time cannot consist of cycles because no subsequent cycle will ever repeat the event. In western civilization, the leading example of a nonrepeatable event is the life and death of Jesus. Was it, as Christians believe, an event that has no parallel or likeness and can never be repeated? It is my contention that it was not. In fact, modern research has demonstrated that it was a rather commonplace life in most respects. For example, his immaculate conception is considered by many to be a unique occurrence. Historical records show, however, that in early times there were many such virgin births among those considered to be saviors.

> The notion that mortal women were impregnated by gods or spirits was a matter of everyday acceptance throughout the ancient world.
>
> Zoroaster, Sargon, Perseus, Jason, Miletus, Asclepius, and dozens of others were god-begotten and virgin-born. Even Zeus, the Heavenly Father who begot many other "virgin-born" heroes, was himself called Zeus Marnas, "Virgin-born Zeus."[2]

There is even a present-day instance of virgin birth. Sai Baba, the great Hindu avatar now living in Puttaparthi in southern India, is thought to have been conceived by God. His mother, Easwarama, is said to have stated, "That morning I went to the well and when I was taking the water out, a great ball of light came rolling toward me. In this way, I became pregnant."[3]

Research also clearly demonstrates that no feature of Jesus' life or accomplishments is unique and unrepeatable. Mithra, for one example, whose religion successfully competed with Christianity during its first four hundred years, exercised the same kinds of powers and abilities as Jesus. "Mithra performed the usual assortment of miracles: raising the dead, healing the sick, making the blind see and the lame walk, casting out devils."[4] Neither was Jesus the only high religious figure to be crucified.

> Uninformed Christians, and that means most of them, believe that only their Savior suffered death on a cross, whereas some sixteen of them died just this way. . . . Jesus—Nazareth / Krishna—India / Sakia—India / Iva—Nepal / Indra—Tibet / Mithra—Persia / Tammuz—Babylonia / Criti—Chaldea / Attis—Phrygia / Baili—Orissa / Thules—Egypt / Orontes—Egypt / Witoba of the—Telingonese / Odin—Scandinavia / Hesus—the Druids / Quetzalcoatl—Mexico.[5]

These historical facts firmly establish that, although Jesus led a distinctive life, it was in no way truly unique and one of a kind. It could equally be shown through a similar analysis there exists no event that is truly singular in history. If any seemingly singular event or person were properly examined, it would soon become clear to an objective observer that there is a number of other instances of that same type that together constitute a class of such things. As the timeworn adage goes, "There is nothing new under the sun."

We have determined, albeit briefly, that linear time cannot be justified on the basis of there being unrepeatable events in history. In actuality, every thing in the world—past, present, and future—has unique properties or characteristics that may never again be precisely duplicated. No two snowflakes are, or have ever been, the same. No two people are, or have ever been, the same. Thus, the basis for believing linear time to be the *real* measure of time is shown to be invalid, or at least not exclusive.

It might be asked, *Why go to all this effort to argue against linear time? After all, it has served the needs of our modern world quite well.* The alternative method of timekeeping, cyclic time, was largely abandoned centuries ago. Why even consider returning to a concept of time now viewed as primitive and unscientific? The answer is that cyclic time is more meaningful than linear time. It is attuned to the natural rhythms of life. It enhances the quest to attain wisdom and understanding in this life. It complements spiritual life.

There are three concepts that underlie the notion of cycles of time. The first concept is that of *patterns*. Although every person, event, and object is unique in at least some respects, there are always basic elements that group things together. The perception of the connecting links establishes the pattern. Consider "tables" as an example. Tables come in thousands upon thousands of different sizes, shapes, heights, materials, paints, colors, decorations, uses, ages, conditions, and design styles. There are miniature tables for dollhouses, small tables for children, and tables made for stage sets. There are utilitarian tables, antiques, tables for show, enormous tables for large groups, broken-down tables, and many, many more types of tables. The linear approach to the wide diversity of tables is to say that there is no overall class called tables. Consequently, each one must be taken separately on its own merits. The perspective of cyclic time is that certain elements common to all tables enable us to create an overall class of such objects. That is the pattern. Within that pattern are unending varieties, but those variations do not negate the fact of the general classification.

In terms of events of time, any event can be linked to other events of its class by perceiving the elements common to them. An example of such a class of events is verbal communication. The different types of oral communication are many and varied, including: conversations, talks, seminars, teaching, explaining, debates, monologues, interviews, military orders, incoherent rambling, arguments, giving directions, motivational speeches, sales pitches, discussions, lies, diplomatic negotiations, bartering, bargaining, preaching, reading poetry to groups, theater performances, laughter and crying, giving instructions, lodging complaints, and so on and so forth. The concept of linear time views all these as separate and unrelated events. It says that every event stands on its own as complete, with no special rapport or connection to other events. The concept of cyclic time views these diverse events as related.

This notion is of key importance to understand the validity and relevance of cycles of time. It is very instructive and meaningful to know the relationships of things. Then, the commonality shared by our example, communication events, can be determined. Consider the following four separate events: conversation, argument, negotiation, then another conversation. Each is meaningful on its own terms (linear time), but much more so if they can be linked (cyclic time). We can imagine, for instance, two people having a **conversation.** Then an **argument** erupts from their discussion, and, in the interest of their friendship, they work to **negotiate** an understanding of their differences. Afterward, they are able to resume their **conversation.** In this manner, four "separate events" are meaningfully linked together as a cycle.

Taken as a group, these four events constitute a very common cycle in human affairs. Throughout life, every person who has a friend will sooner or later have his friendship disrupted by discord that is subsequently resolved, reinstating friendly relations. This is one example of a cycle common to all people everywhere. In cyclic time, it is a given that people go through a cycle like this not just once, but repeatedly throughout their lives—as children, then as teenagers, later as adults, and even late in life. With repetition comes learning. Most of us "do better" as we advance in age. Implicit in cycles, therefore, is the idea of evolution.

The idea of *evolving through time* is the second concept of cyclic time. This is quite different from material progress and advances in technology, which are so dominant in our society today. It is our consciousness that really evolves as we go from cycle to cycle. It is all part of a continuum. Cycles endow purpose and direction toward which to proceed. We go through a great many cycles of every imaginable type in the course of our lives. Some are long, some short. Some are routine, and others test us deeply. As cycles repeat over and over, we progress in our lives. Cycles are the mechanism by which we advance spiritually.

The third concept basic to the understanding of cycles of time is *scale*. As cycles repeat again and again over time, the outward form of events evolves. Even though the essential character remains the same, the scale changes, making it difficult, sometimes nearly impossible, to see all the connections. We have already discussed one cycle of **conversation-argument-negotiation-conversation.** If a communication event is expanded from an hour to, say, a year or a decade, what begins as personal conversation will invariably become something quite different over a long period of time. Its scale will change everything. Let us examine this more closely. Most conversations last some portion of an hour, sometimes as long as two or three. Few conversations have a duration of minutes. Extremely few continue for most or all of a full day. Consequently, the normal cycle length of a *personal conversation* is **one hour.** Now, we need to ask ourselves what form a "personal conversation" might take in the shortest cycle of one second. In order to figure this out, what we need to determine is the initial impulse, which, if nurtured, leads to having a conversation. I would say that at the base of it is the simple *yearning to commune.* That urge is felt in a heartbeat. The event is complete in about **one second,** the very shortest cycle of time, or maybe two or three seconds at the very longest. The next cycle up is **one minute.** At this level, the basic impulse progresses to *initiating a conversation*—speaking, in other words. Now, let's see what form "personal conversation" develops into as it progresses to longer and longer cycles of time. Since conversations almost never last more than a few hours, there will be some change in form when the "personal conversation" persists for a full day. If friendly talk goes on and on, what emerges is *establishing rapport,* the cycle of **one day.** If this kind of communication between two people continues for a full week, the harmony they achieved the first day will develop into something more, the affinity between people we call *companionship,* the cycle of **one week.** Amiable companionship, if continued week after week, becomes *friendship* after **one month.** Admittedly, it is arbitrary to assign friendship to a period of one month as a general rule. I do not suggest any definitive link between cycles and the meanings I assign to them. What I do seek to establish is a reasonable sequence of development to demonstrate the dramatic effect of differences of scale in a succession of forms.

Through the inevitable ups and downs of a relationship, communication inevitably improves and deepens, month by month. Consequently, over a **one year** period, prolonged friendship results in the acquisition of *communication skills.* As these communication skills are honed and refined over the length of **one decade,** they further distill into *principles of communication.* They are no longer simply personal techniques an individual uses. They have become a formal method of communication employed by many.

Notice how far from that "personal conversation" we have come as we advanced from the one-hour cycle to the one-decade cycle! As the cycle of a decade expands to a century-long cycle, there is plenty of time for "principles of communication" to be absorbed into society and to influence the way language is used and people interrelate. So, after **one century,** the progressed form is *modes of communication,* which could be a new form of communication, such as that which developed after the telephone came into common use. Or, they could be a new type of thinking. Consider how common the concepts of psychology have become in daily social intercourse as compared with one hundred years ago when there were very few well-known terms and those were regarded with suspicion. Today, people from all walks of life are routinely familiar with such terms as "low self-esteem," "repressed feelings," "dream symbolism," and so on. As century follows upon century, "modes of communication" develop into elements of language (grammar, vocabulary, syntax, style, and so on) until, over the course of **one millennium,** those elements become a *new language.* The story of Latin is a remarkable illustration of this. Its degeneration into other languages did indeed take place over a period close to nine hundred years! This was the language of Imperial Rome, and it was exported to the many places in Europe the Romans conquered, from present-day Spain to Germany and Great Britain. Latin was the official language of all the different regions of the empire until the fall of Rome in 476 C.E. Previous native languages were suppressed and eventually became extinct. Local variations of Latin developed and emerged, called Vulgar Latin. Differences became quite pronounced as the centuries passed, resulting in dozens of related but dissimilar dialects. From Vulgar Latin eventually emerged the Romance languages, of which the main ones are French, Spanish, Italian, Portuguese, Provençal (a once dominant language of Southern France that became extinct around 1900), Romanian, and Romansch (a language of Switzerland). There was at one time great controversy among the peoples of Europe as to whether their local dialect was Latin or in fact their own language. Eventually, the new languages were finally declared. In about 1300, for example, when the King of Paris conquered surrounding rivals, his dialect became the common tongue of the region, and was subsequently known as French. So, in a period close to a millennium, Latin degenerated into the languages we have in Europe today.

In summary, the cycles of communication we have been discussing are as follows:

One second: yearning to commune

One minute: initiating a conversation

One hour: personal conversation

One day: establishing rapport

One week: companionship

One month: friendship

One year: communication skills

One decade: principles of communication

One century: modes of communication

One millennium: new language

In the previous discussion, I have put together a realistic sequence of cyclic evolvements. They are based on likely outcomes of events that, nurtured over periods of repeated cycles, mature into more complex forms. The form of any cycle springs from the previous one and prepares the way for the more lengthy cycle that follows. There is no single correct answer or course of development in what I have discussed. In fact, there are many possible variations of the aforementioned communication cycles. The key to the validity of a progression of cycles is a continuity that connects them all.

It is important to recognize that cyclic events of different scales, like those discussed previously, are all essentially the same event spelled out in greater or lesser detail. They *appear* to be different, even unrelated, because the form they assume at different cycle lengths cannot be the same. What represents a completed cycle at one second cannot possibly persist unchanged over a decade or a century.

The question now becomes: on what basis are cycles of different length the same thing? In other words, how can a "personal conversation" (one hour), "friendship" (one month), "communication skills" (one year), and "modes of communication" (one century) all be different versions of the same thing? The outward appearances belie the equivalence that underlies and connects all the cycle-events, regardless of their scale. This principle can be explained metaphorically by different fractions that have the same value. There is no proportional difference between the following fractions: $\frac{1}{2}$, $\frac{5}{10}$, $\frac{500}{1000}$, and $\frac{5,000}{10,000}$; $\frac{1}{2}$ may be viewed as "tiny" and $\frac{5,000}{10,000}$ "very large." But no single fraction expresses the truth of this proportion better than another. The "constant proportion" of cycle-events is their *essential nature*. The differing size of equivalent fractions expresses the degree of elaboration of detail. When sufficient detail is added or subtracted from the form of a cycle, an entirely different picture seems to emerge.

A deep study of mathematical symbolism teaches one to perceive patterns. Perception of patterns relies on the ability to recognize the relationships shared by certain elements. Mathematical symbolism is a symbol system consisting exclusively of relationships. Therefore, to master mathematical symbolism is to master relationships. Its numbers are the elements of life. As one works with this symbol system, one comes to discover the fundamental patterns of life called *archetypes of patterns.*

Mathematical symbolism also teaches the *way of evolution.* The sequence of developments represented by the numbers 0 through 9 is among the most fundamental of evolutionary patterns. It is the cycle of cycles that delineates a progression of consciousness. If one can but grasp the subtle essence as it moves through its numerical paces, one can assess one's own cycles and know what is being fomented in what we call "the future." Zero through 9 is the complete, elemental cycle. Larger numbers also represent cycles, such as two-digit numbers (10 through 99), three-digit numbers (100 through 999), and so on. When we go beyond one-digit numbers, we are no longer dealing with the basic elements, but rather combinations of elements. This is why the Pythagoreans in ancient Greece said that after the final single-digit number—9 in modern numeration—one returns to the first number and begins all over again. Ten reduces to 1, 11 to 2, and so on, ad infinitum. Ten begins a different class of numbers, and a different quality of cycle. There is merit in the Pythagorean view as well as in leaving numbers unreduced, as we shall see in the final chapter.

Mathematical symbolism also helps to recognize an event's essence as it changes form at different scales. As we struggle to know the numbers, the mathematical principles that govern their use and their applications to life, we delve more and more deeply into their essence—what they really are. In this manner, an ability to focus on the evolving essence strengthens, while the outer form proves to be less and less distracting.

A major benefit of knowing all of this—pattern, evolution, and scale—through mathematical symbolism is that it is highly organized. The chart on the following two pages illustrates a sample progression of number-cycles from one second to one millennium. The purpose of these examples is to demonstrate a complete sequence of cycles for each number. The event presented for each number is one of an unlimited number that could have been used, just as the evolutionary course of each number could have assumed an endless number of other directions.

	Second	Minute	Hour	Day	Week
0	Conceive a concept	Imagination	Imagination	Imagination	Imagination
1	Experience newness	Contemplate new action	Develop new ideas	Take a personal stance	Make a new start
2	React	Feel emotions	Form attitudes	Make interpretations	Interrelate with others
3	Respond	Have personal thought	Express oneself	Synthesize differing thoughts	Be creative
4	Need to be grounded in reality	Be purposeful	Organize	Perform work	Persevere in duty and responsibility
5	Be curious	Be adventurous	Be free to act	Wheel and deal	Explore and experiment with life
6	Care about others	Listen	Be involved	Give a helping hand	Take responsible social action
7	Wonder	Reflect	Think	Focus attention	Study and research
8	Be determined	Be strong	Persevere	Be decisive	Set goals
9	Be connected with all	See commonality in everything	Give and share	Volunteer	Make self-sacrifice

	Month	Year	Decade	Century	Millennium
0	Imagination	Imagination	Imagination	Imagination	Imagination
1	Make initiatives	Set up progressive programs	Develop new trends in society	Create new elements of society	Establish structure of civilization
2	Form relationships	Formulate concepts of relationships	Establish social policy	Develop social mores	Establish structure of civilization
3	Develop art and social skills	Produce art	Develop cultural movements	Make cultural achievements	Establish social and cultural identity of civilization
4	Build foundation in life	Earn a stable living	Maintain prosperous economy	Establish strong infrastructure	Build enduring institutions
5	Maximize opportunities	Prosper	Make unique achievements	Cause revolutionary developments in society	Inspire civilization with tradition of epic heroes
6	Make social initiatives	Establish social programs	Legislate social politics	Make social reforms	Form values of civilization
7	Analyze	Develop concepts	Develop theories	Make scientific achievements	Create universal world view
8	Compete	Be empowered	Achieve in business and government	Dominate economically and militarily	Be dominant civilization
9	Do good works	Develop humanitarian philosophy	Establish idealistic and humanitarian programs	Develop humanitarian and utopian movements	Establish spiritual traditions of civilization

Today, it is difficult to imagine time being measured cyclically. What would the cycles be? What would they mean to our daily lives? How would they fit in with our present system of timekeeping?

Yet cycles lurk everywhere on the periphery of our consciousness. They cease-lessly intimate meaning into the mechanical beat of linear time. Hints are all around us, once we know where to seek them. The **seasons of the year** are one of the most evident cycles. They are sometimes called the cycle of life. Spring is uni-versally experienced as rebirth and renewal. Summer brings everything to full blos-som, which then withers and fades in autumn, and finally perishes in the desolation of winter. Many people respond to the spirit of the season.

A **second** is our briefest cycle, too short in which to reason anything through. This is a subconscious cycle because the dynamics at play reach completion in less time than it takes to breathe. It is a period of impulse, of instinct, of intuition, and of spontaneous reaction. We speak of split-second timing, which is exceedingly pre-cise. Its successor, the **minute**, is perhaps the first "conscious" cycle during which there is sufficient time to reflect. "Give me a minute to think," we say. It is also a cycle of quick choice and decisiveness. In terms of schedules and timing, we are pre-cisely on time if we arrive within the minute. When time is of the essence, we are relieved to say, "It happened not a *minute* too soon!" If a deadline of any kind is min-utes away, there is virtually no room for hesitation or mistakes.

The **hour** is the shortest cycle that constitutes a "chunk of time." It is inextricably linked to the day-cycle in that it pinpoints either A.M. or P.M., morning, noon, or night. The character of an hour is also largely determined by its position in a day; 3 A.M. is "the dead of night"; 6 A.M. is that very early hour near dawn; 8 or 9 A.M. is when the workday generally begins; noon is synonymous with the "lunch hour"; 4 P.M. is the "happy hour"; 5 P.M. signifies the end of the workday and the middle of rush hour traffic; 7 P.M. is prime time for television viewing. When bedtime for chil-dren is set, it is usually at a certain hour. Midnight to 2 or 3 A.M. are the "wee hours of the morning." The phrase "now is the hour" indicates the arrival of the moment when an important decision must be made. Still, the latitude allowed by an hour gives the individual the dignity of having sufficient time to reach his own conclu-sion. The hour is the workhorse cycle. It is also the cycle we use to plan out our day. Appointments and meetings are set according to one hour or another, as well as schedules, making itineraries, and the duration of short trips. We say, "Oklahoma

City is two hours from Tulsa." An event is often considered too lengthy if it goes on for "hours and hours," just as it can be too brief if it lasts "less than an hour." Many jobs are paid by the hour.

Now consider a **day** and the kind of cycle it is. "The day" is where we live: eating, sleeping, working, dealing with situations, and doing all the activities that make our daily life what it is. It is the longest cycle that is "all in the present." Something that is due to happen eight or ten hours later in the day still falls within "now," when "now" is expanded to its fullest size. Powerful images are associated with the day. It has two parts, daytime and nighttime, which symbolize positive and negative, conscious and unconscious, and good and evil to our symbol-hungry minds. Images of the sun rising and setting have many applications for the beginning or ending of important events or historic periods of time. The phrase "a day in the life" describes what most typifies a person's normal, everyday existence. We go beyond the call of duty if we "arise before dawn" or "burn the midnight oil." Common wisdom has it that we are doing well if we begin the day early: "The early bird gets the worm." The old adage, "Early to bed, early to rise makes a man healthy, wealthy, and wise," is a commonsense approach to each day. Within that period of time, we are quite late if the "eleventh hour" arrives without completion of a task. The phrase "day by day" or "day in and day out" indicates persistence and strength.

The **week** has a distinct image and prominent role in our lives, and it is something of a specialized cycle. We identify no other period so much with the grind and drudgery of earning a living, and so it is commonly known as the *work*week. It is perhaps more aptly described as a cycle of pleasure and pain. Monday through Friday is the painful part for most of us. It begins with the "Monday blues." On Wednesday, we pass through "hump day," and then we finish gleefully on Friday with T.G.I.F.—"Thank God It's Friday." The weekend is the pleasure part when the "weekly routine" is finished. Friday and Saturday nights are for having fun, going out, partying—letting loose, in other words. Saturday is often reserved for doing household chores, indulging in hobbies, going to a sports game, or visiting friends. Sunday can either be spent like a Saturday or it can be considered "the day of rest." Unlike the soothing rhythm of "day in and day out," the lengthier "week after week" points to bearing a heavy burden.

The **month** is a nature cycle, the period in which the moon completes its phases and a woman's menstrual cycle runs its course. The statement "It's that time of the month" pinpoints the difficult nadir of this cycle. Each month is strongly linked to a season. January is synonymous with winter, just as August is with summer. We speak of March winds, April showers, June brides, and so forth. The phrase "a month of Sundays" expresses the curious, indeterminate nature of the month cycle. It is a period of natural rhythms, gestation, and magic.

The **year** is a full and productive period that contains the entire cycle of the four seasons. This defines the year as a time of maturing. The year is the only cycle in which we honor events and people of national significance: Labor Day; New Year's Day; Valentine's Day; the birthdays of Lincoln, Washington, and Martin Luther King; religious observances like summer and winter solstice, Christmas, Hanukkah, and so forth. Personal birthdays and anniversaries are also celebrated on a yearly basis. Many other events typify the rhythm of the year, like the nine-month school year followed by the three-month summer vacation. There are yearly taxes in April, as well as the large exodus of travelers during the summer months, at Thanksgiving, and at Christmas. The year is the cycle with which we most identify, and the one to which all the others refer. In physics, whose scale is frequently gargantuan, we speak of "light *years*" to measure the distance to stars and galaxies. It is difficult to measure our age by any count other than by the year. We wouldn't describe a thirty-seven-year-old woman as being 444 months, 1,924 weeks, or 13,514 days old (including nine days from the leap years), nor would we say she was 3.7 decades or a little more than a third of a century old. "A year in the life" of a person or place makes a significant statement about his or its nature.

The cycle of a **decade** encompasses a phase in our lives. We expect to make a major transition in our lives over the course of ten years. We finally graduate from school, advance in our careers, marry and settle down, and so on. We are children for about ten years, teenagers for nearly another ten years. Each decade thereafter is very descriptive of a phase in life, and what to expect from it. In our third decade, the twenties, we enjoy the freedom of having left home, trying everything, and becoming adults. In our thirties, we settle down, raise families, and take on adult responsibilities. And that decade brings what might be considered the end of youth.

A **century** marks the span of a lifetime. For an individual, it goes from the first moments following birth to the infirmity of old age. It is "the fullness of our days." A century is longer than the lives of most people, and so it includes everything. In history, one hundred years encompasses tremendous change. The last century, the

1900s, saw astounding scientific and technological development, the exploration of space, several world wars, a whole new kind of art, the end of Europe as a dominant world power, and so on and so forth. A century is a monument of history; a decade is a monument of our personal history. We speak of the past most easily in terms of centuries. In Europe, the Renaissance followed the Dark Ages. Both periods were eras in the scale of centuries, along with the Crusades, the Inquisition, the Industrial revolution, Modern Art, and the advent of science. A **millennium** so far surpasses the life span of human beings that it is difficult to relate to on a personal level. This is a cycle of nations and civilizations. In this cycle we speak of the rise and fall of Rome, the emergence of major world religions, the development of mathematics, and the legacy of civilizations like Greece, Egypt, and Sumeria.

In mathematics today, there are ten cycles, the first of which is 0. For those wondering what a "0 cycle" is, it is the initial cycle. When we count from 0 to 10, for example, 0 through 1 is the "0" cycle, 1 through 2 is the "1" cycle, and so on, making 9 through 10 the "9" cycle and the completion of the series. In the second millennium, 1000 through 1999, the first century lasted from 1000 through 1099, and is considered the "0 century." Every year of the 0 century begins with 0. The "1 century," so named because every year of that century begins with 1, included the years 1100 through the end of 1199. While on this subject, we need to address the question of "endings of cycles." At the turn of the third millennium, popular opinion was that the day of change was December 31, 1999, at midnight, and January 1, 2000 was the beginning of the new millennium. Many said the "technically correct" ending of the thousand-year period was one year later, December 31, 2001. The confusion was due to assigning the number 1, instead of 0, to the year of Jesus' birth.[6] In 525, when our B.C.E.–C.E. system of dating the years was conceived, 0 did not exist in mathematics. Consequently, the number 1 was used to mark Jesus' birth year instead of one year later, as we do today. Therefore, the millennium has always

$$0 \ldots 1 \ldots 2 \ldots 3 \ldots 4 \ldots 5 \ldots 6 \ldots 7 \ldots 8 \ldots 9 \ldots 10$$
$$\#0 \quad \#1 \quad \#2 \quad \#3 \quad \#4 \quad \#5 \quad \#6 \quad \#7 \quad \#8 \quad \#9$$

Figure 16. The complete cycle of 10 begins with 0 and ends with 9.

been technically a year "short," and therefore required an "extra year" in order to complete the full 1,000 years. For mathematical symbolism, there was never any question. The beginning of the third millennium came when the year no longer began with 1, but rather with 2 (see Figure 16).

It is of utmost importance that mathematical symbolism be valid not only as an elegant theory, but also in its practical application. The numbers 0 through 9 of any cycle should roughly correspond to the sequential process of evolution that occurs during that time. The numbers of these time periods have deep symbolic meanings that depict the cycles of our lives. But, can it be shown that actual historical events of a particular cycle actually reflect the number of that cycle? I believe so.

In order to demonstrate this, I propose to analyze the centuries of the last millennium as they transpired in Europe from the year 1000 through 1999. This is a humbling and overwhelming enterprise. A period of a thousand years is very long and exceedingly complex, composed of thousands of cycles within cycles that produce endless patterns and permutations. Lengthy volumes have been devoted to individual lives and significant events, not to mention entire periods and large regions. What I present here in these few pages can do no more than highlight the most fundamental of themes. Nevertheless, it will prove to be sufficient for our purposes. Europe offers the pure conditions of a social laboratory in which to examine the unfoldment of a civilization according to the principles inherent in the numbers of the centuries.

In order to accomplish this task within the context of the present work, I will limit the scope of the inquiry in several ways. First, I will examine history as it evolved in central Europe. This includes Spain and Portugal to the southwest; Italy to the southeast; Austria and Switzerland to the east; Germany to the northeast; Belgium, Denmark, and the Netherlands to the north; Great Britain to the northwest; France to the west; plus several additional tiny countries. These countries of Europe collectively constitute a complete civilization. In addition, I also select Europe because it is the home of our system of dating the years from the calculated birth date of Jesus Christ.

The second limitation to our discussion is to examine history in the broadest terms possible. Only in that way can we hope to discern the evolutionary structure from the bewildering profusion of considerations. I will attempt to show a clear pattern of historical development by the numbers, wrought by the march of centuries. I do not claim this to be a scientific analysis, nor do I claim to prove my thesis. Historical interpretation is at best subjective. What I do seek to present is a plausible case for the correlation of historical events with the numbers of the centuries in which they occurred, and to demonstrate a clear progression of those events through the course of the second millennium.

As I mentioned earlier, our present system of dating the years is of relatively recent vintage. At the time of the birth of Jesus Christ, Europe was in the year 753 A.U.C. (*ab urb condita,* meaning "from the founding of the city," that city being Rome). Later, around 1258 A.U.C., a Roman monk by the name of Dionysius Exeguus was given the task of calculating the correct date of Easter. As a devout Christian, he rejected the idea of honoring Rome more than the life of Jesus, so he came up with the idea of using the birth of Jesus for year number 1. That idea was hatched in the year 525 C.E. Acceptance of the new dating system came slowly. It was only in the eleventh century—the 1000s—that it gained universal use and acceptance in Europe.

The eleventh century is when my interpretation begins. An analysis of the past millennium 1000 through 1999—is bound to be the most authentic in Europe because Europe is its "natural home." This dating system did not even reach the Americas until 1492, when Columbus discovered America. While this system is now universally recognized all over the world, many others have been used. Some continue to this day. At the time of writing this chapter, the Jewish people are in year 5762 and the Chinese are in year 4699, for two examples. The Christian dating system is simply the most dominant and widespread among many.

Before beginning the century-by-century analysis, something needs to be said about the 1 millennium of which they are part. This number began every year from 1000 through 1999, and therefore established the overall character of that era. This means that everything that occurred during the ten centuries must be understood as fomenting the development of the 1 character of the millennium in some form or fashion, with the ten unfolding centuries as ten sequential phases of its evolution. In this manner, the essential character of European civilization was established. In summary: Europe matured over the past thousand years from a fractured society still in the grip of the Dark Ages. Nation states did not yet exist and small kingdoms often fought barbarously. Everyone and everything was firmly under the control of the Roman Catholic Church, which subjected the continent to the Crusades (eleventh century through the thirteenth century) and the interminable and infamous Inquisition (beginning in the thirteenth century and ending finally in Spain in 1834). By the middle of the millennium, nation states had formed whose strong, independent identities persist to this day. Nearly continuous warfare prevailed throughout the entire millennium, culminating in two catastrophic world wars, the first of which ended Europe's position as a world power. During the final fifty years of the millennium, Europe was essentially at peace, and beginning to form an economic and political union.

Does this brief sketch exemplify what we would expect from ten centuries of a 1 millennium? The number 1 is a Force that generally manifests as "independence," "taking the initiative," "development of ego," and "strong belief in the self," to name several of its most prominent characteristics. Kingdoms of the year 1000 were centered on privileged individuals who required "fealty to lord and master" from the common people. That has evolved to the present-day equality of citizens whose loyalties are directed largely to their democratic nation states. At the beginning of the period, everyone was subservient to the Roman Catholic Church in their thinking and living. Today, few individuals are still so dominated by the Catholic Church. Rather, the great majority of people and nations have a strong belief in themselves (that is, their egos). The number 1 also indicates "assertiveness," or "aggression" in the negative polarity. The past thousand years have certainly witnessed endless aggression. On the positive side, individuals today are more prone than ever to assert and claim their rights. Finally, the number 1 indicates "inventiveness" and "new beginnings." The past thousand years saw an astonishing new beginning in the Renaissance, in the advent of science, in the decline of religious political power, in the emergence of democratic governments, and in the state of peacefulness that now pervades Europe.

This is my assessment of the millennium just passed in Europe. The region as a whole does appear to have progressed as would be expected in a 1 millennium. Now we will examine the developments of that period century by century. The goal is to determine whether there occurred a step-by-step, sequential evolution during the course of the 1 millennium, one that reflects the number of each century. If this is so, each century will be shown to contribute its part in the evolutionary process, each one birthing events according to the nature of its Force and preparing the way for the subsequent century.

0 Century: 1000–1099

The beginning of this millennium saw invasions and continuous fighting all throughout Europe. Considerable civil discord ensued, and social structure began to shift and crumble. Political power previously known fell apart, and small kingdoms, duchies, and warlords sprang up. A society of classes became more prevalent than ever; the lowest levels were unbearable and led to short life spans. For much of the population, becoming a serf or slave was a step up. The Roman Catholic Church became the unquestioned absolute authority, and was the moving force behind the choosing of kings based on the Christian Old Testament model. Pope Urban II dedicated himself to the notion of the Crusades and to bringing all of Europe to act on this passionate idea.

These conditions, events, and trends correspond to what is likely to transpire in a 0 century. The civilization-self is as yet unformed. It is a time of uncertainty, insecurity, and chaos; a time when the "certainties" of the past appeared to be dissolving and falling apart, opening the way for the new. What developed in this 0 century formed the subtle seed structure of what was to come, although the implications of it were not yet apparent in the fabric of daily life. All this was the case in Europe. Society existed in a loose, fluid, undefined vacuum primed to be reconceived, redefined, and understood in new, unexpected, and different ways.

1 Century: 1100–1199

Political infighting and collapse of the old order forced society into disarray. The Catholic Church became the only governing power. The Holy Roman Empire submitted completely to the Church. The Crusades seesawed for a while, then gained momentum to take back the Holy Land from the Arabs.

This century bore out the influence of the number 1. One is a Force that takes the lead, by aggression if necessary. It is independent, headstrong, courageous, and often rash. Add to this the masculine nature of 1, the number of ego, generally intolerant of cooperation and compromise. This is what happened in Europe. The Roman Catholic Church took the lead by aggressively dominating all opposition and sending many off to war.

2 Century: 1200–1299

France, England, and Spain began slowly and painfully to pull out of the Dark Ages, becoming modern states. The collection and organization of information evolved into royal institutions. The Catholic hierarchy was a harsh taskmaster and demanded to be obeyed, often with cruel efficiency. The Inquisition was founded and began punishing heretics, defined as anyone who might have an opinion that differs from the Church. Far too often, the Inquisition simply went after a person whose property was desirable to the Church. This is the same time period that the very rich and powerful Catholic Church launched a Crusade against the Holy Roman Empire.

These events are representative of the 2 Force. While most of Europe flowed with the spirit of the 1200s, the Church failed to adjust. The dominance that had worked so well for it in the 1 century was out of sync in the 2 century. Two fosters advances in communication, agreements, compromise, cooperation, success in diplomacy, pacts, and treaties, all of which were necessary for nations to form. The priorities of 2 undermined the Church's forceful, uncompromising leadership in this century. In the absence of effective diplomacy and relationship-building efforts, Church relations with the Holy Roman Empire broke down, and a Crusade against the Empire was the result. Two handles details and information capably, thus favoring the rise of royal institutions. Church leadership (or domination) of the peoples of Europe was replaced by the threat of punishment by the Inquisition. Despite the brutality of the trials, this was a weak strategy. It reflected the weakness and indecisiveness of 2, as well as muddled leadership, ineffective use of power, back stabbing, and being bogged down in squabbling and details. Instead of leading Catholic adherents toward the approved way of living, the Church reacted against those who were perceived as a threat.

3 Century: 1300–1399

Running governments was reserved for the nobility, and institutions were used for idea input only. Disorder prevailed, but the Renaissance began in 1304. The Roman Catholic Church lost its power to tax. A split developed between the French and Italian popes in the later part of the century. Rome won, but a contentious division lingered, and thereafter the Church was forced to share power with secular monarchies. This century also saw the beginning of the Hundred Years' War between England and France.

This was truly a 3 century. The essence of the 3 Force is to create a concept of self, whether of an individual or a civilization. It is also the number of self-expression, synthesis, and articulation of ideas. This was all succinctly represented by the achievement of the organization of political life. In the same vein, Europe found its voice in the Renaissance. Thus, in politics, society, and culture, the identity of the European self emerged in the 3 century. For the Church, expression of opinion became opinionated self-expression, which resulted in the Church being divided against itself. Where religious authority had once reigned unquestioned, secular monarchies had significantly replaced many church functions. As we contemplate all these developments, we need to keep in mind that this century was a stage in the evolution of the 1 millennium. The essential character of the millennium was a secular one, and so the Church lost significant power and influence as Europe came to a conclusion about who and what it was. The powerful 1 drive was for the development of ego, self assertion, independence, and leadership. In this context, the 3 century produced bellicose, opinionated, pompous, and prideful attitudes and actions, as well as callous, faultfinding, jealous, and unforgiving ones. This offers some insight into how it was that England and France fought each other for a full century! Similarly, the pervasive disorder of that time gave expression to such 3 characteristics as being scattered, vacillating, irresponsible, and lacking direction.

4 Century: 1400–1499

The aura of the Middle Ages wafted well into the 1400s, yet the Renaissance wound up revolutionizing all aspects of life in this century. Political life became more organized and Humanism developed. Attitudes became more accepting of human nature, and uplifting of dignity and values. History saw Gutenberg invent the printing press, the heroine Joan of Arc lead French armies to triumph, and the genius of Michelangelo and Leonardo da Vinci explode in Italy. In 1492, the Moors were ousted from Spain and America was discovered by Columbus.

This was a true 4 century that set the basic character of the 1 millennium. The 4 Force establishes and follows through on purpose. In the 1400s, that purpose grounded and manifested the self-concept of the 3 century. This resulted in the flowering of the Renaissance. This phenomenal awakening of European society flourished, and Humanism, the philosophy that expressed the hopes and ideals of the time, took hold. Four is the number of building foundation. Today, the Renaissance still serves as the model of the past millennium, when society was at its best. We refer to someone who is cultured, educated, has broad interests, and brings a spirit of inventiveness to his life as a Renaissance person. Leonardo da Vinci set the standard for that ideal. As much as any invention, the printing press made the 1 millennium what it was. Joan of Arc, the capable and inspired military commander who freed France from English control, is today France's national hero. As European civilization gave its vision reality in the physical world, it rid itself of the principal foreign influence (the Moors) and began to look beyond its borders (Columbus).

The astonishing freedom, change, and opportunity of the 4 century would seem to fly in the face of all that characterizes the 4 Force. At first glance, the Renaissance century has all the earmarks of 5, while 4 is conventionally considered the number of stability, structure, order, and resistance to change. The confusion arises from the failure to recognize two very different phases of freedom. Five is the number of the *exercise* of freedom, while 4 is the number of the *achievement* of freedom. Four attains freedom by adhering single-mindedly to its purpose: doing what it must do. Once the focus of purpose is attained, all the rest of 4 follows: the discipline, the hard work, the building of foundation for what is to follow, the creating of structure and order. In retrospect, it is clear that the character of the entire remainder of the 1 millennium was set in the 1400s. Much of what is best in Europe today—democracy, human rights, the importance of individuals, art and culture, individual initiative, and creativity—had its origin in the Humanistic philosophy and the Renaissance of which it was part.

5 Century: 1500–1599

Nationalism was on the rise. Strong kings and strong governments were the norm. The Protestant movement started the Reformation with Martin Luther's protest in 1517. This ended the domination by the Roman Catholic Church. The unity of Christianity was at an end, and modern history began. Calvinism demanded the separation of church and state, while Lutheranism chose the God-given powers of secular rulers. The slave trade began in 1509. Copernicus is credited with starting the scientific revolution in 1543. It was the age of explorers with the likes of Cortés, Magellan, Pizarro, and Columbus sailing around the world.

Five is the Force of exercising individuality, which is well characterized by its two bywords: freedom and opportunity. It is also the number that most loves dealing with the physical world, and is, therefore, the most secular of the numbers. In the 1500s, European civilization flexed its muscles. It glorified kings. Governments reflected the personalities of their rulers, which were often rash, rebellious, egotistical, and self-aggrandizing. Nationalism, which might be defined as "collective individuality," flourished and threw off the shackles of Roman Catholic domination. The bottom-line of 5 is individuation by proving oneself in the crucible of the world. Exemplifying this, European thought broke free of Church doctrine with the advent of the Scientific Revolution. At the very heart of 5 is the drive to prosper, to wheel and deal, to maximize opportunities, to experiment and to take risks, to explore the world, and to seek out new and different possibilities. This is all aptly represented in the burgeoning commercial enterprise and worldwide escapades of this century. On the negative side of 5—opportunism—the slave trade profited unconscionably from human lives. The 1500s definitely reflected the 5 Force!

6 Century: 1600–1699

History records this as the century of the absolute monarch. The previous 5 century was expressed in raucous and freewheeling ways, while the 6 century found balance, and coalitions formed to check the power of aggressive nations. Colonies were set up around the world. A large secular middle class developed, and the Roman Catholic Church and the Holy Roman Empire lost all political authority after the mid-1600s. In 1633, Galileo was the last recognized scientist to undergo an Inquisition trial. Throughout the century, progress was shown through the founding of the first public company, the first public advertising, laws abolishing torture in England, the establishment of newspapers, and improved nationalized postal service operations.

The 6 Force is about determining values and living by them. It is the number of commitment to others, taking responsibility, meeting others' needs, being involved in other peoples' lives, and it focuses on concerns of community life. The primary emerging value in the 1 millennium was secular. In the 6 century, absolute monarchs and nation states came to hold all the power that had once been the domain of the Roman Catholic Church. The scientific approach to reality came to be accepted. The emergence of allied coalitions and the abolishment of torture, two developments virtually unimaginable in previous centuries, strikingly exemplified 6 energy. This century also developed "institutions of the community" like newspapers and postal service. Whereas exploration and conquest were typical of the 5 century (and characteristic of the number 5), conquered lands were settled as colonies in the 6 century (very representative of the number 6).

This century was clearly shaped by the 6 Force. Subservience to dogmatic church authority and unformed political governance early in the millennium had evolved to strong, ego-centered monarchies. The purpose of the 1 millennium was established in the 4 century, combined with the exuberant experimentation of the 5 century, and then consolidated in the 6 century. Governments took care of the business of managing themselves and others.

7 Century: 1700–1799

The 7 of this century triggered the higher intellectual vibration, which was expressed through philosophy, idealism, utopian ideas, and the scientific method. The belief in human reason gave birth to a new Age of Enlightenment and brought about changes in the areas of religion, politics, education, and science. It was recognized that science was beneficial to society as a whole, not just to agriculture and industry. Up to this point in European life, the wealthy elite and nobility had private armies, but henceforth we see the state develop and own armies. The merchant class was the driving force for political change. The disenfranchised demanded to be recognized and treated fairly, and their lot improved. The French revolution is a demonstration of the growing idea of democracy, and represents one of the great upheavals of modern times.

The 7 Force seeks to know truth. Consequently, it is a number of thinking, analysis, understanding, research, and development of theories and concepts. These characteristics certainly were evident in the Enlightenment and the expansion of science. It required a great deal of knowledge and expertise, both characteristic of 7, for the Industrial Revolution to get started. The same qualities were necessary in order to "consciously build" the nation states. Whereas in the 6 century centralized power of the state came into its own, in the next century the very concept of governing was deepened and expanded. On the level of individual people, the same course of thinking empowered and emboldened people with unprecedented self-assertion to lay their claim on political power. This kind of inner development epitomized the 7 century. The trend culminated in the French revolution. Knowledge is power.

All these developments came about as part of the 1 millennium, which provided the overall context within which each of the centuries evolved. That general theme was the *development of the essential nature of European civilization*. With 1, there is always a robust sense of self and belief in self—a strong, independent ego, in other words. This goal was largely reached in the maturity of the 7 century when the violent French Revolution took place. The common people of France destroyed the power of the king and the nobility. The value and rights of individuals, no matter what their station in life, took the ascendancy. Think of it: in the span of 7 centuries, ordinary people progressed from total subjugation by the Roman Catholic Church and feudal lords, to subjugation by the state, and finally to the beginnings of democracy! This was a true 7 century.

8 Century: 1800–1899

The Industrial Age is a perfect 8. While the seeds of the Industrial Revolution had begun to sprout in the 1700s, the flowers and fruit were produced in the 1800s. There was an explosion of construction, manufacturing, and material expansion of all types, earnest and realistic. Inventions and scientific discoveries improved life for everyone. Governments began to play an important role in economic regulation. Populations became more urban as people streamed into the cities for work in factories and large companies. Freedom, democracy, free press, the brotherhood of all peoples, and the notion of voting rights spread throughout Europe.

Revolution and rights of the working class were on everyone's mind. Liberal groups demanded an open-minded government, and religious institutions, controlled by nobility and the wealthy classes, opposed such liberal open-mindedness. The result was the separation of church and state.

The working class was struggling for freedom and trying to rise from poverty. The nobility and the merchant and industrial classes, aided by religious institutions, kept the lower strata of society in pitiful societal and economic conditions. The Communist Manifesto was published in 1848. Socialist groups sprang up, teaching socialism as the only route to a just and fair society. Realism replaced romanticism. Late in the century, the Victorian Era emerged. It had a reputation for severe and strict morality on the surface, yet underneath the facade of primness and propriety there were alternative religions and philosophies emerging.

The 8 Force is all about power and achievement. It accomplishes its goals. This is clearly evident in the triumph of the Industrial Revolution as well as in the profusion of scientific developments and products of the 1800s. It was during this time that the upgrading of material life was achieved through industrialization. How fitting that an aggressive, empowered man like Napoleon was so highly regarded throughout Europe. Eight is "all business." Its drive is to compete and to achieve pragmatic goals. It is thus truly expressive of 8 that in this century, society reorganized itself along economic lines, producing large commercial enterprises plus the workforce necessary to operate them. Eight can be a demanding and domineering number, which manifested in this century in the many harsh and abusive labor conditions of that era. The serious, ambitious, usually humorless 8 had little tolerance for the fanciful, idealistic Romantic Movement. It was replaced by a far more sober, practical search for certainty, definitely an 8 kind of choice. Finally, 8 works hard to bring about justice. It is a managing energy that takes charge of situations, makes key decisions, assigns responsibility, and so on. One area of management was one that had been too audacious even to consider earlier in the millennium—the separation of church and state. This course of action demonstrated the degree to which governments had become empowered. Also, when broad social ills could no longer be ignored, governments of that century felt it was their role to resolve those kinds of situations. The reaction of the time to social inequality and economic deprivation was to develop utopian ideals and communities. This century manifested the 8 Force to an amazing degree!

9 Century: 1900–1999

The beginning of this century saw World War I, a horrific struggle that ended the Renaissance vision of hope, bright possibilities, and the continuity of culture. Attitudes of world dominance and economic superiority declined in Europe. Common working-class people continued to be the driving political force, and democracy came into its own. World coalitions to promote peace were born, first with the League of Nations in 1939, then with the United Nations in 1945, both following worldwide conflagrations. In 1958 the European Economic Community was formed along with the European Common Market, and toward the end of the century the United States of Europe. The development of public welfare assistance following World War II, the refining of the science of psychology, women's rights, civil rights, protection of the environment, the Olympic Games, and international financial and trade agreements brought the world closer together in a New World Order.

After World War II, the wealth and worldwide predominance that Europe held for centuries went into decay. The tide went against colonial powers.

Democracy came into fashion. The common people were a political force, and Europe assumed both centralized government and totalitarian regimes. With the League of Nations and the United Nations, an era of peaceful coexistence began. In 1958, Europe came together as a community. First, there was the European Economic Community, then the Common Market, which resulted in the elimination of borders, the adoption of the Euro, and joint economic ventures. The welfare state began after World War II. The science of psychology became widely understood and accepted. Europe participated in a number of international movements like the Olympic Games, protection of the environment, women's' rights, and the International Monetary Fund.

This was a true 9 century. The positive drive of the 9 Force is to be one with all of life. Thus, it is the number of humanitarianism, compassion, tolerance, building on links of commonality, and living on the basis of a universal philosophy. Nine transcends the self-interest of ego in favor of the common good of all. These attributes are strikingly reflected in much of what happened in this century: the political power of common people; the prevalence of democracies; participation in worldwide movements; establishment of a European union; emergence of the welfare state; international cooperation; the growth of psychology.

To the extent that egotism obstructs 9 energy, its Force is diminished. If it is sufficiently blocked, then 9 is known as the number of "pain and loss." This is exactly what happened to Europe in the 1900s. The universal potential of the Renaissance was shut down by the negative elements of European society that had been part of European life from the very beginning of the millennium. In typical 9 fashion, the consequence of Europe's Big Ego was the two world wars that cost it everything.

The first half of the twentieth century can therefore be summed up as pain and loss. As a direct result of these two self-inflicted catastrophes, European civilization learned a spiritual lesson: to renounce its destructive ways and henceforth to pursue humanitarian ideals. This was a positive and unexpected outcome for the Europeans. They could well have continued on a belligerent course in the aftermath of World War II. Instead, these people learned their lesson—a very important lesson, and one they had resisted many, many times before.

These conclusions are mirrored in the Encyclopedia Britannica's essay on the history of Europe:

> In such a state of affairs (the chaos, the uncertainty, the lack of hope and of direction of the 20th century), only one supposition may be possible: European man has thrived for half a millennium on the principles of individualism and has exhausted all its possibilities. A new type of man, actuated by a different principle, is required to cope with the conditions created by his predecessor. If he arises, a new culture—art, science, philosophy, social and moral relations, and political state—will follow.[7]

This new type of man did emerge in Europe. The promise of the 1 millennium was fulfilled.

Endnotes

1. G. J. Whitrow, *The Nature of Time* (New York: Holt, Rinehart and Winston, 1972), 14.

2. Barbara G. Walker, *The Woman's Encyclopedia of Myth and Secrets* (San Francisco: Harper and Row Publishers, 1983), 1049.

3. Marcelo Berenstein, *Sai Baba for Beginners* (New York: Writers and Readers Publishing, Inc., 1998), 20.

4. Walker, *The Woman's Encyclopedia of Myth and Secrets*, 663.

5. Lloyd M. Graham, *Deceptions and Myths of the Bible* (New York: Bell Publishing Company, 1979), 352.

6. Modern-day scholars have subsequently determined that the actual year of his birth was in 749 A.U.C. (*ab urb condita*)—4 B.C.E.

7. Robert P. Givin, Chairman, Board of Directors, *The New Encyclopedia Britannica* (Chicago: Encyclopedia Britannica, 1990), vol. 18, 725.

chapter 11

Through the Eye of the Needle

. . . Initiation . . . is simply condensed evolution . . .

—Dion Fortune, *The Cosmic Doctrine*

We think of the minutes and hours of our day as concrete chunks of time. Our lives are timed and scheduled by the clock and the passing of the days and years from the second we're born to the second we die. Nothing we do changes the automatic cadence of the march of time, or so it seems. So, it is all well and good, you may say, to speak philosophically of time as "units of meaning," but in the end, sixty seconds must tick by before a minute has elapsed, and a full sixty minutes must pass before it can be said that an hour has gone by.

But this is not the reality of time. Time is elastic. It ceaselessly slows or quickens. It can be compressed by conscious intent.

It is difficult to conceive of time apart from events whose durations it measures. They are fundamentally linked together in a symbiotic relationship. Our association of things that happen and the amount of time they require to reach completion is highly standardized in today's world. We have strong, even rigid, ideas about how long most events last. Deviations from the norm catch our attention. They impress us as being out of the ordinary, strange, or even impossible. A meal in a restaurant, for example, generally lasts thirty minutes to an hour. If it were reported that a group of people consumed their entire meal in six or seven seconds, we would seriously question whether we had heard correctly. It is not possible, we think, to eat dinner that fast. If someone spent one second brushing his teeth, we would logically conclude he had not had enough time to grab hold of the toothbrush. There are, of course, endless examples from every area of life that would make the same point. All the events of our days are tagged with an "expected time of duration." Those are approximations, of course. Few things begin and end in the same number of seconds. Beyond those general parameters, however, we find it confusing or confounding if the length of time varies too greatly from what we reasonably expect.

This is obvious. It is factual. Nonetheless, I assert that these commonplace expectations with regard to an unalterable standard of time are an illusion. Further, as I will demonstrate shortly, it is quite possible to complete a task or a process in a fraction of the time now believed possible. This is the concept of *time compression*. I contend that the link we perceive between an event and a particular duration of time is a deeply held convention that is arbitrary. I further suggest this is a self-imposed limitation of our imagination and that, once we are free of this unyielding standard, it will be found there is no automatic correlation whatsoever between an event and the amount of time required to complete it.

One of the most fascinating instances of naturally-occurring time compression is the so-called "life-review" that occurs as part of the near-death experience. In a flash, the individual's entire life passes before his mind's eye in complete detail. Scenes going back to the first moments of childhood are reexperienced in full color, in complete detail, followed by every other moment of the individual's life, from beginning to end! In that instant of time, the entire life is relived. One man who had the experience of a life-review during a failed parachute jump said, "It's like a picture runs in front of your eyes, like from the time you can remember up to the time, you know, what was happening . . . in the matter of a second or two."[1] In his book, *Life at Death, a Scientific Investigation of the Near-Death Experience,* the author concludes, "What stands out in these accounts is the tremendous rate at which these images seem to be processed—experienced as millions of 'frames' within seconds. Even allowing for exaggeration, such rates utterly confound one's sense of time."[2]

How long would it take to make a full review of one's life under normal circumstances? Well, it takes a full lifetime to live it through the first time. To touch once again on every experience, every thought, and every feeling of every day of all our years would surely require at least a year, probably more. It defies understanding how such a life-review could be done in one to two seconds!

Amazing instances of time compression are also found among people who have Savant Syndrome. These are individuals whose IQ is generally between 40 and 70, and who often suffer from other disabilities like blindness and cerebral palsy. Despite their limitations, they have astounding abilities that enable them to accomplish tasks in periods of time that seem impossibly brief.

> George and his identical twin brother, Charles, are simply astounding. They are calendar calculators. Give them a date and they can give you the day of the week over a span of 80,000 years . . .[3]

Others have exceptional mathematical abilities and are called "lightning calculators."

> . . . Fleury determined the cube root of 465,484, 375 (which is 775) in 13 seconds.[4]

Another common skill area is that of musical ability.

> Leslie has never had any formal musical training. Yet upon hearing Tchaikovsky's Piano Concerto No. 1 on the piano for the first time in his teen years, he played it back flawlessly and without hesitation.[5]

These individuals are able to perform feats in a fraction of the time normally thought possible. Science may someday explain the basis of Savant Syndrome. That is irrelevant to my point, however. It does not matter *why* they are able to act so fast. My purpose is to demonstrate that our fixed association of an event with a certain duration of time is not inevitable or reality. Rather, it is our *idea* of how long an event or a process requires to reach completion that is rigid.

Everyone experiences time compression or time expansion in his own life, when time seems to drag by ever so slowly or to rush by with inexplicable quickness. When we are seriously bored or awaiting a crucial decision, time passes with excruciating lethargy. Likewise, times of euphoria or ecstasy go by so fast they are, as they say, "over before they begin." Agonizingly slow periods are epitomized by the adage, "A watched pot never boils." Other instances of slow-time include waiting for test results or waiting to find out the status of a loved one after a dangerous surgery, having a dull and laborious task to finish, having to read or study an exceedingly dull book, or waiting in line for a long period. In each of these instances there is some degree of helplessness, fear, or vulnerability that causes time to drag end-lessly. The opposite is the case when we feel empowered, joyous, or just plain happy. Examples of fast-moving experiences include watching a breathtaking dramatic per-formance or musical, reading a wonderfully engrossing book, going through an uplifting wedding ceremony, working on a favorite hobby, being in a state of reverie during a long drive, being extremely *busy* all day long, or having an intimate conver-sation with a lover. We often say of slow-moving experiences, "I never thought the time would pass." And of the latter group we might comment, "I simply lost track of the time" or "I just don't know where the time went."

Time compression is reminiscent of *peak experiences,* a term coined by famed psychologist Abraham Maslow. During a peak experience our whole being comes together in upwelling feelings of joy and fulfillment. They are ". . . moments of great awe, happiness, or rapture, during which the individual loses all his self-con-sciousness and becomes one with the world. Some individuals report that during peak experiences they have penetrating insight into the mystery of life."[6] Such per-ceptions are significant and under ordinary circumstances require long periods of gestation. Here, they occur in an instant. It appears that in these kinds of sublime moments we develop ideas in a flash that generally take far longer, perhaps years or even decades.

Some people respond to these phenomena as distortions of an individual's think-ing caused by his state of mind. Many ignore these facts, believing that mental, emotional, or physical factors make time *appear* to quicken or slow, or to enable people to perform certain feats with astonishing rapidity. But is it possible that time itself is altered, and not simply our sense of time? I believe it is.

Our sense of time is universally perceived to speed up as we age. As a child, time "lasts longer." Do you not recall rising early any Saturday morning with the whole day ahead, and evening so far away in the future it never came to mind? Fifty years later, Saturday has shrunk to a few scraggly hours, barely enough time to finish a chore or two before nightfall. Children play on and on and adults wonder, *Where did the time go?* I believe the explanation for these differences is that there is no single standard of time governing both young and old. In youth time is expanded, while in maturity it is compressed.

Another form of such "time distortion" is what I call *spontaneous time compres-sion.* This is the sudden, inexplicable completion of an event that ordinarily takes considerably longer. We have all heard of the spontaneous remission of disease that sidestepped a prolonged period of healing or deterioration. Many a tobacco smoker has quit the habit painlessly and without a second thought rather than struggle for a long time to give up the addiction. Puberty causes astonishing physical, mental, and emotional changes in children "overnight." Among the most stunning instances of time-compression are those of spiritual enlightenment. Spiritual and religious awakenings sometimes occur in the blink of an eye, conferring on the astonished individual a degree of understanding and insight that normally requires decades of devoted study, thought, effort, and discipline. This happened to Mohammed, prophet and founder of the religion of Islam. Around the age of forty, he had an "awakening" experience in which he learned an entire realm of knowledge and spent many years thereafter writing it down in the Koran. Unexpected life-transforming experiences also occur in the mundane world as well. I personally know of a man who lived with deep anger against his mother for over three decades. During those years, he had often tried to resolve his rage. He spent time in therapy, and participated in self-help groups. He read books about honoring his inner child, and on how to release anger. Nothing touched his pain and loathing. One day, during a fifteen-minute conversation with his wife about his mother, he experienced complete forgiveness. His anger totally disappeared. For the first time since early childhood he viewed his mother affectionately and with love. There may well be scientific or psychological explanations for these kinds of extremely fast accomplishments. Whether valid or not, they do not change my point. I maintain there is no definitive connection between an event and the amount of time necessary for its completion.

The above instances of time compression are striking examples of the human disconnection with clock-time. The case could equally be made for time-expansion experiences. These are happenings that last far longer than ordinary. While I was writing this chapter, I talked to a young woman who had been a boxer some years earlier. When I told her about my ideas of time expansion, she related an experience every boxer has. When a punch is thrown that is going to land squarely, the boxer sees it coming *in very slow motion*. To the boxer the blow is significantly delayed in its delivery, yet for an observer it is over in a split second! Whose pace of time is correct, the boxer's or the observer's? People categorized as mentally retarded think and act very slowly relative to the norm. It is a proven fact that they learn as well as anyone else, but at a slower rate and more superficially. It may well be that what people of average intelligence learn or accomplish in an hour is expanded to a day or a week, or more, for the slow-witted. Is it not possible their life experience is lived in slow motion? At the other extreme, it may also be that the geniuses of the human race are individuals who live subjectively at a far greater speed of time than that of the norm. It is quite possible that highly gifted people who create civilization-changing art, science, or culture achieve in a short time what so-called normal people might accomplish fifty or a hundred years later. It is often said of geniuses that they are "ahead of their time."

We do not live, then, on the plodding loom of time. To the contrary, it appears that time is an exceedingly elastic substance. It further appears that our state of being causes time to shrink and grow erratically. We are not aware of these fluctuations because everything in our lives happens at the tempo to which we are accustomed. But then, it is not time per se that goes faster or slower. It is events that are compacted or expanded, and that therefore finish in a shorter or longer span of time than we expect. Think about it. The validity of clock-time is based on the existence of regular rhythms in nature, like day and night. We humans assigned a time-value to those basic natural events and, from then, to everything else that goes on. Thereafter, I think, time took on a life of its own in our minds, as though it were an objective standard to which our lives, and events, conform. Consider what would happen to our sense of time if the earth were shifted into an irregular orbit and rate of rotation. If we no longer had that reliable standard on which to base time, it is questionable whether we could maintain any system of time keeping.

The reality is that events and clock-time have no objective correlation. *However long an event lasts we accept as normal.* It's a bit like watching the scenery go by as we drive to work. We start and stop, accelerate, and cruise along at various speeds. The rapidity (that is, time) with which each scene (that is, event) passes depends on how fast we're driving (that is, whether we are compressing or expanding time). If we wait at a railroad crossing for fifteen minutes while a train passes through town, time is expanded. Later on the freeway, if we're speeding along at 75 mph, the countryside passes by almost too fast to see, and time is compressed. Regardless of the speed, time inside the car passes at the "normal" rate. The scenery has no inherent amount of time associated with its passage. We, the drivers, determine how long a particular vista remains in view by how fast we go. Linear time—what Bob Lancer calls "Sequential Time"[7]—asserts that each scene passes by in a certain amount of clock-time, without paying any heed to the speeds traveled past the scenery. In contrast, cyclic time—termed "Harmonic Time"[8] by Bob Lancer—takes into account the slower and faster speeds (that is, expanded and compressed time), while disregarding a standardized measure of the passing scenery.

Time is elastic because its essence is *meaning,* and meaning cannot be confined by the standardized norms of the minutes and the hours of our days. Meaning is not bounded by time and space. It adapts to the conceptual form it fills, just as water assumes the shape of its container. A particular significance, whether applied to a minute, a week, a year, or to any length of time, is virtually the same and unchanged. "We live, then, not within the boundaries of a physical world, but within the boundaries of our perception of it . . ."[9]

Meaning can be transferred from one *conceptual form* to another. Units of time have certain meanings. Events have particular meanings. Time compression consists of extracting the meaning of an event from its "natural" cycle and identifying it with a factor cycle of time. The sticking point in this process is that meaning, and the form that signifies that meaning, are bonded together as securely as two materials joined by a strong adhesive. We customarily imagine the form to *be* the meaning, when actually it is not. Any form can represent widely differing meanings. My wife, Evelyn Moss Pither, wrote the following poem after we talked about this concept:

> One man's trash
>   Is another man's treasure;
> One man's chagrin
>   Is another man's pleasure;
> One man's drink
>   Is another man's poison;
> One man's excuse
>   Is another man's reason;
> It's yin and yang,
>   Black and white;
> A chance for courage
>   Is another man's fright.

Earlier, I mentioned "dinner" as an example of a one-hour event. To eat dinner in a minute or a day stresses the very idea of what it means to dine. This is because we view the meaning of dinner "the same as" the form of dinner. Why, there's so much to do! There's relaxing at the table, spreading the napkin on the lap, the camaraderie, sweetening the drinks, drinking the tea or other beverage, seasoning the food, eating and savoring the distinctive tastes and flavors, and feeling full and satisfied. All that is the form of dinner; none of it is the meaning. Of course, the experience could be shriveled down to a minute or so by removing all the elements that make dinner what it is: no napkin, no leisurely conversation, no adjusting flavors with seasonings, no savoring beverages, and certainly no satisfaction from the dining experience. You would also have to eat a small amount as fast as you can with no distractions and no pauses. It can be done, but that is not time compression. It is an extremely rushed dinner from which every extra is removed to save time, and this has nothing to do with compressing time. When we compress time, we strive to finish the full event in a complete, satisfying, and normal manner in less time than usual. In order to compress the dinner experience to a minute, it is necessary to discern its *abstract quintessence*. This does not mean determining "what dinner means to us." That only serves to lock us into "dinner as we know it." Rather, I would say its *pure meaning* is about *satisfaction of nourishment*. But here words fail because, being form themselves, they preclude expressing meaning in its formless state. Once this meaning-essence has been conceived in the imagination, it can, in its entirety, reemerge in material form in one minute or in any other length of time. That is what it means to transfer *meaning* to a shorter or longer cycle. To an observer, it might appear that the one-minute dinner falls far short of being a "full and complete meal." If executed properly, however, the compressed dinner will be as satisfying as the one that lasts an hour or two.

I chose the example of dinner because it is one to which everyone can relate. It is also flawed. Sure, it is possible to have a complete dinner experience in a minute, but who wants to do it? Everyone enjoys a pleasant, leisurely meal. The idea of voluntarily giving up all but one or two minutes of the pleasure is immediately rejected. What's the point? This resistance blocks any possibility of time-compressing dinner. You have to *want* to compress time in order for the process to work.

If time is meaning, then what is the significance of linear time? The highly routinized nature of clock-time suggests its meaning is *habit*. Habit—the tendency to repeated action—characterizes so much of our lives: our activities, our decisions, our thinking, our attitudes, and our emotional responses. Generally, we eat at certain times, often the same foods with the same people conversing about similar topics. We work according to schedules, use the same kinds of skills day in and day out, retire to bed and arise at the usual times, and so on and so forth. Linear time expresses the broad extent to which life on earth is patterned.

Thus far, I have described cyclic time as a meaningful alternative to linear time. Whereas I characterize linear time as signifying habit, in contrast, cyclic time is *evolution*. If we approach the cycles of our lives purposefully and constructively, we grow. If we work them with spiritual intent, we transcend our limitations. To study a spiritual symbol system is to have one foot in cyclic time. To master a spiritual symbol system is to be fleet of realization. The very act of acquiring proficiency in the art changes our perception of life's meaning. We see differently. We live differently.

We also experience time differently. This is so because time is a perception that we bring to reality; consequently, it is within our capability to act the speed of its passage. Modern science has already established this concept to a limited degree. Physics has proven that the relative speed of objects causes time to pass at different rates for each one. The greater the speed, the less time that passes in comparison with slower objects. Metaphysical science teaches that we exercise personal control over the passage of time. "It is the focus of our consciousness that creates the sensation of time passing rather as looking through the window of a train creates the sensation of scenery passing, although we know the world outside the train is in fact standing still."[10] What this is really about, of course, is the rate at which meaning flows past that train window.

A key element of the ability to compress time is knowing the relatedness of different phases of an event. It is realizing that ice, snow, water, steam, and vapor are all *one* substance. It is recognizing that the acorn, the sapling, the mature oak, the old and gnarled tree, and the weathered and rotten log are all different stages of the *same thing*. In terms of time, the "phases of an event" are its cycles, which, when sufficiently repeated, consolidate into longer cycles that eventually unite into still longer cycles. All such cycles have a subtle connectedness, if it can be discerned. To see the acorn is to see the fallen and rotting log, so to speak.

This knowledge is the basis of time compression. It is, I believe, a latent talent of human beings. In the future, there will be those individuals who hone this skill to a high degree of proficiency. They will have the adeptness to shorten traumatic experiences significantly and to acquire complex skills in a fraction of the time now required to learn them. Instead of needing years to acquire fluency in a language, to be proficient in higher mathematics, or to play a musical instrument well, some people will do so in hours or days. Mental and emotional conflicts and difficulties will be resolved in a matter of minutes or seconds rather than months or years. This will occur in part because humankind will learn how to live according to higher symbolic mathematics.

In mathematics, time compression is calculated by fractal geometry. This is the ". . . geometry of nature . . ."[11] conceived by Benoit Mandelbrot in 1975. It is an astounding innovation that gives mathematical expression to a wide variety of patterns that occur in the world that were once considered too irregular and chaotic to be formalized into equations. Now, however, such structures as coastlines, clouds, rivers, trees, flowers, islands, lakes, waves, snowflakes, and moon craters can be stunningly and realistically replicated. Natural and cultural processes can also be expressed as fractals, like price changes, economics, population growth, fluid mechanics, and linguistics.

Two aspects of fractal geometry have remarkable implications for time compression. First, fractal designs are developed through successive calculations of a formula that incorporates its own previous result. The same is true of a progression of cycles: every new cycle in part derives its attributes from cycles that came before it. In this manner, they build up endlessly into fractal patterns. Second, fractals are self-similar, meaning that ". . . with a certain scale of magnification, the pattern will repeat itself."[12] In other words, if any detail of the pattern is sufficiently enlarged, the entire design will emerge whole from it! The size of a design, relative to patterns at larger or smaller scale, changes nothing. The scale-size on which one focuses will contain the full design in every respect, no different from any other scale-size! This is most astonishing to see in computer-generated animation. As a tiny aspect of the fractal design begins to grow larger and larger, the initial scale-size becomes too big to see in its entirety. Then, what was merely a speck in the complex original pattern looks just like what was first visible. This demonstrates conclusively that differences of scale do not alter the nature of an event. William Blake got it literally correct in his poem, *Auguries of Innocence:*

To see a world in a grain of sand
And a heaven in a wildflower,
Hold infinity in the palm of your hand
And eternity in an hour.[13]

These ideas, so far removed from daily experiences, bring us to a startling conclusion: any cycle *a* = any cycle *b*. This means that there is no difference between cycles of different lengths. They are the same, just as different scale-sizes of fractal geometry are the same. This astounding conclusion means that what happens in a one thousand year cycle is the same—exactly the same—as what happens in a one second cycle of the same event. What are we to make of this? Clearly, this will not be borne out through a comparison of their respective facts. What we need to focus on instead is *that which makes an event what it is*—the intrinsic nature of each cycle, in other words. This essence remains unaltered no matter how long or short the cycle is, like fractal patterns. This defies mundane logic and reason, so we will need a symbolic explanation for our answer.

I think Pythagoras had an understanding of the relationship between long and short, big and small. He considered single-digit numbers to be the Elements of Life from which everything emerges. Large numbers, he thought, were nothing more than accumulations of the Elements whose fundamental nature could be determined by adding them together. Thus, the numbers 37 and 64, for example, share a rudimentary equivalence because they both reduce to 10, then to 1, and 1 = 1. So regardless of size and complexity, every *thing* has, in reality, its Elementary nature. This principle is found in chemistry, also. Water is composed of two elements—hydrogen and oxygen. Its nature is the same whether it's a tiny drop of dew or the Atlantic Ocean.

In mathematical symbolism, the Elemental nature has always been determined by reducing large numbers to a single digit. This method does not lend itself directly to the determination of the Elements of time. Here, the Elements are the basic units of time: second, minute, hour, day, and so on. Each cycle represents *a complete experience*. This is possible because meaning has no inherent length of duration and can, without alteration or modification, be applied to any size cycle of time. When any cycle is repeated enough times, it evolves into the next larger unit, in accordance with the principles of fractal geometry. Its essential nature is identically repeated at larger and larger scales.

Time compression is a natural part of living for everyone. It is rarely recognized for what it is, though, because, however compressed or expanded an event is, it "seems normal." Rarely do we find ourselves thinking, "Gee, that event should have taken fifty times longer than this!" Yet, if this event does normally take fifty times longer, something extraordinary has happened. To be able to complete a lengthy task in a brief amount of time is to be spiritually empowered. Thinking and analysis, strong feeling and understanding are all integral to what is required to compress time, but in and of themselves they are insufficient to accomplish this task. Time compression is an experience. It is something that happens to you.

When we set out to compress time, it must be engineered precisely. A closely approximated experience will not produce the desired effect. After all, if we are to compress a year or a decade into, say, a minute or an hour, the corresponding significances must be true and exact. The successful completion of time compression is absolutely definitive, and its resolution is as final as though it had been struggled through week in and week out, month after month, even year after year, until at last it ended.

The process of compressing time begins with identifying the challenge. What is the experience to be foreshortened? When this has been determined, it needs to be fully examined in order to know every aspect of its nature, intimately and thoroughly. Once the concept is fully understood, it should be expressed succinctly in one sentence, if at all possible. The length of cycle of this experience also needs to be figured out. Next, the experience in question needs to be written out in as few words as possible for every shorter cycle down to one second. This provides unique insight into what this experience is all about.

The next step is to select the cycle at which to compress the experience. Although the experience at the shorter cycle is identical to the one at the longer cycle, we think of them as being totally different. So, here again, there is the need to explore the compressed experience from every perspective until we are intimately familiar with it. Now we have the full scope of the problem, but don't know what to do about it. Goals need to be set. This means thinking long and hard about the solution to the challenge. Once the goal has been tersely expressed in one sentence, the same needs to be done for every shorter cycle down to one second. Every aspect of the chosen goal needs to be embraced with affection and devotion. Once the compressed challenge and solution are thoroughly known and understood, considerable effort needs to be spent imagining the goal as it applies to every aspect of one's life.

Finally, the decision to act is made. If the chosen cycle is that of one minute, then it will take about that long to finish. Then it's over! Time has been compressed.

It should be kept in mind at all times that even though the process for time compression is presented simply and clearly, it cannot be worked by plugging in set or memorized concepts. It is not a paint-by-the-numbers canvas. It is anything but a rote exercise. It is spiritual creativity at its best.

Let us turn our attention now to our old friend, Wilma Dawn Thomas, to see how this works in practice. With the numbers in her chart—5, 7, and 9— we can easily imagine Wilma feeling troubled and thinking to herself, "I am so scared and miserable and upset! I've been without a husband and lover all my life. I haven't seen anybody from my family for over seventeen years. I'm isolated just about all the time, and when I do things with friends, it you want to call them friends, it's always some exciting adventure, nothing ever intimate. Everything's so impersonal. Nobody cares about me, and I . . . I don't know. In a way, I've never really cared if I had anybody close to me or not. Too much trouble. Suddenly, after all these years, I feel so alone and lonely I can't stand it. I am overwhelmed."

This is Wilma's challenge. Once the challenge has been stated, the next step is to determine which cycle it is. A year? A decade? Wilma said her loneliness has been going on "all her life." Given the standard lengths of cycle, Wilma is clearly describing a decade cycle. Her situation has been going on for nearly three decades, much too long to be categorized as a year cycle and far too short for a century cycle. Wilma's initial statement of the challenge now needs to be carefully worded in one sentence. The purpose is to define the quintessence of the cycle, succinctly and exactly. It may be occasionally necessary to state the challenge in several sentences or even a short paragraph. The thing to avoid is any discussion—state the bare bones only, no elaboration. After considerable thought and deliberation, Wilma concludes that "I live a secretive life of isolation and high-stakes risk." As brief as this is to encapsulate a lifelong behavior, it states her truth with the same extreme economy of a line of Haiku poetry.

Step 1:
State the experience to be foreshortened in one sentence, and determine its cycle

Step 2:
State the
challenge in
one sentence
for each
shorter cycle

Once the problematic cycle has been identified and the challenge put succinctly into words, the same needs to be done for each of the cycle lengths down to one second. This is necessary in order for the full cyclic picture to emerge. Also, it would be extraordinarily difficult to grasp any of the very short cycles if the intermediate ones were ignored. This requires a lot of soul searching from Wilma. She is exploring the unknown. It is scary and painful. She is facing the truth about herself, no doubt for the first time. What she eventually comes up with is as follows:

Decade: "I live a secretive life of isolation and high-stakes risk."

Year: "I lead an eccentric life with nothing in common with anybody else."

Month: "I live in seclusion, and my life outside consists of fast-paced thrills."

Week: "I keep my time for myself, and I'm freer that way."

Day: "I don't relate to other people."

Hour: "People cramp my style and they intrude into my personal life."

Minute: "I make the decision to have total freedom and to be alone."

Second: "I instinctively shun intimacy."

Step 3:
Select the
cycle length
at which to
compress the
challenge

The next step in the process is to select the cycle length at which Wilma resolves her problem. When making this choice, keep in mind the meaning of each cycle length. A **second** provides a truly quick resolution, but I suggest leaving this one to the experts for the time being. It is an unconscious cycle, so it requires instinctive action. It is over almost as soon as it begins, leaving no time for adjustments. In a **minute** cycle you have to be businesslike and clear on exactly what you want—no doubt or conflict. An advantage of longer "short" cycles—the hour and the day—is that they offer the learner sufficient time to work the process with deliberation. Both hours and days have significant connotations depending on their position in the next larger cycle and other factors. These should be carefully considered. If an **hour** is chosen, 6 A.M. would be an appropriate time. That is the hour of first light and dawn. Another beneficial hour is noon, when the day is at full strength. And since they represent the start of the workday, when we are accustomed to begin our daily labor, 8 A.M. and 9 A.M. are also strong. Midnight to 1 A.M. is considered by some to be the ideal time. This is zero hour, and the day ahead is still a dream. It contains the very opening moments. The air is quiet and filled with anticipation. The hour to be chosen might also be selected for its number. One and 8 are particularly effective because 1 is the number of new beginnings, and 8 is the number of achievement. But any number can be potent if properly understood. Using a number that is strong and prominent in the numerology chart can enhance success as well. Seven would be ideal for Wilma because of its position in her chart and because the purpose of 7 is to find and live by the truth. On the other hand, 5 might be her most opportune hour, since 5 maximizes opportunities and time compression is an incredible opportunity.

If a day cycle is to be used, Monday is powerful. It is universally experienced as the beginning of the week, and because work begins on Monday for the majority of workers. On the other hand, it is sometimes difficult to adjust to the demands of the job after the leisure of the weekend. So Tuesday might be more conducive, since by then we are generally in the swing of the workweek. Saturday or Sunday is the Sabbath for some religions, and can therefore be considered spiritual days on which to reach a meaningful goal. Saturday may also be viewed as the day for personal projects. Sunday is thought of as the "day of rest" or, to put it in metaphysical terms, the "day of meditation."

An additional approach to choose a particular hour or day cycle is to calculate the number for each day, and to use the number that is strongest in the numerology chart or that provides the greatest motivation. Those numbers are:

Sunday: 3 (self-discovery)

Monday: 9 (transcendence)

Tuesday: 5 (maximizing opportunity)

Wednesday: 1 (new beginning)

Thursday: 8 (achievement)

Friday: 9 (transcendence)

Saturday: 1 (new beginning)

The point here is to explore all aspects of the cycle to be used for compressing time until one of them "feels right." I personally like the minute cycle, so we will use that for Wilma's time compression.

Step 4: State the goal in one sentence for each shorter cycle

It is essential to identify not only the difficulty to be overcome but also the solution. We need to know what we're trying to accomplish, so a goal needs to be established for every cycle. It might be wondered, *Why go to all the trouble to figure out eight different cycles when only one is going to be used to compress time?* The answer: even though both challenge and solution of *every* cycle of length are the same, we think of them very differently. Working out *all* the challenges and *all* the solutions creates a comprehensive grasp of the task to be accomplished, and provides continuity from cycle to cycle. This must be done carefully and accurately. If any important element of the challenge or solution definition is missing or imprecise, the desired result will not come about. Instead, the longer cycle will continue, perhaps in a modified way. If that is the case, more than likely the missing element(s) is the one (or ones) that caused the problem in the first place. Later, there will be plenty of time to piece through the "missing element," detail by detail. One way or another, all the difficult issues will be have to be faced. It will no doubt take Wilma a good while to figure out her goals. This is unfamiliar territory for her that she has habitually avoided her entire life. At long last, she comes to the following conclusions for her goals:

Decade: "I live a fulfilling life of intellectual and emotional companionship, and adventurer comrades."

Year: "I enjoy unique pastimes with my beloved spouse and good friends."

Month: "I have exciting, meaningful relationships."

Week: "I involve others in intellectual activity and outdoor adventure."

Day: "I enjoy relating personally and intimately."

Hour: "All kinds of people attract me, and I interrelate with them in personal, dynamic ways."

Minute: "I decide to share the adventure of living with others."

Second: "I naturally seek out intimacy."

So, Wilma has decided to compress her challenge down to the one minute cycle: "I make the decision to have total freedom and to be alone." She has also set her goal: "I decide to share the adventure of living with others." Now she immerses herself in both dynamics. She concentrates on the "feel" of them from every perspective. She recalls experiences throughout her life that have had a bearing on the problem, as well as the times she has briefly transcended it (and there have been some). She dwells on her thoughts and feelings of past times, as well as those of the present. She mulls over habits, beliefs, attitudes, expectations, needs and fears, anything that may have locked the problem in place within her being. Likewise, she examines all her resources and experiences she can draw on to reach her goal. Her numerology chart is helpful in this endeavor. The reading made her aware of her inherent disposition toward isolation and freedom.

When Wilma has developed a fluent, conscious awareness of the entire dilemma and no longer needs words to ponder it, she turns her reflections to the solution. She hungers for it and visualizes practical applications of her aspirations. She demands compliance from her powers of imagination, as a director firmly guides a young actor to an inspired performance. She experiments with various approaches and situations. She draws clues from those fleeting past moments when, for no apparent reason, she was hot on the trail of intimacy and caring. "How did I *do* that, exactly?" she muses insistently, much like an actor struggling to see into the motivations of a character she can't seem to grasp. She will have succeeded in her efforts once she feels the lure of those yearnings for relationship. With that primal impetus in hand, she can readily visualize in her imagination scene after scene in which she dresses "the adventure of living" with vivid details of enjoying the company of others. To do that, she draws upon the stuff of her present life for raw material. She uses people she knows and familiar places to help make it all real to her, and she visualizes outcomes she would like, *with* those people *in* those places. She is ready for the final step when, at any moment of her day in any situation, she can mentally picture "sharing the adventure of living" with whomever is there.

Having spent so much time and effort in preparation, Wilma is now ready to do the deed. This is the moment of decision when she applies the solution to her life. This is not hypothetical. Her solution must be applied to a real situation or condition in her life if she is to compress time in reality. Perhaps there is someone she frequently encounters at the library or at her favorite restaurant to whom she is strongly attracted. Perhaps her most immediate concern is opening up a close relationship with a female coworker. It could be that she has a deep desire to communicate intimately with her parents.

She chooses one. When this moment arrives, she makes the decision. This is a leap of courage. She thinks it over for one minute, then *Bam!* It's done. She changes her life. She ends three decades of avoiding relationships. Just like *that*.

Endnotes

1. Kenneth Ring, Ph.D., *Life at Death, a Scientific Investigation of the Near-Death Experience* (New York: Coward, McCann & Geoghegan, 1980), 116.

2. Ibid., 118.

3. Darold A. Treffert, M.D., *Extraordinary People: Understanding the "Idiot Savant"* (New York: Harper & Row, Publishers, 1989), 36.

4. Ibid., 65.

5. Ibid., xi.

6. James P. Chaplin, *Dictionary of Psychology* (New York: Dell Publishing, 1985), 328.

7. Bob Lancer, *Inner Freedom Through Qabala* (Phoenix, Arizona: Limitless Light Publishing, 1986), 70.

8. Ibid., 70.

9. James N. Powell, *The Tao of Symbols* (New York: Quill, 1982), 165.

10. J. H. Brennan, *Time Travel: A New Perspective* (St. Paul, Minnesota: Llewellyn Publications, 1997), 35.

11. Benoit B. Mandelbrot, *The Fractal Geometry of Nature* (New York: W. H. Freeman and Company, 1983), 1.

12. Jan Gullberg, *Mathematics from the Birth of Numbers* (New York: W. W. Norton and Company, 1997), 626.

13. William Harmon, Editor, *The Top 500 Poems* (New York: Columbia University Press, 1992), 368.

chapter 12

Initiation and Your Worldview

I did not write this book starting from a preconceived theoretically or emotionally based opinion. . . . I experienced the insights which are collected in this book, as, say, a settler in an uninhabited wilderness must collect and master his observations and experiences if he wishes to survive.

—Wilhelm Reich, *People in Trouble*

There are three broad classes of symbolic numbers. The first and most common is *Generic Numbers,* the mainstay of Pythagorean numerology that are generally referred to as "reduced numbers." This class consists of 1 through 9, and 0 in very rare instances. The second category is *Elemental Numbers,* 0 through 9. These are philosophical concepts that represent the Elements of which the universe is constructed. The third class is *Natural Numbers,* 1 through infinity, plus 0. We will be concerned with 0 through 999,999,999 because of their significance for spiritual seekers. This latter group of numbers represents the experience of living on the earth plane and the evolution of consciousness to the point at which the soul is liberated from the Wheel of Karma.

Together these three types of numbers have great significance for that process of spiritual growth called Initiation.

We have already discussed Generic Numbers extensively. They have proven to be very useful for deep understanding because they conveniently summarize the multiple, complex meanings of life. They are broad generalizations, and this is also their great limitation. All detail and subtlety of polydigit numbers are lost, leaving only a faint glimmering of the total scope of meaning. All of the following numbers reduce to 5: 59, 680, 3,992, 14,801, and 777,452. It should be evident that those numbers cannot be adequately represented by 5. The more digits a number has, the greater the loss of meaning when it is reduced. Still, Generic Numbers can be extremely useful as general indicators. They permit us to work with many numbers at a time that, in their longer forms, are cumbersome to work with.

There are ten Elemental Numbers, the same as Generic Numbers, but the likeness ends there. Generic Numbers concern mundane life. They are essentially psychological dynamics. Elemental Numbers, on the other hand, are philosophical principles, the fundamental laws of our existence. As we discuss the Elemental Numbers, you may feel confused at first trying to distinguish between the two types of numbers. This is partially because throughout the book I have combined the meanings of Elemental Numbers with the meanings of Generic Numbers in order to present a fuller discussion of numbers than is available in present-day Pythagorean numerology. As I have said before, Pythagorean numerology basically provides psychological insight. It can only be used as a spiritual symbol system if its numbers and principles have a philosophical basis. Lacking that, this numerology is permanently limited to being an interpreter of the mundane.

Both kinds of numbers have related meanings, but their differences are readily apparent when compared side by side.

Elemental Numbers	Generic Numbers
0 Nonbeing	**0** Void
1 Being	**1** Oneself
2 Duality	**2** Others
3 "I" concept	**3** Self-expression
4 Physical reality	**4** Realism
5 Individuality	**5** Freedom and opportunity
6 Values	**6** Commitment and Responsibility
7 Truth	**7** Analysis and understanding
8 Empowerment	**8** Achievement
9 Oneness of life	**9** Humanitarianism

Just as there is a connectedness between Elemental and Generic Numbers, there is also an integral relation between Elemental and Natural Numbers. Natural Numbers stand for the *experience of living*. From 0 through 999,999,999, there are nine fundamentally different life experiences, or *Levels*, based on the number of digits in a number. The nine Levels are as follows:

Level 1: 0 through 9 (all the positive, whole numbers consisting of one digit)

Level 2: 10 through 99 (all the positive, whole numbers consisting of two digits)

Level 3: 100 through 999 (all the positive, whole numbers consisting of three digits)

Level 4: 1,000 through 9,999 (all the positive, whole numbers consisting of four digits)

Level 5: 10,000 through 99,999 (all the positive, whole numbers consisting of five digits)

Level 6: 100,000 through 999,999 (all the positive, whole numbers consisting of six digits)

Level 7: 1,000,000 through 9,999,999 (all the positive, whole numbers consisting of seven digits)

Level 8: 10,000,000 through 99,999,999 (all the positive, whole numbers consisting of eight digits)

Level 9: 100,000,000 through 999,999,999 (all the positive, whole numbers consisting of nine digits)

Each Level reflects the qualities of an Elemental Number. Thus, the 2 Level, for example, consists of all two-digit numbers, 10 through 99. They engender a wide variety of experiences, all of which share a certain quality unique to Elemental Number 2. In other words, those ninety numbers make a complete statement about the nature of duality. Similarly, numbers consisting of eight digits—10,000,000 through 99,999,999—represent all possible dynamics and permutations of Elemental Number 8. Those ninety million numbers are all connected with 8, and have a certain way of dealing with life that is not to be found in any other Level. Together, the nine Levels represent the complete life of the ego, or lower self, from inception (the 1 Level) to transcendence (the 9 Level).

Each of us experiences life from one particular Level of numbers. Everything in our life bears its stamp. We think, feel, understand, and act within the context of that Level. *That* is what we know. It determines what we think Reality is, causing us to create the worldview that we have as well as the nature of our spiritual philosophy. Thus, if our Level is that of five-digit numbers—10,000 through 99,000— then virtually all of our experiences exemplify some aspect of Elemental Number 5. This is so even if all the numbers in our numerology chart seem to conflict with 5. In some respect, *every* experience whatsoever is the working out of an Elemental Number.

When we live and breathe on a certain Level, the Levels listed below are experienced as known quantities and mastered skills. We have been through them before and we have mastered the lessons. To a great extent, the known and understood Levels make up the bulk of circumstances in which we find ourselves. To continue with the earlier example of the five-digit number, let's say you are having a 76,294 experience in the current period. Your Level of experience is 5 because this number consists of five digits. Everything that happens in your life has something to do with developing and exploring your individuality. Within the scope of this 5-Level number are four "lesser" Levels:

The 4 Level: 6,294

The 3 Level: 294

The 2 Level: 94

The 1 Level: 4

Since your 5-Level number encompasses those lower Levels, you know how to handle all of them in their own terms. You've been there, done that. They have all been mastered in their own terms, but not as part of five-digit numbers. Five provides a new slant on old themes. Consequently, in meeting the challenge of 76,294, you also learn more deeply about the four more basic Levels.

Thus far, I have been speaking of nine Elemental Levels. Every such "major" Level contains nine "minor" levels, based on the number with which it begins. Since 76,294 starts with 7, this is a five-digit number at the 7 Level: for short, *5 at the 7 Level*. To say that 76,294 is a five-digit number is very broad. It includes a tremendous number of possibilities. To know its level narrows down the range of experiences. It makes the interpretation more useful because it is specific.

Above the Level on which we are experiencing life are "higher" Levels. These are aspects of life that are beyond what we know or understand. We have never "been there," and don't know how to go there. Through study of the numbers, we may develop deep and insightful understanding of those higher Levels, but we will only know them in terms of the Level on which we function. The real key to those experiences remains inaccessible and beyond our reach. They are mute mysteries not in our awareness. In the example 76,294, there are the experiences of 7, 6, and 9, but *only* as they manifest up through the 5 Level. We may *imagine* those higher Levels vividly, but until we have crossed into their territory, *that* is not ours. To make the major transition from one Level to the next is called *Initiation*.

You may be wondering what connection you could possibly have with Natural Numbers in the tens or hundreds of millions. It is not so much of a stretch as you might imagine. There are many ways to attain high numbers by applying mathematical functions to the numbers of your numerology chart. Consider the result if the numbers of Wilma's name are all multiplied together:

5 x 9 x 3 x 4 x 1 x 4 x 1 x 5 x 5 x 2 x 8 x 6 x 4 x 1 x 1 = 20,736,000
W   I   L   M   A   D   A   W   N   T   H   O   M   A   S

That number 20, 736,000 is 8 at the 2 Level. If her birthday is multiplied in the same way, the result is 6 at the 4 Level:

1 x 7 x 9 x 9 x 3 x 1 x 6 x 1 x 9 x 5 x 1 = 459,270
A   P   R   I   L   1   6   1   9   5   1

If her participation number is cubed, the result is also a very high number—10 at the 7 Level:

$$1996^3 = 7,952,095,936$$

Such mathematical manipulations are definitely possible for individuals to do, but they require extraordinary measures to bring about in real life. We generally live on the basis of far more modest mathematical functions in our daily experience. We add, subtract, multiply, and divide, for the most part. If, however, we know how to proceed, it is certainly possible to find and activate more potent mathematical functions. One example of a higher number that we all work with is the *block of futurity* every person brings to his life through his Participation number. When the birth month and birth day are added to the birth year, a number is produced that is the same as a particular year of the future. In effect, each individual brings an aspect of the future to the world of today, and thereby contributes to the process of evolution. Wilma was born on April 16, 1951. With the addition of her month, day, and year of birth—29 + 16 + 1951—her Participation energy is 1996, forty-five years "ahead" of her birth year of 1951. This was the level at which she has actually functioned throughout her life. So, while the world plodded through the years following 1951, the energy that Wilma contributed year after year was characteristic of the year 1996. Her block of futurity was 45. In this manner, the world, and everyone in it, is always "ahead of itself."

Every number has infinite potentials and qualities. Every number has the attributes of every other number. In the earlier example of 76,294, for instance, this 5-Level number actually expresses characteristics of 7, 6, 2, 9, and 4. Those numbers are usually thought to conflict with 5, not to form part of what 5 is all about. Yet here, those very numbers express part of Elemental 5, a very natural and normal part. This is boundless diversity. Natural Numbers organize the myriad contrasts and differences according to mathematical principle. The method of interpreting Natural Numbers is similar to that of Generic Numbers. It is also far more complex for several reasons. First of all, as we have discussed, the number of digits in a Natural Number indicates its Initiatory Level. The single-digit number 7 is related to the Initiation of the 1 Level because it consists of one digit. Seventy-six is part of the 2 Initiation, being a two-digit number. The five-digit number we've been using as an illustration for the past few pages, 76,294, is an experience of the 5 Initiatory Level. Second, the internal organization of Natural Numbers contains a great deal of information. The order in which the numbers occur is significant. If just two digits of 76,294 were switched—7 and 4—a vastly different experience would emerge: 46,297. Third, and of particular significance, are *number series*. These are sets of numbers consisting of the same number of digits that all begin with the same number followed by 0 through 9. Thus, 10 through 19 is called a number series, the 1 series at the 2 Level. One hundred through 199 is also a 1 series, but at the 3 Level.

Each Level contains nine number series. The 2 Level, for example, includes 10 through 99 and contains nine number series: 10–19, 20–29, 30–39, 40–49, and so on through 90–99. The 3 Level also contains the nine number series: 100–199, 200–299, 300–399, 400–499, to 900–999. Further, any number series consisting of two or more digits contains nine "sub" series within it. The series 100–199, for example, contains within it the following ten subseries: **100–109, 110–119, 120–129, 130–139,** and so forth through **190–199.** In this book, we are concerned with the basic number series of 1 through 999,999,999. Their interpretations can be found in the appendix of this book.

The importance of number series lies in the depth of their meaning. They add considerable insight to the number of the series. The number 1, for example, has certain meanings associated with it, but there are always deeper, more inclusive meanings to be discerned. The 1 series at the 2 Level (10–19) spells out those meanings in greater detail than is possible with a single-digit 1, and does so in an organized manner. Thus, when 10 is interpreted for meaning, it involves determining how 0 modifies 1. This is called *1 at the 0 level.* Since 0 is "potential," 10 expresses 1 in "the formative stages." Similarly, 11 (1 at the 1 Level) represents what 1 is like when modified by 1; when, in other words, the focus is on the "oneness" of 1. When the entire 1 series is studied in this manner, a deeper and more complete concept of the number 1 is the result. The 1 series at the 3 Level—100 through 199—probes the meaning of 1 more deeply than is possible at the 2 Level.

It will be recalled that, earlier in this book, I wrote against the concept of Master Numbers and Karmic Debt Numbers in Pythagorean numerology. Master Numbers are two-digit numbers in which both digits are the same: 11, 22, 33, 44, and so on through 99. The four numbers—13, 14, 16, and 19—are said to represent karmic debts due to activities of the soul in prior lifetimes. It is generally believed that the soul must rectify its earlier erroneous ways by overcoming extraordinarily difficult challenges in this incarnation. But again, I believe there is no mathematical basis on which to single out these thirteen numbers from the 2 Level for special significance. One is the number of the ego. *Any* aspect of 1, from 10 through 19, involves ego issues and is inherently challenging, not solely 13, 14, 16, and 19. As far as the Master Numbers go, there is no unique dynamic that singles them out from the other nine numbers of its series. Yes, they are highly challenging. Master Numbers represent the *test* of a given series, while the final number is the *achievement* of that series.

So if a person overcomes the rigorous difficulties of 11, he has successfully faced the key challenges of this series. But mastery of this series is not really attained until he works through the dynamics of 19. Careful contemplation of all ten numbers of any number series will demonstrate conclusively that every number in the series is a significant step along the way of spiritual evolution. Every one is challenging in its own right and has its own rewards; none emerges as the special number of the series. A final word about the so-called Master Numbers: it should also be apparent that two-digit Master Numbers are not the only ones. From a mathematical perspective, the same dynamics that make 11 a Master number also apply to 111; 1,111; 11,111; and so on. Given the greater depth of meaning of larger numbers, Pythagorean numerologists would do well to investigate Master Numbers consisting of nine digits instead of the relatively simplistic two-digit versions.

Advancement through a particular number series—10 to 19, for example—is personal growth. Stepping up to the next series—20 through 29—represents a *Minor Initiation*. The individual moves to a higher perceptual level of living within the same Level. He has had a profound insight that alters the way he understands himself and the world in which he lives. A Minor Initiation, therefore, means acquiring greater expertise in the skill of living. Progression from one number Level to the next number Level is a Major Initiation, and represents a new vision of what it means to be alive. It confers a higher, more inclusive degree of empowerment, knowledge, insight, ability, understanding, wisdom, and responsibility than was possible at the previous Level. Anyone who lives on the 2 Level has a certain inherent understanding of what life is all about, including specific kinds of capabilities as well as particular types of limitations. When he advances to the 3 Level, the problems and difficulties of the 2 Level lose their power over him. He has "graduated" to a different arena where he plays out a more meaningful destiny.

Together, the three classes of numbers—Generic, Elemental, and Natural—are a powerful aid to spiritual growth. These numbers pinpoint where one is in his evolution, which goals and challenges he faces on his way, and how to proceed. They take the ignorance and confusion out of the task of following the spiritual path. The relationship between Natural Numbers, Elemental Numbers, and Generic Numbers is this: Elemental Numbers are *philosophical principles;* Natural Numbers are *lived experiences* based on the philosophical principles; Generic Numbers are *summarized statements* of lived experiences.

The proper interpretation of Natural Numbers is very helpful in spiritual work and evolution. Every number from 0 through 999,999,999 is intense with meaning. The brief descriptive statements given here with regard to a particular Natural Number or Elemental Number should be taken only as indicators. They do not define the numbers. They refer to them only, and are always incomplete. A particular interpretation must be understood in the context of the number being described, as well as fully integrated with one's personal experience, before that interpretation can have any real meaning. The full import of meaning can only be gained through analysis, contemplation, and action. In this way, the significance of a Natural or Elemental Number can gradually be gleaned over time.

The techniques of interpreting Natural Numbers are essentially extensions of those of interpreting Generic Numbers: identify and compare. They involve understanding the Level of a number, the combination of digits that compose the number, and their order. The first number always sets the *theme* of the interpretation, and the number(s) that follow *modify* the theme. Thus, in the cases of 78, 783, 7,830, and 78,304, all four of these numbers have meanings with regard to 7. Virtually all the experiences of 78; 783; 7,830; and 78,304 are linked together in the number 7 in a basic, thematic way, that being "the search for truth and understanding." Seventy-eight narrows the broad meaning of 7. The question becomes, what is 7 at the 8 level? The answer involves assessing 7 in the light of 8. This is virtually the same process of assessment we do for ourselves every day of our lives. With each new piece of information we learn about anything—any person, thing, or situation—we *refine* or *adjust* our thoughts on the matter accordingly. Consider Wilma Dawn Thomas once again. If we say "she works," that is *one* piece of information. It is also unrestrictedly broad. There are many forms her work could take. If we then add to this that Wilma is an "advertising executive," that is *two* pieces of information, and our understanding is significantly modified. It doesn't change the fact that she works, but we certainly know more. A still more complete picture emerges if, adding a *third* bit of information, we learn Wilma has "decided to retire from advertising." If we then learn that she intends to "open a retail shop," a *fourth* piece of information, this adds a whole new perspective on what we know of Wilma's working life.

What we have when we put all four facts together is this: Wilma, an advertising executive, is retiring to open a retail shop. Even though we have combined the meanings of four elements into a single, composite meaning, this interpretation method is not the same as reducing numbers by addition. Interpretation of Natural Numbers builds up a consensus of all the factors. Nothing is eliminated. Reducing indiscriminately downsizes multiple complex factors into a single simple factor. It might say of Wilma, "she sells."

How, then, shall we apply this process to 78 in order to understand its meaning? Well, 7 represents the search for truth. Eight represents achievement. Since 8 modifies the 7, the interpretation will involve an achievement with regard to finding truth. With these two numbers understood together as a unit, we can say 78 means "achievement of discovering the truth." If an additional digit is added to form 783, we have "one further bit of information" that narrows the meaning of 7 still further. Now we are faced with determining the combined meaning of three numbers—7, 8, and 3—in descending order of importance. Again, 7 is the search for truth and 8 is achievement. To this we add that 3 is creativity. Seven is now modified by 83—8 at the 3 level—and means "achievement brought about through creativity." When we merge this modifying influence with 7, it produces "achieving knowledge of truth in creative ways."

Going further with this, let's consider an even larger number—7,830. We need to begin by examining the meaning of 3 at the 0 Level. Three is creativity, modified by 0, which represents potential. Zero also indicates a Minor Initiation. So, 3 at the 0 Level can be interpreted as "discovering the capacity for creativity." When this is applied to the 8 it signifies "learning creative ways to achieve." Finally, interpreting the full 7,830, it means "learning creative ways to achieve knowledge of truth." In this manner, any number consisting of two or more digits may be interpreted. The key is to discern the internal logic of the combination of numbers.

In addition to interpreting the combination of numbers that compose a Natural Number, it is also necessary to consider the Level of that number. The combination of numbers and their order provides the meaning. The Level indicates the *context* of that meaning. In this manner, the innumerable combinations and permutations of Natural Numbers can be interpreted.

The meanings of the nine Levels of Natural Numbers are summarized as follows:

1: Experience of the Unity of Being

2: Experience of the Differentiation of Things

3: Development of the "I" concept

4: Coping with World Reality

5: Experience of Individuality

6: Living by Values

7: Finding the Truth

8: Being Empowered

9: Being One with Life

Previously, I interpreted 78 to mean "achievement of discovering the truth." Now we also need to understand 78 in the context of the 2 Level. Two has to do with the ability to experience the differentiation of things. This is based on *discernment*—knowing what a thing *is* and what it *is not.* Therefore, at the 2 Level, the self's "achievement of discovering the truth" is a function of its capacity to perceive and to understand the differences between things. Putting this all together, we can say that 78 means "the self ascertains the truth." The number 783 was earlier interpreted to mean "achieving knowledge of truth in creative ways." The 3 Level has to do with developing the "I" concept—answering the question, *Who am I?* So the number at this Level is about self-awareness and how the self figures out how to achieve knowledge in its own terms. In light of this, the full interpretation of 783 becomes "learning personal, creative ways to achieve knowledge of truth." The same process continues at the 4 Level. The interpretation of 7,830—"learning creative ways to achieve knowledge of truth"—now needs to be understood as it applies to living in the physical world. The 3 Level is subjective. Now, the self must function in objective reality. When 7,830 is understood in the context of the world, the interpretation becomes "learning creative ways to achieve knowledge of the truth in real-life situations."

We are concerned in this book with Natural Numbers up through those consisting of nine digits—0 through 999,999,999. These are the numbers that concern the personal ego, or lower self. With each Major Initiation, the spiritual aspirant transcends certain types of challenges and limitations, and thereby frees himself from certain restrictions of being. The number 1,000,000,000 (1 billion) marks a significant departure because it is the end of the struggle with ego/separateness/Wheel of Karma/Spiritual Ignorance. At the same time, it is just another advance of the self as it treads the spiritual path throughout eternity. *Every* Major Initiation is profoundly freeing to one's being and adds certain empowerment and responsibility to the process of living. Every Minor Initiation is a crucial insight into life and hones an individual's skill of living.

Much contemplation needs to go into these matters. Otherwise, one risks having to reckon with a great deal of very complicated information without intimate meaning.

When we analyzed Wilma Dawn Thomas' chart earlier, we focused exclusively on Generic Numbers. Now, let's examine her chart briefly in terms of Natural Numbers:

$$9 \ + \ 1 \ + \ 1 \qquad + \qquad 6 + 1 \qquad = 18 \text{ Heart's Desire}$$

$$\text{W I L M A} \quad \text{D A W N} \quad \text{T H O M A S}$$

$$5 \ + \ 3{+}4 \ + \ 4 \ + \ 5{+}5{+}2{+}8 \ + \ 4 \ + \ 1 \qquad = 41 \text{ Personality}$$

$$5{+}9{+}3{+}4{+}1 \ + \ 4{+}1{+}5{+}5 \ + \ 2{+}8{+}6{+}4{+}1{+}1 \qquad = 59 \text{ Character}$$

$$29 \ 16 \ 1951 \ = 1996$$

$$\text{April 16, 1951}$$

It should be immediately apparent that much more meaning is conveyed here than with Generic Numbers. Wilma's 18 Heart's Desire, 41 Personality, and 59 Character put a whole new light on her 9–5–5 Generic-Numbered positions. Her 59 Character—5 at the 9 level—is at the "mature" end of the 5 series. The 5 series has to do with "living one's individuality." Nine is the number of "selfless giving." With 59, therefore, "the self applies its individual talents in humanitarian ways." Her Heart's Desire—18—is 1 at the 8 level. The 1 series has to do with "evolution of the ego." Eight is the number of "resolving karma," and has a strong drive for "doing what needs to be done." Together, then, 1 modified by 8 "resolves issues of the ego with strength and pragmatism." The nature of the personality—41—is the solid, reliable 4 at the 1 level. Four is all about being "serious, dutiful, and hard working." The 1 level makes the 4 focus on "independence and belief in the self." So, with a 41 Personality, Wilma comes across as "stable, reliable, and industrious in her own self-assured way." Wilma's Participation number—1996—begins with 1, just as that of everyone else born in the preceding millennium. This fundamental commonality contributed greatly to the creation and maintenance of the world community, making that age what it was. The transition from the 1 series (the 1000s) to the 2 series (the 2000s) is sure to be significant and to bring about a fundamental shift from "individuality" to "the needs of others." For Wilma personally, 1996 is first and foremost about her ego and her belief in herself, since 1 is the lead number. The two 9s are numbers of purification and release. The 6 means that this final cleansing is about "refining ego values." In other words, 1996 is a very important spiritual moment for Wilma's ego, when "she fully harmonizes her innermost standards and attitudes with Spirit."

Now, you may wonder how my interpretation of 1996 for Wilma applies to the state of the world in that year. Am I suggesting that the world was "spiritualizing its ego" in 1996? No, not exactly. Like all numbers, the meaning of 1996 can be viewed from many perspectives. It can assume very different forms. I formulated my interpretation to be relevant to Wilma's nature. To apply the meaning of 1996 to the world, I would need to begin my analysis from scratch. Every consideration is different—the diverse cultures, the interrelation of nations, the great complexity, the vast scale, so on and so forth. The world is not an individual with an ego. It is a civilization in a phase of history. Individuals face personal problems and pursue goals. The world copes with social movements, economic and political crises, and struggles to improve the lot of humanity. It is far more demanding to generalize about the entire world than characterize an individual.

It should be abundantly clear by now how much more involved it is to interpret Natural Numbers than Generic Numbers. The ease and convenience of that symbolic shorthand is replaced by some very complicated considerations. The process of analyzing Natural Numbers is essentially the same as with Generic Numbers: identify and compare. There is no objective, factual formula that can be used. It is entirely a judgment call, based on knowledge, wisdom, and understanding. To some extent, Generic Numbers can be learned and defined as factual information. This is not possible with Natural or Elemental Numbers. To understand their interpretations as objective data is to miss the point. Statements made about them can do no more than point one's thinking in a certain direction, or serve as a point of departure in meditation.

Previously, I pointed out how an individual's numbers could be raised to the hundreds of thousands or hundreds of millions. These kinds of mathematical results reveal much about an individual's spiritual potential, and what is required to reach it. They permit us to select a spiritual goal, then to find a mathematical way to accomplish it. Below are additional examples of mathematical calculations using Wilma's chart. For interpretations of the results, consult the Table of Interpretations in the appendix.

Multiplication of the Character number by the Participation number:

$59 \times 1996 = 117,764$

(1 at the 6 Level)

Multiplication of the numbers of Character, Heart's Desire, Personality, and Participation:

$59 \times 18 \times 41 \times 1996 = 86,909,832$

(8 at the 8 Level)

Squaring the Character number:

$59^2 = 3,481$

(3 at the 4 Level)

Cubing the Character number:

$59^3 = 205,379$

(2 at the 6 Level)

Squaring the Participation number:

$1996^2 = 3,984,016$

(3 at the 7 Level)

The Character number squared times the Participation number squared:

$59^2 \times 1996^2 = 13,868,359,696$

(1 at the 11 Level—no interpretation given)

The Participation number divided by the Character number:

$1996 \div 59 = 33.8305085$

(3 at the 2 Level)

The Square root of the Participation number:

$\sqrt{1996} = 44.6766158$

(4 at the 2 Level)

The simplicity of the previous calculations conceals the profoundly difficult spiritual challenge of translating those numbers into personal experience. I cite them as examples of how mathematical symbolism can serve as an aid to the understanding of our spiritual potential for growth and evolution.

One of the most significant numbers to determine is that representing the Soul's Ultimate Purpose for this incarnation (see the appendix for a complete list of interpretations). The complete number consists of nine digits. It encompasses the entire duration of a life and is, so to speak, the hoped-for result once the life has been completed. Imagine the time before birth when we were still in the Spirit Realm planning the upcoming incarnation. We had many ideas for things to accomplish and karma to account for. Underlying all the many specifics was a general purpose, which I call the Soul's Ultimate Goal. It is an encompassing context in which all that occurs during the incarnation is meaningfully linked. This number has no day-to-day, year-to-year, or decade-to-decade application. It represents an experience that is abstract for us because it can only be fully known after our lives on earth have been completed.

The nine numbers are derived from the following positions:

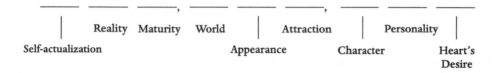

We will use Wilma's data to illustrate the production of this number. Her Character, Heart's Desire, and Personality positions provide the first three numbers:

The second set of three numbers is developed by adding the numbers of the city, state, and country of birth. The complete, formal name of the country should be used in its native language and spelling. The Attraction number is figured by totaling the numbers of the vowels; the Appearance number is the sum of all the consonants; the World number is the sum total of the numbers of both vowels and consonants. Wilma's birthplace was Bloomington, Indiana, The United States of America. (Refer to the conversion chart below.)

1	2	3	4	5	6	7	8	9
A	B	C	D	E	F	G	H	I
J	K	L	M	N	O	P	Q	R
S	T	U	V	W	X	Y	Z	

Attraction:

6 6 9   6   9 9 1 1   5 3 9 5   1 5   6   1 5 9 1   = 97/16/7

BLOOMINGTON INDIANA THE UNITED STATES OF AMERICA

Appearance:

2 3   4 5 7 2 5   5 4   5   2 8   5 2 4 12 2 1   6   4 9 3   = 91/10/1

World:

2 3 6 6 4 9 5 7 2 6 5   9 5 4 9 1 5 1   2 8 5   3 5 9 2 5 4   1 2 1 2 5 1   6 6   1 4 5 9 9 3 1   = 188/17/8

_____ _____ _____, 8   1   7   , _____ _____ _____

| Appearance |

World   Attraction

The final set of three numbers is determined by adding combinations of the Character, World, and Participation numbers. For Wilma, these numbers are as follows:

Maturity number: Add and reduce the Character and Participation numbers.

Character: 5
Participation: +7
                    12/3

Reality number: Add and reduce the Character and World numbers.

Character: 5
World: +8
                    13/4

Self-actualization: Add and reduce the Maturity and Reality numbers.

Maturity: 3
Reality: +4
                    7

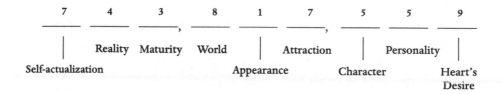

7	4	3	8	1	7	5	5	9
	Reality	Maturity	World		Attraction		Personality	
Self-actualization				Appearance		Character		Heart's Desire

This nine-digit number represents the Ultimate Spiritual Goal toward which Wilma's soul progresses during this incarnation. It is a Vast Meaning. She is not, however, working all of it with equal emphasis. Wilma, like each of us, is focused primarily on one of the nine Levels, which symbolizes her *Level of Consciousness*. It therefore represents how she creates her worldview and how she actually functions in life. To figure this number Level, add and reduce the Participation and World numbers. For Wilma, these are:

Participation: 7
World: +8
Level of Consciousness: 15/6

This establishes that Wilma's Spiritual Goal in this life is a six-digit number. Since the sixth number is an 8, we therefore say that her Level of Consciousness is 8 at the 6 Level: 817,559. The 7th, 8th, and 9th Levels are beyond Wilma's conscious awareness because they are above the 6 Level. The Levels below the 6 Level characterize 8 in particular ways.

The first three numbers of the Soul's Ultimate Purpose—Heart's Desire, Personality, and Character—represent the *subjective* levels of our experience in life. The second group of three numbers—Attraction, Appearance, and World—symbolizes the *objective* levels of our experience. The third group of three numbers—Maturity, Reality, Self-actualization—relates to *spiritual consciousness.* So in this lifetime, Wilma is resolving the interaction of subjective and objective aspects of her being from the perspective of spiritual consciousness. It should be borne in mind that even though the third group of three numbers is defined as "spiritual consciousness," *all aspects* of a spiritual symbol system are fully and equally "spiritual." The usual criteria of judgment we use to make assessments—good/bad, high/low, advanced/beginning, and the like—are not applicable here. Such judgments are the stuff of the 2 Level, not the symbol system as a whole.

The interpretation for Wilma's Ultimate Goal—8 at the 6 Level—is as follows: "the self teaches principles of loving, responsible behavior to others by example." This means that, in some way, *everything* that Wilma does and experiences in her life, from beginning to end, promotes that goal. This includes all the things that she *thinks* contribute to the goal, as well as those things that *seem* unrelated or in conflict with the goal. *Every last thing* in her life is part of realizing that goal. The above interpretation for 8 at the 6 Level is for a life that is lived positively. If a person leads a negative life, then an outcome of "bad karma" is the result. For Wilma this would mean: "the self enforces negative, limiting modes of behavior on others in social interaction."

As I bring the twelfth and final chapter of this book to a close, it is a soulful moment for me. This project has been my constant fascination for nine years, my "greatest intellectual adventure of a lifetime." Now it is finished at last.

The work on mathematical symbolism has barely begun. Sacred geometry is based on the principles of Euclidian geometry, and uses traditional concepts. It has not been updated to include modern developments like elliptic geometry, hyperbolic geometry, topology, and Fractal geometry. While it may have validity on its own terms, it, like Pythagorean numerology, has very limited applications in our day and time. Vast areas of mathematics are virtually unexplored. The meanings of trigonometry, statistics, vector analysis, chaos theory, algebra, physics, probability, calculus, and other forms of mathematics are unresearched and unknown.

Their time will come.

If this book helped you in your spiritual quest, it has served its purpose.

Spirit is pure creativity.
Every number is infinite.

Table of Interpretations

1 through 9—one-digit numbers—the 1 Level

Initiation to Being (or) Nonexistence

1   +   Consciousness is aware of All That Is
          −   Consciousness is aware of All That Is

2   +   Consciousness discerns the nature of infinite
               diversity with Perfect Understanding
          −   Consciousness does not discern the nature of
               infinite diversity

3   +   Consciousness expands to connect with the
               diversity of which it is aware
          −   Consciousness does not expand to connect with
               the diversity of which it is aware

4   +   Consciousness names the meanings of the diverse
               forms of which it is aware
          −   Consciousness does not name the meanings of the
               diverse forms of which it is aware

5   +   Consciousness becomes self-aware
          −   Consciousness does not become self-aware

6   +   Consciousness evaluates the relationships
               between the diversity of forms of the Oneness
          −   Consciousness does not evaluate the relationships
               between the diversity of forms of the Oneness

7   +   Consciousness understands its nature
          −   Consciousness does not understand its nature

8   + Consciousness evolves according to its self-awareness
    − Consciousness does not evolve according to its
     self-awareness

9   + Consciousness becomes all that it has evolved
    − Consciousness does not become all that it has evolved

10 through 99—two-digit numbers—the 2 Level

Initiation to Having Choice of Action (or) Initiation to Being in Opposition

10–19   + Consciousness develops positive self-concept
      − Consciousness develops ego

20–29   + The self develops skills of relationship with others
      − The self develops fear/desire of others

30–39   + The self learns the mechanics of
       expressing itself
      − The self represses self-expression

40–49   + The self deals with physical reality
      − The self lives according to its own ideas without
       regard to physical reality

50–59   + The self discovers the nature of its individuality
      − The self fears taking risks

60–69   + The self sets and lives by values
      − The self lives according to personal wants and needs

70–79   + The self analyzes the differences between things
       to know them
      − The self lives in ignorance

80–89   + The self develops techniques of achievement
      − The self refuses to act

90–99   + The self embraces the qualities of self and nonself
      − The self plays favorites in life

100 through 999—three-digit numbers—the 3 Level

Initiation to Self-Awareness (or) Initiation to Fantasy

100–199	+	The self declares its nature to the world in a bold, uninhibited manner
	−	The self withholds itself from the world
200–299	+	The self formulates its self-expression to meet the needs of others
	−	The self communicates according to others' expectations
300–399	+	The self formulates and expresses its "I am" concept
	−	The self is splintered between inner and outer
400–499	+	The self organizes and relates to the world
	−	The self does not face reality
500–599	+	The self discovers and expresses its uniqueness
	−	The self expresses extremes of attitude and behavior
600–699	+	The self loves and cares for others
	−	The self works to have its needs and wants met by others
700–799	+	The self develops awareness of its inner nature through interacting with the world
	−	The self reacts to the appearance of things in the world
800–899	+	The self takes responsibility for its views and its interactions
	−	The self passes judgment on others
900–999	+	The self is loving
	−	The self is dogmatic

1,000 through 9,999—four-digit numbers—the 4 Level

Initiation to Purposeful Activity (or) Initiation to Servitude

1,000–1,999	+ The self initiates action to realize its goals
	– The self acts on goals with fear and negativity
2,000–2,999	+ The self learns the skills of functioning in the world from others
	– The self is ruled by the ways of the physical world
3,000–3,999	+ The self develops a philosophy of living
	– The self has an identity crisis
4,000–4,999	+ The self works to meet its needs
	– The self depends on others for its physical well-being
5,000–5,999	+ The self triumphantly profits from the world
	– The self acts on temptation and greed
6,000–6,999	+ The self meets others' needs
	– The self manipulates others to meet its own needs
7,000–7,999	+ The self educates itself for living
	– The self develops a delusional mythos with which to live in the world
8,000–8,999	+ The self deals with all situations it encounters, the positive and the negative alike
	– The self manages through authoritarian power
9,000–9,999	+ The self transcends fears and limitations of the world
	– The self adheres tenaciously to the principles of physicality as the basis of reality

10,000 through 99,999—*five-digit numbers—the 5 Level*

Initiation to Experiencing the World as Opportunity (or)

Initiation to Fear of Envisioning The Freedom to Be

10,000–19,999
+ The self zeros in on all opportunity using every available resource in complete freedom of attitude and behavior
− The self refuses to go beyond the known

20,000–29,999
+ The self actively researches the nature of life with specific purpose
− The self is self-centered, vainglorious, and full of itself

30,000–39,999
+ The self sharpens its social skills through discourse and debate
The self develops ideas and attitudes based on the thinking and actions of others

40,000–49,999
+ The self actualizes a plan of action to live prosperously in the world
− The self schemes opportunistically to advance in life

50,000–59,999
+ The self, acting on the impulse of love, adventure, and high-spiritedness, actively seeks out its destiny in life successfully and maximizes the potential of all that it encounters according to the dictates of its inner nature
− The self avoids dealing with its individuality and its destiny in the world

60,000–69,999
+ The self initiates and experiments with innovative social programs
− The self undermines society with organized criminal activity

70,000–79,999
+ The self analyzes life in order to enhance effectiveness of action
− The self devises means of escaping from its destiny

| 80,000–89,999 | + The self masters living in the physical world for its own purposes |
| | – The self succeeds in the world as the master criminal |

| 90,000–99,999 | + The self devotes its resources and ingenuity for the greater prosperity of others |
| | – The self uses the world for self-serving purposes |

100,000 through 999,999—six-digit numbers—the 6 Level

Initiation to Responsibility Toward Others (or) Initiation to Be a Conscienceless Con Artist

| 100,000–199,999 | + The self develops a social contract |
| | – The self develops a rationale for needy behavior |

| 200,000–299,999 | + The self embraces the yearnings and aspirations of the human heart |
| | – The self proclaims support for publicly accepted values without personal commitment |

| 300,000–399,999 | + The self takes personal responsibility in its interactions with others |
| | – The self adheres to self-interest in social interaction |

| 400,000–499,999 | + The self works to maintain a high ethical standard in social interaction |
| | – The self works to exert control over social interaction |

| 500,000–599,999 | + Perceiving opportunity, the self risks and grows by teaching and healing others |
| | – In social interaction, the self is indifferent to the common welfare |

| 600,000–699,999 | + The self, seeking to give form to impersonal love, blesses and heals others |
| | – The self betrays others |

| 700,000–799,999 | + The self relies upon its intuition and its understanding of truth for guidance in social situations |
| | – The self creates negative or fearful delusions that limit or confuse social interaction with others |

800,000–899,999
+ The self teaches principles of loving, responsible behavior to others by example
– The self enforces negative, limiting modes of behavior on others in social interaction

900,000–999,999
+ The self, sacrificing personal need, works to uplift the lives of others
– The self, claiming the authority of high principle, strives to use personal dogma to dominate the lives of others

1,000,000 through 9,999,999—seven-digit numbers—the 7 Level

Initiation to Know and to Be Its True Spiritual Nature (or) Initiation to Develop and Live by Limiting or Inaccurate Knowledge of Its Inner Nature

1,000,000 1,999,999
+ The self envisions its personal spiritual vision
– The self denies the truth of its inner nature

2,000,000–2,999,999
+ The self heeds the still small voice of Spirit
– The self lives according to its personal understanding

3,000,000–3,999,999
+ The self formulates a spiritual philosophy of living
– The self lives in spiritual confusion or adheres tenaciously to an arbitrary selection of spiritual principles while disregarding others

4,000,000–4,999,999
+ The self grounds its spiritual belief system in its inner being
– The self grounds its mix of beliefs, fallacies, and illusions in its inner being

5,000,000–5,999,999
+ The self views its entire inner existence with a single eye, prospering every experience with wonder and daring
– The self modifies its inner existence according to the nature of its lower self

6,000,000–6,999,999
+ The self attains to spiritual standards of inner being through commitment, discipline, and purification
– The self, thinking to conceal error from the All Seeing Eye of Spirit, weaves a web of intractable self-deception

7,000,000–7,999,999

+ The self models its entire inner existence on the Divine
− The self focuses its inner being on the world of the five senses

8,000,000–8,999,999

+ The self sets goals of spiritual consciousness and devotes its inner resources to their attainment
− The self uses its dynamic inner resources to develop lower impulses into Illusions of Reality

9,000,000–9,999,999

+ The self acts to know Spirit before all else
− The self places ultimate importance on the temporal and the illusory

10,000,000 through 99,999,999—eight-digit numbers—the 8 Level

Initiation to Know the World is Illusion, which the Self Creates in Cooperation with Divine Purpose (or) Initiation to Know the World Is Illusion, which the Self Creates in Order to Achieve Personal Ambition

10,000,000–19,999,999

+ The self sees in every force and circumstance of its environment a symbol of and a reflection of its own nature
− The self establishes supremacy over every force and circumstance in its environment

20,000,000–29,999,999

+ The self, upon assessing forces and circumstances in its environment, perceives the means to achieve its goals
− The self is stymied in living purposively due to force and circumstances in its environment

30,000,000–39,999,999

+ The self achieves consensus of purpose among people in order to realize its goals
− The self depends on others for direction and purpose

40,000,000–49,999,999

+ The self organizes and builds the physical vehicle through which to realize its goals
− The self is content to talk and dream about its goals, lacking the commitment to build the physical vehicle through which to realize its goals

50,000,000–59,999,999

+ The self vigorously and ingeniously achieves its goals, maximizing opportunities and solving problems
− The self balks at accomplishing its goals by picking and choosing which opportunities it cares to maximize and which problems it cares to solve

60,000,000–69,999,999

+ The self uplifts the lives of others to higher levels of reality
− The self regulates the lives of others, setting expectations and assigning responsibilities

70,000,000–79,999,999

+ The self finds and deals with the truth in all things
− The self incurs negative karma due to acting on illusion

80,000,000–89,999,999

+ The self, at peace with life and spiritually empowered, is unrestricted in living according to its purpose
− The self abuses power wantonly and without conscience

90,000,000–99,999,999

+ The self, as a gift of spiritual love, improves the lot of humanity
− The self leads crusades to achieve its personal ambition, bringing pain and loss to all concerned

100,000,000 through 999,999,999—nine-digit numbers—the 9 Level

The Self Transcends Ego (or) The Self Perceives Elements of Ego as Truth

100,000,000–199,999,999

+ The self commits to the Spiritual Path
− The self rallies others to its idiosyncratic version of truth

200,000,000–299,999,999

+ The self exercises good spiritual judgment in making choices
− The self makes spiritually correct and incorrect choices depending on circumstances

300,000,000–399,999,999

+ The self develops a spiritual philosophy that is a True Symbol of Divinity

– The self formulates abstract concepts of a philosophical nature derived from illusion

400,000,000–499,999,999

+ The self refocuses its purpose to the spiritual in all aspects of its daily, mundane life

– The self acts on dogmatism to judge others good and evil

500,000,000–599,999,999

+ The self, self-effacing, discovers moment by moment how to live its spiritual philosophy

– The self uses spiritual principles to its own advantage

600,000,000–699,999,999

+ The self becomes Perfect Love, selflessly healing and raising the consciousness of others

– The self fully commits to the negative, leading the vulnerable into ignorance and death

700,000,000–799,999,999

+ The self knows the True Nature and Purpose of All Things and the Spiritual Principles upon Which Manifestation Occurs

– The self lives a life of illusion, blind to reality

800,000,000–899,999,999

+ The self, fully awakened to Spirit, is empowered by Spirit to realize Purposes of the Divine

– The self, an afraid soul and lost, commits sacrilege against the sacred

900,000,000–999,999,999

+ The self, having mastered every dynamic of human existence, perfectly embodies Spirit in every aspect of its life

– The self, awakened to Divine Love and Truth, judges and destroys the corruption of its being

Bibliography

Barry, Kieren. *The Greek Qabalah: Alphabetic Mysticism and Numerology in the World.* York Beach, Maine: Samuel Weiser, Inc., 1999.

Berenstein, Marcelo. *Sai Baba for Beginners.* New York: Writers and Readers Publishing, Inc., 1998.

Brennan, J. H. *Time Travel: A New Perspective.* St. Paul, Minn.: Llewellyn Publications, 1997.

Caine, Renate Nummela and Geoffrey Caine. *Making Connections: Teaching and the Human Brain.* Menlo Park, Calif.: Innovative Learning Publications, Addison Wesley, 1994.

Campbell, Joseph. *The Masks of God.* New York: Penguin Books, 1976.

_____. *Transformations of Myth through Time.* New York: Harper and Row, Publishers, 1990.

Capra, Fritjof. *The Tao of Physics.* Boston, Mass.: Shambhala, 1991.

_____. *The Web of Life.* New York: Doubleday, 1996.

Cassirer, Ernst. *The Philosophy of Symbolic Forms—Volume 1.* New Haven, Conn.: Yale University Press, 1953.

Castaneda, Carlos. *The Power of Silence: Further Lessons from Don Juan.* New York: Pocket Books, 1987.

Chaplin, James P. *Dictionary of Psychology.* New York: Dell Publishing, 1985.

Cohen, John Michael, ed. *New Penguin Dictionary of Quotations.* New York: Viking, 1992.

Davidson, John. *The Secret of the Creative Vacuum: Man and the Energy Dance.* Essex, England: C. W. Daniel Company Limited, 1994.

Decoz, Hans with Tom Monte. *Numerology: Key to Your Inner Self.* Garden City Park, New York: Avery Publishing Group, 1994.

Fortune, Dion. *Cosmic Doctrine.* New York: Samuel Weiser, 1976.

_____. *Sane Occultism*. London: Inner Light Publishing Company, 1938.

_____. *The Mystical Qabalah*. York Beach, Maine: Samuel Weiser, Inc., 1989.

Freeman, Arnold. *Meditation Under the Guidance of Rudolf Steiner*. Sheffield, England: The Sheffield Education Settlement.

Gérardin, Lucien. *Le Mystère des Nombres*. St.-Jean-de-Braye, France: Editions Dangles, 1985.

Givin, Robert P., Chairman, Board of Directors. *The New Encyclopedia Britannica*. Chicago: Encyclopedia Britannica, 1990.

Gleick, James. *Chaos: Making a New Science*. New York: Penguin, 1987.

Goodwin, Matthew Oliver. *Numerology: The Complete Guide*. North Hollywood, Calif.: Newcastle Publishing Company, Inc., 1981.

Graham, Lloyd M. *Deceptions and Myths of the Bible*. New York: Bell Publishing Company, 1979.

Gullberg, Jan. *Mathematics from the Birth of Numbers*. New York: W. W. Norton Company, 1997.

Hancock, Graham. *The Sign and the Seal: The Quest for the Lost Ark of the Covenant*. New York: Touchstone, 1992.

Harmon, William, ed. *The Top 500 Poems*. New York: Columbia University Press, 1992.

Harner, Michael. *The Way of the Shaman: A Guide to Power and Healing*. San Francisco: Harper and Row, Publishers, 1980.

Harvey, Edmund H. Jr. *Reader's Digest Book of Facts*. Pleasantville, New York: The Reader's Digest Association, 1987.

Hawking, Stephen. *A Brief History of Time*. New York: Bantam Books, 1990.

Hope, Murry. *The Sirius Connection*. Rockport, Maine: Element Books, 1996.

Jensen, Eric. *Brain-Based Learning and Teaching*. Del Mar, Calif.: Turning Point Publishing, 1995.

Kaku, Michio. *Visions: How Science Will Revolutionize the 21st Century*. New York: Anchor Books, 1997.

Lancer, Bob. *Inner Freedom through Qabala*. Phoenix, Ariz.: Limitless Light Publishing, 1986.

Mandelbrot, Benoit B. *The Fractal Geometry of Nature*. New York: W. H. Freeman and Company, 1983.

McClain, Ernest G. *Myth of Invariance.* York Beach, Maine: Nicholas-Hays, Inc., 1984.

Menninger, Karl. *Number Words and Number Symbols: A Cultural History of Numbers.* Cambridge, Mass.: The M.I.T. Press, 1970.

Morse, Joseph Loffan, ed. *Funk and Wagnals Standard Reference Encyclopedia.* New York: Funk and Wagnals, 1962.

Myss, Carolyn. *Anatomy of the Spirit.* New York: Harmony Books, 1996.

Osborn, Diane K. *Reflections on the Art of Living, A Joseph Campbell Companion.* New York: Harper Collins Publishers, 1991.

Powell, James N. *The Tao of Symbols.* New York: Quill, 1982.

Ravens, J. E. *Pythagoreans and Eleatics.* Chicago, Ill.: Ares Publishers, 1966.

Reich, Wilhelm. *People in Trouble.* Rangely, Maine: Orgone Institute Press, 1953.

Ring, Kenneth. *Life at Death: A Scientific Investigation of the Near-Death Experience.* New York: Coward, McCann and Geoghegan, 1980.

Scofield, C. I. *Scofield Reference Bible.* New York: Oxford University Press, 1945.

Stowe, Everett M. *Communicating Reality through Symbols.* Philadelphia, Pa.: The Westminster Press, 1996.

Treffert, Darold. *Extraordinary People: Understanding "Idiot Savants."* New York: Harper & Row, Publishers, 1989.

Voss, Sarah. *What Number Is God?* New York: State University of New York Press, 1995.

Walker, Barbara G. *The Woman's Encyclopedia of Myths and Secrets.* San Francisco: Harper and Row, 1983.

Webster's Encyclopedic Unabridged Dictionary of the English Language. New York: Gramercy Books, 1994.

Whitrow, G. J. *The Nature of Time.* New York: Holt, Rinehart and Winston, 1973.

Wilhelm, Richard. *The I Ching or Book of Changes.* Princeton, N.J.: Princeton University Press, 1971.

Williamson, Marianne. *Illuminata.* New York: Random House, 1994.

Wilson, Edward O. *Consilience: The Unity of Knowledge.* New York: Alfred A. Knopf, 1998.

Zukov, Gary. *The Dancing Wu Li Masters.* New York: Bantam Books, 1986.

Index

Llewellyn publishes hundreds of books
on your favorite subjects.

Look for the Crescent Moon

to find the one you've been searching for!

To find the book you've been searching for, just call or write for a FREE copy of our full-color catalog, New Worlds of Mind & Spirit. New Worlds is brimming with books and other resources to help you develop your magical and spiritual potential to the fullest! Explore over 80 exciting pages that include:

- Exclusive interviews, articles and "how-tos" by Llewellyn's expert authors

- Features on classic Llewellyn books

- Tasty previews of Llewellyn's latest books on astrology, Tarot, Wicca, shamanism, magick, the paranormal, spirituality, mythology, alternative health and healing, and more

- Monthly horoscopes by Gloria Star

- Plus special offers available only to New Worlds readers

To get your free New Worlds catalog, call:
1-877-NEW-WRLD

or send your name and address to

Llewellyn
P.O. Box 64383, Dept. 0-7387-0218-8
St. Paul, MN 55164-0383

Visit our website at www.llewellyn.com

LLEWELLYN
New Worlds of Mind and Spirit